Don't Roll Your Eyes

Other Books by Dr. Ruth Nemzoff

Don't Bite Your Tongue: How to Foster Rewarding Relationships with Your Adult Children (2008)

Don't Roll Your Eyes

Making In-Laws into Family

Ruth Nemzoff

palgrave
macmillan

First published in 2012 by
PALGRAVE MACMILLAN®
in the United States—a division of St. Martin's Press LLC,
175 Fifth Avenue, New York, NY 10010.

Where this book is distributed in the UK, Europe and the rest of the world,
this is by Palgrave Macmillan, a division of Macmillan Publishers Limited,
registered in England, company number 785998, of Houndmills,
Basingstoke, Hampshire RG21 6XS.

Palgrave Macmillan is the global academic imprint of the above companies
and has companies and representatives throughout the world.

Palgrave® and Macmillan® are registered trademarks in the United States,
the United Kingdom, Europe and other countries.

ISBN: 978–0–230–33899–9

Library of Congress Cataloging-in-Publication Data

Nemzoff, Ruth E.
    Don't roll your eyes : making in-laws into family / Ruth Nemzoff.
        p. cm.
    Includes bibliographical references and index.
    ISBN 978–0–230–33899–9
    1. Parents-in-law. 2. Married people—Family relationships. 3. Families.
    I. Title.

 HQ759.8.N46 2012
 346.01'7—dc23   2012004243

A catalogue record of the book is available from the British Library.

Design by Newgen Imaging Systems (P) Ltd., Chennai, India.

First edition: September 2012

10 9 8 7 6 5 4 3 2 1

Printed in the United States of America.

To women's friendships, to which I am indebted for my success in raising four children and writing two books.

With special thanks to Elinor Yudin Sachse, my college roommate, who helped me through Economics 101 and has been steadfast in her support since then. She has been my confidant, my interior decorator, my editor, and my friend for 50 years.

To my husband, Harris Berman, superb father, expert proofreader, and extraordinary companion through life's changes.

Contents

VIIICONTENTS

DISCLAIMER

All of the characters and stories in this book are composites. If the characters and vignettes seem familiar to you though you have never met me, or even if you have had long talks with me, be assured, they are not you. They are familiar because the situations are so common that the stories were repeated to me in one version or another by many people. I hope, however, you will gain insight into yourself by looking at these composite characters. Enjoy the book.

Acknowledgments

Elinor Sachse, Phd, my Barnard college roommate, and economist, has once again edited, added her ideas, and generally supported me as I wrote this book. Melanie Grossman, MSW, my friend from my days in India with the Peace Corps, has shared her knowledge, edited, and contributed many ideas. Ellen Offner of Offner Associates, Healthcare Consultants, and Jessica Lipnack of NetAge Consulting, both friends from Newton, MA, took time from their work to edit and add insights and were always available in my panics. Ellen even tracked down some pesky footnotes. Marcia Boumil was ever ready with a quick response, a good edit, and a great deal of legal experience, which she shared freely. How lucky I am to have smart women friends!

In the spirit of this book, I communicated with each of my loved ones and am acknowledging them. Although none of the stories in this book is from these relationships, my loved ones have helped inform my expertise on the topic and provided me with love and support during the writing of *Don't Roll Your Eyes*.

Once again, Luba Ostashevsky of Palgrave Macmillan encouraged me and helped me shape the contents. She is unparalleled as a supportive and insightful editor.

Many colleagues at the Brandeis Women's Studies Research Center contributed stories or led me to sources. Specifically and alphabetically, they are Helen Berger, Sarita Bhalotra, Marguiete Bouvard, Jennifer Coplon, Andrea Dottolo, Diana Durham, Nance Goldstein, Laurie Kahn, Linda Paloli, Rosie Rosensweig, Roberta Salper, and Georgia Sassen. Elizabeth Markson helped me compile the list of films. There are others who wish to remain anonymous.

Members of my community from many aspects of my life also contributed their stories and ideas, including Jay Albany, Alan Becker, Mila Bronstein, Carol Cardozo, Betsy Connolly, Father Walter Cuenin, Dede Draper, Lynda Fink, Lois Finn, Robert Frank, Barbara Gaffin, Lisa Goodman, Carole Levine, Shawn MacLean, Betty Solomon

Madoff, Connie and Haig Mardikian, Kayla McAuley, Carol Singer, Carol Tannenbaum, Laura Wilson, and Chuck Yanikoski. My thanks are heartfelt to all of the other people who helped but whose names I will not include so that they may remain anonymous.

The hundreds of people who have attended my lectures and shared their lives and their dilemmas generously were the inspiration for this book.

Student partners at Brandeis and beyond who copyedited and did library research for me include Tommy Arnott, Leah Edelman, Miriam Gleckman-Krut, Adam Hollenberg, Nathan Koskella, Samantha Paternoster, and Marielle Temkin. Please send job offers to these wonderful students.

It takes a village for me to write a book!

Don't Roll Your Eyes: Making In-Laws into Family

In-laws are not related to us by blood, but they are family. Or are they? Who is family? Does it include just parents and siblings, or the whole tribe of cousins, second cousins, grandparents, and great-grandparents? Why do we roll our eyes and minimize our in-laws? Why are in-law relationships so difficult? In *Don't Roll Your Eyes*, I examine the forces that make in-law relationships troublesome, but I also explore how multiple generations can benefit from these essentially voluntary associations. Every coupling involves more than just two people. Technically, in the West, in-laws are the spouse of one's child (son- or daughter-in-law) or the parents of one's spouse (father- or mother-in-law). However, in some extended families, the two sets of parents of the couple consider themselves in-laws. The siblings of both spouses, too, become part of the extended family, or in-law sibs. To complicate matters further, the frequent reconfiguring of many Western families brings stepparents, stepsiblings, unrelated former spouses, and current companions into the in-law circle. Aunts and uncles may or may not become part of the family constellation. One might ask, how am I connected to siblings-in-law? What about my spouse's parent who left the family years ago? How do all the cousins, uncles, and aunts fit into my life? Are they part of the extended family or not?

LANGUAGE CONFOUNDS

We are uncertain who counts as in-laws. In English, we don't have the vocabulary to describe the various in-law relationships. Other languages have words to describe the parents of your in-law child, including Yiddish (*machatonim*), Spanish (*consuegros*), and Armenian (*khnami*). In Chinese, different words denote maternal and paternal grandparents, making specific the differing relationships. Vocabulary serves to explain and distinguish certain relationships from others. In English, we lump all persons related by marriage together under one umbrella word: *in-law*. We do not differentiate. It is up to each one of us to determine who is family and who is not. In a multicultural society, definitions of extended families differ. We each must decide what being family means. Many first-generation immigrants to the United States assume that the family is a vertical multigenerational unit: parents, children, and grandchildren. Resources of time and money belong to all three. Those who have been here longer may think that the family is more horizontal: only the nuclear family, two generations—parents and children—deserve intimacy and financial support.[1]

Nor has our language caught up with the changes in our social customs. What do we call the surrogate mother who is also the aunt of a grandchild? Or the sperm donor of your child/grandchild? Is one still an in-law if one is divorced? Is one an in-law if one is in a long-term partnership but not legally married? Are in-law relationships defined by love or by law?

Either generation may include couples in long-term relationships, which are sanctioned by neither the clergy nor the state. People marry or choose not to for a wide variety of reasons. Sometimes the law does not allow them to marry. For others, the rules and regulations of their pensions make legal coupling an economic disincentive, or estate-planning concerns may discourage marriage. Others have seen so much divorce that they wish to be free from any legal entanglements. Both generations find great ambiguity around their roles vis-à-vis these partners and their families. All involved may be uncertain how much to invest emotionally in these "in-laws by love." Yet some of these relationships are effectively permanent. The lack of language reflects our lack of agreement on who actually is an in-law. No wonder we find in-law relationships tricky.

TRADITION AND JOKES SET US UP FOR TROUBLE

No matter how open-minded we've become about the structure of contemporary families, negative attitudes still prevail.[2] Some people dislike their in-laws simply because they feel they are supposed to. Others truly believe their in-laws are crazy. Others have given up even trying to relate to their spouse's parents or their child's spouse. Many experience hurt and anger in their interactions with their in-laws without understanding the root reason. It's all very confusing. Uncertainty leads to insecurity, and insecurity makes us particularly touchy about our roles.

While today Internet dating and ease of travel enable contact and marital choices beyond borders, stereotypes die hard, as do our actions and attitudes based on these stereotypes. For most of history, parents and matchmakers, not children, chose spouses from their own communities. Marriages traditionally forged alliances between warring parties or supplied families with free labor or expanded family wealth.[3] The aim was to create progeny and gain status. Such motivations created very ambivalent and often negative feelings between the generations. Daughters-in-law were often little more than servants or baby machines. Husbands and their families were meal tickets. Natal ties weakened or dissolved when a child entered the circle of another clan. Affection and love between the couple or their families were irrelevant.

Although in many parts of the world marriage is now based on common interests and personal preference, remnants of the past live on in today's humor. Jokes portray the ambivalence between the generations.

Mothers-in-law are portrayed as meddlesome:

Two men were in a pub. One said to his mate, "My mother-in-law is an angel." His friend replied, "You're lucky. Mine is still alive."

Fathers-in-law are depicted as ridiculously bereft at losing their daughters:

Question: *Why would you rather deal with a vicious dog than your father-in-law?*
Answer: *A vicious dog eventually lets go!*

Mothers and daughters-in-law have little love between them[4]:

When I die, I want to be buried next to the Krispy Kreme. At least my daughter-in-law will visit me there.

Sons-in-law are shown as inadequate but loveable oafs:

A golfer hits a ball and it misses the green by inches. His partner says, "That's called a son-in-law shot. It's not what you expected, but you'll take it."

Some jokes hint that what people feel about their in-laws is a matter of perspective:

Two old men are sitting on a bench. One says to the other, "My daughter married the most wonderful man: he cooks, he cleans, and he gets the kids off to school." The other says, "My son married the laziest woman: she makes him cook, clean, and get the kids off to school."

For in-law parents, in-law relationships are so problematic that when I spoke to audiences about my first book, *Don't Bite Your Tongue: How to Foster Rewarding Relationships with Your Adult Children*, the most common and troubling questions were about relationships with in-law children. For parents, it is hard to accept a person they have not chosen. It is hard to readjust their dreams for their children. It is hard to incorporate a new person into the family they have created. Parents asked questions such as "How do I relate to my daughter-in-law? How do I relate to her relatives?" and "My son doesn't get along with his sister's husband. What should I do?"

Mothers-in-law and fathers-in-law feared commenting on just about anything lest they be considered interfering. They wanted to continue as an important part of their own children's lives but were uncertain how to do this.

Jokes from the perspective of adult children show their ambivalence:

Question: *What is the definition of mixed feelings?*
Answer: *When your Maserati goes over a cliff with your mother-in-law in it.*

Comments by the adult children expressed uncertainty and negative feelings as their in-laws attempted to become part of their lives.

"I have a mother-in-law from hell. She can't let go of her son. How do I deal with her?"

* * *

"My father-in-law tries to run our lives."

Like their parents, in-law children have difficulty coping with lifestyle differences, differences in belief, and differences in expectations. In many blogs, young in-laws seek guidance. The blogosphere is filled with the uncertainties of in-law children. Good relationships between siblings and in-laws can increase the nuclear family bonds while bad relationships can tear them asunder. The ease or difficulty of these relationships depends mostly on the willingness of all to make things work. Most of us do not want to be seen as the wicked mother-in-law or father-in-law, and no one aspires to be the inadequate son- or daughter-in-law. Jokes may help us blow off steam and allow us to comment on taboo feelings. They may even create a bond among fellow sufferers, but they also set the stage for future problems. We fear being defined by these stereotypes.

These jokes live on because they encapsulate grains of truth. While most marriages in the West are no longer merely business agreements, they do require readjustments on the part of both individuals and families. Parents must be flexible to incorporate new family members, and children must adjust to a plethora of new requests and family customs. Expectations of problems, on the one hand, prepare us to make allowances and to understand that melding two or more families will have its rough spots. On the other hand, negative expectations set us up to be wary of one another, to approach each other with suspicions.

HIDDEN EXPECTATIONS

The generations often blame each other when expectations they don't even know they have are not met. Only when one finds oneself angry when an in-law child decides it is too much of a hassle to come to his sister-in-law's championship game do parents realize they expect all their children to be present for each other's shining moments. When no gift arrives, we realize we expected one. Only when we are insulted that someone arrives late or wears the wrong clothes do we know that we anticipated something else. We may not have mentioned to the person the dress code or the expectation of promptness, yet we are upset. Emotions often come before our realization of what we want. Little remains static as life progresses. Things can improve or worsen. People change. The environment changes. Life events intervene. Throughout all of these transformations, in-laws can add or detract, making transitions easier and more joyous or more difficult. The constantly moving picture forces us to continually reconsider our relationships and makes finding permanent solutions complicated.

GLOBALIZATION COMPLICATES

It won't surprise anyone to hear that family traditions are disrupted as the world becomes more global. Family obligations change as career opportunities and intercultural marriages detach us from home communities and send us to destinations far way. This lowers the chances that children will live nearby in order to care for aging parents. Grandparents won't be able to care for grandchildren on a daily basis. The extended family is dispersed. Moreover, increased mobility has many of us interacting with people whose customs differ from our own. Parents who expected to be waited on hand and foot as is the local custom on one continent now find themselves serving as babysitters or cooks in another.[5] Parents who had hoped their children and children-in-law would take care of them in their old age find themselves dealing with in-law children who have no such expectations. The cost and time of travel prevent many from both generations from sharing holidays and life's peak moments together. Both generations develop ties with neighbors and friends. Their own family members may become jealous as these unrelated persons become like kin, celebrating holidays and helping out in the small and large crises of life.

GENDER ROLES MORPH

Changing gender roles also confuse expectations. New opportunities for women make many no longer willing to assume all the traditional familial obligations. As they enter the workforce, their brothers or husbands pick up some of their former duties. If they live nearby, a father-in-law may be doing the babysitting while the mother-in-law works. The son-in-law may be in charge of the social calendar or of cleaning the house. Families with children of only one gender often call upon their in-law children to assist with duties formerly relegated to the other gender. Thus, your in-law child may be doing house repairs or picking your nursing home. Both parents and children hold onto nostalgic expectations of well-defined family roles when all of these roles are changing. The dissonance between expectation and reality can cause problems.

The stereotypical American family of a married mother and father and two children is not the only family configuration.[6] Many children have grown up with only one parent or two parents of the same gender or one parent to whom they are related by blood or adoption and another with whom they are related by shared experience and affection. With this shift in family composition goes a shift in expectation and obligation. On the positive side, many families have experienced incorporating new members into their circle. On the more challenging side, everyone is inventing new roles as they go along.

Some families find joy and a sense of expansiveness in welcoming new members into their families, and others find them problematic and stressful. Some parents and adult children find themselves immediately attracted to their new families, and others are horrified, are jealous, or find nothing in common with the people to whom they are suddenly related. For most of us, these relationships evolve over time.

MY STORY

Of all my careers—teacher, administrator, state legislator, and professor—mothering has been the most rewarding and the most long-lived. As my children stepped forth from school to work, my relationships with them changed. I was no longer the one responsible for their safety and their decisions. My role turned to one of advisor, a shoulder to cry on, trusted friend, and "go to" person in emergencies. As they coupled, I moved from the center stage in their lives to the wings. Their partners were their primary interest; later, their children occupied that spot. Throughout all these changes, I drew on what I had learned from my other careers. As a teacher, I found that each of us learns differently and at our own pace. As an administrator, I learned that when I delegate a task, it will be done differently from the way I might have done it-sometimes for the better, sometimes for the worse. If I micromanaged, I lost the creativity of my team. As a legislator, I learned that everyone has good reasons for what they think. Some believe people are essentially good and should be trusted. Others believe humans are essentially bad and must be controlled. Some believe in carrots and others in sticks. All of these insights helped me write my first book on fostering rewarding relationships with adult children and have contributed to this book on in-law relationships.

My relationships with my own four in-law children are very satisfying. Over the years, we have all learned that, though our opinions and customs may differ, we do not need to control each other's choices. My family, like yours, is similar to others in the twenty-first century in some ways and different in others. My husband and I have been married for more than 45 years. He is now at his third major professional position since "retirement," and I am in my first postretirement career. In these years, we have faced and overcome the challenges of illness and—more recently and more unusual—of a fire that destroyed our home. Over the past 15 years, all our children have met and married their soul mates. Our three oldest children married people with recent roots in different countries. Ethnically, culturally, and religiously, their in-law families differ sharply from ours, yet despite these differences, our family and theirs share common values. These common values have turned out to be much more significant than conventional definitions of similarity. Our youngest child only recently married. We now have seven grandchildren. Only one of the four families lives nearby. The others are scattered over the globe.

After the house fire, the whole family rallied from the four corners of the earth. One or the other bought us clothes online, arranged housing, and flew in to help deal with a thousand and one details. They filled the house with groceries. They fended off the insurance adjusters who flock to such disasters. They called regularly until we told them that life had taken on a sufficient degree of normalcy.

My in-law relationships have been an invaluable source of support and much enjoyment. The parents and siblings of our children's spouses bring additional pleasure, as do their aunts, uncles, and cousins. All of the in-law parents add richness to my life. They offered their homes after the fire. They share the joys of family achievements. They pitch in when help is needed and offer support in facing whatever challenges life brings. They spend time in our home, and we enjoy going out to dinner together. We see their other children when they are in town. Our interactions are pleasant and convivial.

It could have been otherwise. Had we expected our children to drop their own lives after the fire and tend to us exclusively, or had we expected the other grandparents to treat our mutual grandchildren exactly the way we do, we could have had plenty of tension. Our in-laws could have thought I was annoying or messy. The list of all my faults could be long. But as simple as it sounds, all of the children and all of the in-law parents make an effort. All of us are uncritical of one another, and all of us love our children, each other's children, and our mutual grandchildren. We send cards for each other's holidays. We enjoy being together, just the parents-in-law, when they are in town. We respect the gifts the others have to give the grandchildren. One set of grandparents teaches the kids chess and has the patience to rock the babies. The others teach crafts and a second language. I can do none of these things. But everyone seems to appreciate my boundless energy for family yoga and excursions.

Because my in-law relationships have so enriched my own life, I know that these associations do not need to be unpleasant. My experience has been reinforced by those who made positive comments in the interviews or focus groups conducted for this book:

"My son is far nicer to us because of his wife."

* * *

"My mother-in-law is a real source of support."

* * *

"My kid's parents in-law are lovely people, which I would expect because they raised a great kid."

Like their parents, the in-law children have difficulty coping with lifestyle differences, differences in belief, and differences in expectations. In many blogs, young in-laws seek guidance. The problems seem greatest early after marriage, with the birth of a child, and then around the illness and death of either generation. However, the minor traumas of life also dominate the blogosphere. Do in-laws have a right to comment on how you raise a child? Who determines what sorts of gifts are acceptable? What are my obligations to the parents and siblings of my new spouse?

Each family and each individual in it is trying to figure out whether they consider in-laws as family. The ease or difficulty of these relationships depends mostly, but not only, on the willingness of all to make things work. On reflection, I realize that both generations want to be appreciated and acknowledged for their efforts. Neither wants to be taken for granted or judged. Most often, the angry feelings are over hurt—hurt about being cast aside, hurt about feeling inadequate, hurt about not being understood, and hurt about not understanding the new rules of the family. *Don't Roll Your Eyes* will help families gain insight and will suggest behaviors so that some of this hurt can be avoided. Relationships between siblings and in-laws can increase the nuclear family bonds or escalate rifts.

Parents who want to continue as part of their children's and grandchildren's lives must have good relationships with their children's spouses, their sons- and daughters-in-law. In-law children gain practical help and emotional and sometimes financial support when they have good relations with their spouse's parents. All of us win when we increase the circle of caring around us. However, in-laws have the potential to cause trouble in marriages. Because in-law ties are so important and can be so troubling, I wanted to start a constructive conversation about in-laws. Few of us challenge our friends' perceptions of their extended-family relationships. We don't want to infringe on each other's privacy or be insensitive to cultural nuances. However, each of us views situations differently. We can learn from each other how to solve problems. The scenarios in *Don't Roll Your Eyes* are based on comments by the hundreds of people who attended my lectures and on interviews with many others. The insights and composite vignettes from this random, but not randomized, sample are meant to provide impetus for either generation to share their views on their newly extended families.

Before I started writing, I explored bookstores, libraries, and blogs to see what help exists for fostering positive children-in-law relationships. Not surprisingly, given the jokes I have quoted about in-laws, most of what I found was downright silly. It reinforced old clichés and provided little useful advice. I then read the few academic studies of in-law relationships. I found even the most trivial of filial obligations vary by culture, location, and economics.[7] There are no uniform expectations.

Good relationships between the in-laws can be a wonderful social safety net, and conflict between the generations can lead to strife and even divorce. Or, put another way, in-law relationships can provide wonderful social insurance, or they can suck energy from a marriage or relationship. In-law relationships are not trivial. Joking about them, discounting them, or ignoring difficulties will not help any of us forge new bonds. These relationships take work and many years of effort. Capturing the upside potential in these associations benefits individuals, families, and societies.[8]

DON'T ROLL YOUR EYES: THE CONTENTS

This book focuses on the multiple perspectives of various in-laws and on specific issues that can cause tension or bring in-laws together. I will begin by sharing the perspective of the older generation. Most want to remain part of their children's lives. Next, I will share the younger generation's desire and struggle for independence. I will then examine how in-law siblings can disrupt or reinforce both generations' connections. After this, I will explore the potential tensions and jealousies between the two (which could actually be more than two) parental units of in-laws. I will address the pain I heard in countless comments from both in-law parents and in-law children on the salient issues of interacting with ex-in-laws, grandchildren of divorce, commingling of finances, and end-of-life planning. Embedded in each chapter will be examples of how many families manage to create caring relationships from the base of their own love.

Chapter 1, "Why We Make In-Laws into Outlaws," looks at how history, jokes, and pop culture conspire to make us wary of one another even before we have met. Couple all of this with the fact that in-laws are related by neither blood nor choice, and we are faced with a stage set for animosity. There are no prescribed roles. Each person may have a different view of appropriate gender roles and customary obligations. We all encounter misunderstandings because we do not understand all of the implications of economic disparities and each other's varying needs for independence or connection. We forget that each one of us is on our own life course. We are constantly growing and changing, and the circumstances around us are also changing. Any one of these factors can lead us to blame the in-law for trouble in the relationship. *"If only Suzie were warm like our family,"* or *"If only Billy did not talk about sports all the time,"* or *"If only your mother would stop calling all the time"*... *"then we could get along."* These explanations are far too simplistic. Insight alone will not mitigate the difficulties or end the blame game. However, insight can help all in-laws understand why they are not necessarily a perfect fit from the get-go.

Because in-law relationships are a tale of multiple perspectives, the next four chapters examine the views of the major players. Chapter 2, "Where Do I Fit in? The In-Law Parents Speak," delineates the in-law parents' view. Parents may differ in the degree of closeness they want. Some feel they have devoted so much of their time, money, and effort to their kids that to be dismissed seems incomprehensible and terribly hurtful. Others feel that their job is completed and wish to devote their time to fulfilling their own dreams they had put on hold. Or they do not want to devote time and energy to an in-law child who seems less than ideal. Many parents think, *"That woman [or man] has kept my child from visiting us,"* or *"There is no role for me in my child's life."* These perceptions, right or wrong, lead to a misinterpretation of many situations. Shared experiences, new routines, and affection take a long time to develop.

In chapter 3, "How Many People Did I Marry? The Adult Children Speak," I explore the view from the child-in-law's perspective. Many brides and grooms think they are marrying one person, not a family. They are surprised by the extent to which each spouse comes with a whole series of commitments. Many just want to create their own family identity without interference. Some like their parents-in-law and maybe even cherish them; others don't. Whether actually present or not, the parents-in-law guide or misguide the young couple at every turn. The couple blames the in-law parent for flaws they see in their mate.

Hostility among the siblings can tear families asunder. Chapter 4, "Have I Been Displaced? The Siblings Speak," tackles the impact of sibling approval or disapproval of in-laws of both generations. Even if the newcomer has been around for a long time, the formalization of a relationship introduces new elements into sibling interactions. Siblings find themselves sharing resources with a newcomer. Those resources may be material, or they may be the time and attention of their sibling or their parents. All face the challenge of dealing with a new center of attention. Tensions erupt. When siblings are also in committed relationships, the complexities compound. The other in-law sibs may like each other, or not. Each possibility implies another set of challenges or benefits. Parents who had hoped their children would be close forever are brokenhearted when their kids lose their former closeness. And of course, if there were tensions between the siblings before the newcomers entered the picture, the in-law can alleviate old tensions or create new ones.

The two, and sometimes many more, sets of parental in-laws can cooperate or compete. Some find themselves immediately attracted to their children's new families, and others find nothing in common with these people with whom one day they may share grandchildren. Chapter 5, "Dueling and Other In-Law Games: The Two (or More) Sets of In-Laws," focuses on the interactions and animosities between the various parents-in-law. When there are but two in-law parent couples, these relationships can feel like contests, and when there are more, they can feel like war on many fronts. Parents vie for priority in time, money, and perks with both the children and the grandchildren. For some parents, being an in-law is a competition. Imagine the complexity when more parents are involved! This chapter focuses on the importance of building your own connections with the children and grandchildren, regardless of others.

About 41 percent of American marriages end in divorce.[9] Relating to all these family members—past, present, and potential—can be exhausting. Juggling all these relationships without stepping on feelings is thorny. Emotional attachments do not always follow legal patterns.[10] Divorce, death, gay relationships, and long-term couplings of any type affect the extended family. Is the person who accompanies a family member to holidays and other family events really family? Chapter 6, "In Love, but Not in Law: Unrelated 'In-Laws,'" explores relationships complicated by divorces, deaths, and remarriage or cohabitation of either generation. Whether these relationships are temporary or permanent, any version of the two-person partnered units affects all three generations.

The rest of *Don't Roll Your Eyes* explores specific contexts and problems. Chapter 7, "Diversity Comes Home: Intermarriage," focuses on the disappointments and joys that intermarriage can bring to families. Among the other changes in American families are the rates of intermarriage. More than 50 percent of Greek Orthodox[11] and Jewish people are "marrying out,"[12] and Asian intermarriage is increasing.[13] The multiracial and multicultural population is growing.[14] In many families, religion is becoming an individual rather than a family choice.[15] Individuals are torn between their upbringing and their new alliances. Sometimes they are at odds with the teachings of their religious institutions. This chapter focuses on how families can grapple with the pulls of family and individual beliefs, complicated by marriage to people with different beliefs. It also covers the disappointment that comes when children choose to bring up their own children with a different belief system from that of their parents and grandparents. It will also give examples of families that manage to blend their belief systems or become enriched by learning new customs.

Chapter 8, "Whose Child Is This? Grandparents, Parents, and Grandchildren," explores the tensions between the two generations of in-laws in setting rules. Grandparents enrich children's lives.[16] They can help parents as crises arise. However, they can be a source of aggravation. Facilitating and maintaining these intergenerational ties can be tricky with an in-law and even more problematic with an ex-relative. In divorce, grandparents may no longer be part of the parents' family legally. However, their affection and blood ties remain. Many grandparents have found a way through the morass of anger and disillusionment of their children's divorce to remain a part of their grandchildren's lives. Others have not. The evolving territory of grandparental rights to visit their grandchildren gives little protection. Many parents have benefitted by turning their ex-in-laws into extended family.

Chapter 9, "More Money, More Problems, Less Money, Still Problems," suggests how and why families need to talk about money. Some in-laws come from families in which these topics are taboo. Others discuss all the details of their lives and future deaths, making the in-law children or parents uncomfortable. Either generation or either individual within the generations may be making very different assumptions about what financial contribution is appropriate when the other comes upon hard times. The younger generation may not want to jeopardize their current status or their children's welfare for the parents' needs. Or the older generation may not want to jeopardize their retirement to help out a struggling younger family. One in-law thinks we are each other's social safety net, the other thinks each generation should take care of itself. Too often, neither children nor parents have accurate ideas about what money the other has, what needs they must cover, or how to distribute what remains, if any does.

Much as we hate to face it, all good things come to an end, including our own lives. Chapter 10, "Until Death Do Us Part: Prepare for Illness and Death," focuses on disability, death, and dying. Grief and loss are all among the most difficult topics to face. But face them we must. In some cases, in-laws may be the legal next of kin, making decisions about our lives and the lives of our children and grandchildren. Or they may be the ones providing the care, while our own children remain distant. Because their values and beliefs may differ from ours, family members must discuss their wishes for end-of-life care. There is potential for a clash of cultures. Doing the paperwork of illness, living wills, advance directives, powers of attorney, and guardianship plans provides families with opportunities for open, candid conversations before any decline is imminent.

Finally, in chapter 11, "Do Unto Your In-Laws," I summarize habits that can help improve your relationships with your in-laws. We *can* change ourselves and our attitudes.

I hope that this book will lead everyone involved to a greater understanding of why in-law relationships can be difficult, and that it will expand everyone's capacity to accommodate to new family members.

Since this book is intended only to start discussions, I have provided a bibliography, annotated film list, and some websites to help readers who want to explore further. All of these lists will be useful to therapists, clergy, teachers, and professors, as well as in-laws. My hope is that readers will gain insight into themselves and their new family members. To that end, I conclude each chapter with questions that you can contemplate by yourself or discuss in a group.

Here are some questions to help you begin to understand the assumptions you bring to your in-law relationships:

- What is my goal in my relationship with my in-law child?
- How much closeness do I want with my in-law child?
- How much closeness do I want with my in-law child's parents?
- What is my goal in my relationship with the in-law parents?
- How much closeness is too much?
- What expectations do I have?
- How does reality differ from my expectations?
- Who was I before I was an in-law? Who am I now?
- What did my own in-laws do well?
- What could they have done better?
- What did I do well with my in-laws?
- What could I have done better?
- Did my spouse or partner have different relationships from mine with the in-laws?
- How did my spouse or partner help or hurt these relationships?
- What did my in-laws do that I would like to continue with my in-law children?
- What could he or she have done better?

CHAPTER 1

Why We Make In-Laws into Outlaws

FAMILY TIES WITHOUT THE BONDS

Any family relationship is complex, but in-law relationships are particularly difficult because they have the obligations and expectations of family without the benefits of intimacy, comfort, and support. This is especially true when the relationships are new. In-laws do not know each other's personality quirks and passions. They have little idea which buttons they can push, what happens when they push one, and which buttons the new person will push in them. They have not survived disagreements and arguments. In-laws do not share a common history. They are virtual strangers.

The expectation that these strangers will immediately become loving members of our clans is unrealistic. It takes years to merge a newcomer into the family. Many misunderstandings may be suffered before in-laws can trust that they can truly work together, and many never do. On the positive side, in-laws also lack the "baggage" that comes from years of less-than-positive family interactions. That can make the new in-law easier to deal with than one's own offspring or one's own parents.

Nonetheless, from the very beginning, in-laws are expected to be present at events only open to family. Or in-laws may be imposed upon for favors or commitments usually reserved for close friends. Sometimes they are asked for financial or personal sacrifices greater than they would request from their closest friends. Either generation might resent these requests from someone related by neither blood nor choice.

NEITHER PARENTS' NOR ADULT KIDS' CHOICE

We become an in-law by a decision made by someone else. The younger generation makes the choice of partner, but they have no say in all the relatives who come along with their mate. The older generation often has no input. Both generations feel resentful that they are saddled with relations and obligations they did not choose. Those who wish to control their own fates are frustrated. Parents assumed their child would marry someone from their own socioeconomic, cultural, national, or religious group, but the child chooses differently. Or the parents assume their child would marry a perfect superstar, but instead he or she marries a mere mortal. In short, the reality does not measure up to the parents' fantasy. The in-law child, too, faces disappointment. Some have barely met the in-laws before they find themselves enmeshed in their spouse's family. The new family differs in ways large and small. One family may be closer, the other more distant. The new in-law family may have all the friction of one's own family plus some new and unfamiliar problems. How easy it is for everyone to be disappointed. Other times, parents are thrilled at first and disappointed later. The disillusionment can come for any number of reasons. Perhaps the parents had hoped they would be included in the lives of their grandchildren and they are not. Or perhaps siblings are asked to babysit more than they want. Sometimes parents become irate at the in-law child because they cannot protect their own children from mistakes and so they fault the in-law child. Parents often blame the in-law because it is too painful to admit that their own children and grandchildren are just as imperfect as their own families. In brief, they have their own version of ideal, and they blame the in-law for the imperfections that are part of life.

In-law children may have expected no relationship with the parents of their new spouse and discover that they are embedded in a whole circle they did not bargain for. They may be expected to help out their spouse's parents and siblings on the weekend or socialize with family, when they don't have time for their own friends and family. Or they may have expected the in-laws to fill in all the holes their parents left and they do not. They may have wanted the perfect parents who are all-forgiving and who give money and time generously, only to find their in-laws are just as flawed as their own parents. The parents-in-law may be completely involved in their own lives and have little time or interest in getting to know the new family member. Both generations must cope with the imperfect.

WHEN THE SUBTEXT IS GENDER

Women are still held responsible for fostering kin bonds.[1] Mothers-in-law often assume that their daughters-in-law will take on what were the sons' responsibilities toward his parents.[2] They expect their daughters-in-law to be the family communicators because at one time they were required to be. However, the role of daughters-in-law has changed. Now families divide communication, if for no other reason than the advent of personal communication devices.

Today, many of us have our own cell phone and e-mail account. The young couple negotiates how and who will be responsible for their social connections. Some couples divide the responsibilities for social life along gender lines, others divide along affiliative lines, and still others divide by time: he's in charge of the weekend calendar; she's in charge of the weekdays. The woman is no longer the only one responsible for family life. Mothers-in-law are hurt when their daughters-in-law do not remember birthdays or anniversaries or call to chat. When the son does not call, the parents assume the daughter-in-law failed to remind him, though she may figure her husband has taken care of the communication. It's easy to blame the daughter-in-law.[3]

Complaints about in-law children often are based on outdated notions of what is appropriate for each gender. Most frequently, mothers complain, "*My daughter-in-law raises the children with too many [or too few] rules.*" Fathers complain, "*My son-in-law is not a good provider*" or "*My son-in-law can't fix anything around the house.*"

But gender roles have changed. Many fathers participate in child rearing and influence their children's characters and behaviors. More and more women work outside the home. Some earn as much or more than their husbands.[4] Gender-based criticisms miss the mark today.

Daughters-in-laws' expectations, too, can affect the quality of the relationship along gender lines.[5] If daughters-in-law expect a second mother or a readily available babysitter and the mother-in-law wants to forge ahead in her own career and has limited time for family responsibilities, both will be dissatisfied. Mothers in the parent generation may also be working outside the home or be engrossed in their own activities, or they may simply feel that they raised their own children and have no desire or feel too old to repeat the experience.

EACH FAMILY IS ITS OWN NATION

When a person marries into a family, it is as if he or she is entering a new culture. Gradually we teach the outsider our inside jokes and our ways of doing things. However, the new in-law will inevitably step on a few toes while figuring out the values, customs, and traditions of his or her in-law family. It is easy to judge the new family member as lacking or unfeeling, when he or she may merely have different boundaries, manners, values, expectations, and rewards. Newcomers are likely to miss the cues telling them which subtle behaviors are acceptable and which are not important in the new family. It can take years to figure this out. The family must decide whether to see the new member's *faux pas* as part of a learning process or as an insult. They can choose to be gracious and assume the best of intentions on the part of the new family member, or they can assume the offender had malicious intent. Their attitudes can set the stage for stressful relationships or build the foundations for good ones.

The truth is that most of us cannot even articulate exactly what our sacred traditions and subtle boundaries are. Indeed, we often only realize them once they have already been overstepped and we feel hurt or disrespected. Newcomers notice habits that we take for granted. Seeing ourselves and our families through the eyes of an outsider can be disquieting.

Marianne hated Sunday lunches at her in-laws. It seemed to her that the family only argued and yelled. They discussed everything controversial—money, politics, religion. They constantly turned to her for her opinion. She felt they were rude and pompous. Her husband,

Andy, was confused. How could Marianne possibly consider these stimulating intellectual discussions rude? How could she think his family was intruding on her private thoughts by asking her opinion?

At first, Andy was upset that Marianne would call his family rude. When Marianne revealed her thoughts to her husband, she realized that in her family, mentioning any controversial topic at the dinner table was taboo. It never occurred to Andy that a newcomer might find his family discussions threatening. When he saw things through Marianne's eyes, he realized he had never questioned his family's mode of communicating. He could now see how a person could interpret his family's fiery discussions as arguments. He also now understood how Marianne might interpret his family's request for her ideas as pressure to respond. Had anyone asked Marianne before, she would not have thought of herself as reluctant to share her opinion. Neither partner had been fully conscious of their respective family's assumptions, but both realized them through each other's perspective. Even when people are from the same religion or the same nationalities, they have different family cultures.

*   *   *

The in-laws blame one another when unspoken expectations are not met. This blame can manifest itself around small social interactions, or it may be the grounds for more substantive disagreements. For example, in a family in which all relatives hug and kiss when they arrive or leave, a newcomer who prefers to shake hands is seen as cold. Those who come from families that share every detail with all members do not understand those who see such communication as a personal infringement.

Shandra comes from a blended family with a mother and father and two stepsisters. Her parents divorced when she was nine. Shandra has spent her life carving out privacy for herself. Her stepsisters, from her point of view, would completely run her life if she gave in even on the smallest issue. She marries Martin, who comes from a large extended family. They make her uncomfortable when they get close, but she has no idea why. Their constant hugging and kissing and sharing what she considers secrets make her hate family gatherings. Initially she attends these and stands aside, not participating. Her mother-in-law considers her a cold fish. She does not realize, however, that Shandra protects herself out of fear of being taken over by the family. She and Martin's family speak two different body languages, and they have different definitions of what should remain private.

Shandra has learned to protect herself in her stepfamily by keeping all of her news to herself. What her husband's family tells as news, she hears as sharing intimacies, and that makes her uncomfortable. She is also unaccustomed to showing social warmth by physical contact. Thus, she cringes when extended family members greet her in a manner that to them denotes friendship and caring but to her feels like an invasion of her personal space.

*   *   *

Sometimes, the clash of cultures stumbles on what seems like trivial social customs but are really about deep-seated values. Other times what seem like really important issues are really quite trivial. One family considers every act, including what they eat, as an important political statement, and another family sees family meals as a time to socialize and bond. Consider the experience of Phyllis, a mother-in-law and a gourmet cook.

Pascal, who works for an animal rights group, is a strict vegan and finds the very thought of eating animal products repugnant. His mother-in-law, Phyllis, is a gourmet cook who always has a huge meal prepared when he and her daughter visit. Her family has always relished these mealtimes together. Phyllis thinks she is being thoughtful by including at least two vegan dishes so that Pascal will have plenty to eat. But Pascal is so completely repelled by the sight of meat that he refuses to sit with the family. He feels that his diet is morally superior to that of his in-law family and will not be a part of any rite that includes animal food products. Phyllis is not only hurt by Pascal's lack of acknowledgment of her efforts, but also worried that her daughter will not get the protein necessary for good health. The family is insulted by his refusal to eat with them.

It is not surprising that food becomes a battleground. All of us eat. Food is fundamental to every culture, as it helps define national identities. It maintains ethnic ties and is one way individuals define themselves.[6] We all know people who have little knowledge of their ancestral country but who eat and serve its food. We differentiate ourselves through food and its presentation.

For Phyllis, the meal and her family are the top priorities. To Pascal, the issue of animal rights trumps family relationships. Neither fully understands why they are so annoyed with each other. They obviously have different ideas on when and where to express political views and what constitutes a good-faith effort in accommodating the needs of others.

Phyllis, for her part, escalates her frustration with Pascal into a worry about her daughter's health. She worries that living on Pascal's low-protein vegan diet will make it hard for her daughter to get pregnant. She has read that protein is important, and she knows that animal products are the most readily available source of that protein. True or not, Phyllis believes Pascal might harm her daughter. She also fears that Pascal's definition of self as an animal savior will crimp her daughter's ability to participate in her beloved family meals and, thus, that Pascal will alienate her daughter from her nuclear family. She conflates these concerns with the immediate issue of how to satisfy her other children's cravings for her home cooking with her desire to incorporate her vegan son-in-law into family gatherings.

Phyllis has options that she may not realize. Phyllis could and should learn more about vegetarian and vegan diets. In this way, she can show Pascal that she respects his ideas on animal rights and diet enough to learn about them. Perhaps he will return that honor in kind by joining the family. At any rate, she will be modeling behavior that demonstrates that differences can be an impetus for new knowledge. She can suggest that Pascal prepare the meal for the whole family. However, because she likes to cook, this will likely feel like a real sacrifice, and she would need to be willing to make it. Or she could invite him to cook a vegan meal for the family with her. In this way, she would build a relationship based on their shared interest in food. The family might have to sacrifice their favorite dishes, and Phyllis would have to be willing to share her kitchen. Everyone would get the proverbial part of the pie. Or she could suggest that Pascal join the family after dinner. Again, she would have to be willing to forego her dream of having all her children and their spouses gathered at the table for a whole meal. She would, however, avert her children's disappointment in not having their favorite foods. She might even be averting a crisis between her daughter and the siblings.

Right now Pascal has rigid boundaries. His whole self-concept is tied to being sensitive to animals. It may not be so forever. He may continue his passion for animals and vegan eating but also become a father. Then, the extended family may take on a more important place in his thinking. He may incorporate many definitions of self into his persona, as many of us do. He may learn many new tools to encourage others to become vegans. He may be forced to eat with nonvegans at his next job and thus become more flexible. As a result, he may decide to bring his own food with him and eat beforehand or at another table, but in the same room as the family. As Pascal becomes more confident that his mother-in-law is not trying to convert him into a meat eater, he may be more comfortable sitting at her table.

Phyllis could decide that while her own story is bound up in the importance of family gatherings, the exact type of food is less important than the being together. As Phyllis and Pascal begin to share their stories, they may be able to build a new chapter that will link them and the family. As we invite others into our worldviews, we strengthen the possibilities for fruitful interactions.

Phyllis understands that food is both political and social. She also senses that she may need to wait to take this up with Pascal. She may find that Pascal does not change with time, in which case Phyllis will need to discuss with her daughter where she is willing to compromise and where she is not. The family may decide to share outings together and divide at the end of the day for meals. The family may find that they enjoy many activities together in addition to eating. Over time, they may build enough trust and affection to share with Pascal the meaning and warmth embedded in their family's soul food. In short, they may need to try many options if they want to include Pascal. Social situations are at once minor and at the same time symbolic of deeper cultural and personal definition.

* * *

Examples abound of different interpretations of behaviors. One family thinks traveling to new venues is enriching and another family considers it an extravagant escape from the duties of life. One family thinks watching football is a waste of time while another thinks it's a bonding experience. One family expects thank-you notes for every kindness and another finds it strange that a family member would write a note for what they consider normal convivial family interactions.

> *Vivette's son and new daughter-in-law visited with their new baby. Vivette was upset that the new daughter-in-law, Betty Ann, did not write a thank-you note after their visit. For her part, Betty Ann felt that writing a note was not necessary. She had gone out of her way to bring the new grandchild to his grandparents. She had thanked her mother-in-law verbally for her hospitality, just as she would her own mother, but thank-you notes, in her mind, were to acknowledge strangers and gifts that had arrived by mail. Betty Ann explained to her husband her notion of proper thank-you notes. He, however, felt that his mother was intractable on manners and that his wife must cave in to please his mother even if she's unreasonable and write a note every time they visited.*

The social graces were of critical importance to Vivette who saw thank-you notes as a sign of good breeding. Betty Ann could have bowed to her mother-in-law's request, since it only takes five minutes to write a note, but she felt overwhelmed with her job and her new baby, and she resented Vivette's attitude about her upbringing. She suggested to her husband that he write the note, but he said that his mother would find that unacceptable. Perhaps if Betty Ann's husband had been willing to run interference with his mother, it would have blown over. Or, if Betty Ann herself had dared to politely explain her views to Vivette, the distance between them might have narrowed. Instead, Betty Ann felt unsupported by her husband and, as a result, limited the frequency of her visits to the grandparents and requested that no gifts be given to the grandchild. This small disagreement about manners led to a much bigger rift than any of the parties wanted. Had Vivette realized that her demands would lead to a disagreement between the couple and to her own distance from her grandchild, she might have reevaluated her thinking. Her son did both of the women in his life a disservice by thinking that the problem was about a note and not the feelings behind the writing of one. Helping family members understand each other's viewpoints is an important part of paving the way to closer bonds. Sometimes the spouse does a service by acting as cultural translator.

WHEN YOU JUST DON'T LIKE EACH OTHER

Tension in in-law relationships may also arise from individual temperaments. Some in-law matches are more compatible than others. I often hear parents say, "*I get along so well with one of my children's spouse, but the other I just don't like.*" For the shy, the outgoing seem overbearing, and for the exuberant, the reserved seem positively cold and phlegmatic. Those who are from small families may be overwhelmed by the sheer size of their spouse's contingent. And those from large families may have no idea how to focus their attention on one member at a time. It would be wonderful if all family members understood the different coping mechanisms of each individual; however, these insights often elude us. Since both generations and both individuals are on their own life journey, each prioritizes time and energy differently. One person devotes time and energy to a career, while another focuses on relationships. It is rare that everyone involved places the same priority on work or family obligations. The young couple focuses on becoming a new independent unit. They may not have the desire or energy for building relationships with a whole raft of people who are the family of their spouse. The parents may want to focus elsewhere and enjoy their newfound freedom, or they may want to spend their efforts incorporating the newcomer into their lives. Or they may harbor ambivalence, at one moment insisting on their freedom and the next beseeching the new in-law to spend time with them.

All of this is difficult enough with one family, but the high remarriage rates of either generation in contemporary America call on in-laws to figure out the intricacies of several families, often families with conflicting values.

Ashley had spent her childhood negotiating between her divorced and remarried parents. She knew she had to give equal time to each set. When she marries Luke, she feels that she now has three families to please. She is so exhausted by the thought of sharing every holiday in a way that suits everyone and finding equally meaningful gifts for all of the family members that she withdraws from everyone.

Ashley's mother-in-law, Elaine, was disappointed. She had three sons and had hoped to be close with her daughter-in-law. She trusted her instinct that Ashley did not dislike her. Finally she asked her son whether she or his dad had offended Ashley. He explained her history, and his mother backed off and decided to give her daughter-in-law time to figure out how to incorporate yet another set of parents into her life. Elaine assured her son that she and his father would not expect equal time but would welcome whatever attention Ashley would give them. Elaine took the long view. She knew life has its moments when one needs help, and she knew she would be willing to help Ashley when that time came. She could and would be patient and understanding. In this case, Ashley's family structure, not her personality, created the difficulties. She, like so many in-law children, did not want to be disloyal to her own family and feared that giving her new family more time would cause jealousy.

* * *

Family structure can create new needs, some of which are temporary and some of which are permanent. It could be the older generation that has the temporary period in which extra support is needed. A recently widowed or divorced parent may require more attention than a married one, particularly when the death or divorce is new. Or parents of children with disabilities may need more practical assistance than those without. The opposite is also true. There are periods when one generation or the other wants less contact.

> *In the early years of her marriage, Marlene was happy to be cordial to her in-laws, but she had plenty of friends and a great extended family of her own. Her mother-in-law, Andrea, would frequently ask her to go shopping and to lunch, and to various family gatherings. Marlene never accepted the duo activities and only went to the important family events—never to casual get-togethers. Andrea felt Marlene didn't want to become a real part of her husband's family. After many attempts to set up shopping and hiking trips, Andrea gave up. However, three children later, Andrea was pleasantly surprised to see that Marlene fully welcomed her as a grandmother.*

Not all in-laws have the same goals for relating. In this case, Marlene regarded her mother-in-law's attempts to bond as trying to become another mother, which she did not want. However, once she had children, she was happy to have Andrea as the grandmother of her children and include her as a big presence in her life. Marlene never disliked Andrea. They merely had different needs for closeness. Assumptions of ill will or active dislike are often untrue.

PINING FOR THE BAD OLD DAYS

In traditional societies, expectations are all laid out. Everyone knows the family obligations. Any breach is obvious. Now we invent as we go along, which means that there is more opportunity for misunderstanding and more opportunity for negligence. Now our inner compasses tell us what our obligations are to our in-law children or our in-law parents. Sadly, these compasses are not calibrated universally. The ambiguity leads to more hurt and more disappointment, and there are few ways to talk about them.

We no longer have the old system of obligatory care. Yet the needs for care and support have not disappeared, nor have the indirect or direct benefits that come from the satisfaction of providing that support.

However, the family—nuclear and in-law—remains the source of such service. Some feel they are required to take care of their in-law parents or to pitch in and help the children. Others do not feel required to do anything. Obligation has given way to relationships based on affection and voluntary assistance. Both generations must work to earn that affection. Because it is so unclear exactly what the role of in-laws is today, we are crafting and refining our roles as we go along. Our relationships are unlikely to be perfect, but over time, they can become workable.

> Carmen and Roy were about to have their first baby. Both sets of grandparents were thrilled—that is, until they were informed that they were not to visit for the first two weeks after the birth. The young couple reasoned that the father only had two weeks of paternity leave and that they should use the initial time to bond as a family. All of the grandparents were deeply hurt and interpreted the young couple's decision as insulting. They felt excluded. Becoming grandparents was a huge marker in their own lives. The paternal in-laws assumed their daughter-in-law was laying claim to their son and excluding them. The maternal grandparents thought their son-in-law was doing the same. In fact, the new mother felt that she did not know how she would feel after giving birth, and she did not want to have to entertain or even be nice to anyone, including her own mother.

History, personal and cultural preferences, family structure, and gender expectations all make in-law relationships difficult. Personal quirks and cultural prescriptions can cause problems. Family interactions, too, make in-law relationships a challenge. While we can readily acknowledge that these forces impinge on our relationships, we don't have to let the complications stymie our dealings. Understanding the forces greater than ourselves that affect us can mitigate the instinct to blame the newcomer.

IRRECONCILABLE DIFFERENCES

There are times when family members dislike each other so completely that there may be no obvious set of fixes. Even in these situations, you are not impotent. You can be kind, gracious, generous, and even loving though your overtures are spurned or unrecognized.

The trick is to set goals for yourself that focus on your own behavior. You can meet these goals. But if you set goals based on how other people behave, you have no chance of meeting them. In other words, put the focus on your own behavior and not on the in-law's behavior, which is totally beyond your control. It does take practice, though. However, it is better than constantly reacting to the negative stimuli hurled at you. Over time, perhaps intractable situations will change. They may not, but unless you continue to be polite, there is little hope of transformation. With continued vigilance, many a family has healed their rifts as new family members enter and old ones die. Give peace a chance by creating a foundation on which to build a future. It is easy to assume that our in-laws will always remain forever outside the family circle. A healthy dose of ignoring some behaviors, choosing not to be annoyed, and continuing to embrace any small invitation might eventually heal an unpleasant relationship. You do not need to constantly put yourself in hurt's way; neither should you escalate the problems.

Markella's mother-in-law did not like her. She was from the wrong side of the tracks; she was also Greek, not Italian; and she had not gone to Harvard like their son. She was, in short, not good enough for the family. Her mother-in-law never used her name, instead referring to her as the "dark one," unlike her husband's brother's wife who was blond. This joke became stale in short order. Markella remained polite and dutiful. She liked her father-in-law and did not want to make her husband choose between her and his family. Although it was painful to be looked down upon, she attended all of the family events. When her daughter was not declared valedictorian at her sixth-grade graduation, her mother-in-law sent an e-mail to the extended family criticizing Markella's mothering. A cousin forwarded the message to Markella, who became enraged. She waited until her initial anger had subsided before calmly mentioning to her mother-in-law that if she felt Markella was doing something wrong to please tell her rather than discuss the problem via e-mail with the whole family. She did not want to feel like a doormat, but she did not want to cause a huge rift.

Later, 15 years into her marriage, Markella's mother-in-law became too frail to host the Seven Fishes Christmas celebration, an event that was very important to her Italian mother-in-law. Markella offered to host all 70 of her in-laws' customary guests. She made a delicious and gracious event with all of her mother-in-law's recipes. To her surprise, her mother-in-law was incredibly complimentary and bragged about her and her children to everyone at the party. Her mother-in-law's attitude notably and permanently shifted.

Markella showed great restraint in not escalating the animosity toward her mother-in-law. She was able to brush off her mother-in-law's disrespect in part because she felt like a worthy person herself. She realized that her husband had gone against his mother's wishes in marrying her and understood that it might take a while for her mother-in-law to accept her. She thus did not require him to confront his mother. Rather, she was satisfied by his affirmations to her that her actions were not the cause of the dissention. However, his mother remained a source of tension, if not of outright disruption. His mother may or may not have realized that in showing her disapproval she was causing trouble not just for her daughter-in-law, but also for the young couple. Many parents do not realize that their disapproval reverberates beyond the in-law child and into children's marriages. Markella would have, early on, if she had been included, honored her mother-in-law's culture. However, her mother-in-law may not have been willing to bury her hatchet until she faced her own decline. Only then did she realize that her daughter-in-law would be the one to help her live on in the family traditions. Markella would have accepted any olive branch rather than endure years of snide comments and snubbing. Markella's willingness to help was the catalyst for her mother-in-law's reevaluation.

It took Markella quite a while to get over her anger about the egregious e-mail, but she was glad that she had not yelled at her mother-in-law. Markella made her point and then dropped the subject. She was happy that she had never stooped to her mother-in-law's level of rudeness despite her hurt feelings. Now that she was in her mother-in-law's good graces, she made a decision to forget the past. Although her mother-in-law never actually apologized, Markella chose to accept her current compliments as an apology. She could make room for family happiness now. Though Markella did not deny her hurt and anger, she swallowed her pride in order to keep family peace.

This story also warns us all about the dangers of complaining via e-mail. Her mother-in-law's attempt to discredit her with the family was certainly beyond the pale of politeness. E-mail tar and feathering is always inappropriate. Markella showed enormous self-control in not completely cutting off her mother-in-law. Clearly her mother-in-law would have been well served if she herself had exercised caution.

Not all families reunite, but all of us can, like Markella, keep our self-image intact by focusing on being the best person we can be and not focusing on rude and insulting behavior. Not all people are wonderful, kind, and forgiving. Some people are cruel, insensitive, and unyielding. There are those who would rather be right (as they determine right) than congenial. Their self-righteousness may come from their personality, their long-held beliefs, or the beliefs of their community. They may feel so dedicated to their ideals that they cannot allow any person who deviates from their mold into their lives. In these cases, after you have done your part in attempting to get along and in being civil, you have the freedom to know that nothing more can be done. You have done the right thing. You are not the problem. Only then can you liberate yourself from the aggravation of being shunned or hurt by an inconsiderate, selfish, or cruel in-law. One type of behavior that cannot be ignored, however, is abuse.

ABUSE MUST BE ADDRESSED

There are times when we must speak up. With 25 percent of women experiencing abuse at some time in their lives, it is essential that any book about marital relationships touch on this surge.[7] We all hope that our family members will marry wonderful, caring people. Whether due to circumstances, upbringing, or personality, not all people do. Our own family member might be the abuser or the victim.

If you see or sense abuse, you must address it whether the abuser is from your side of the family or is an in-law. If you notice that a child, sibling, or parent has bruises or constant "accidents," you should inquire whether everything is OK at home. These could be signs of physical abuse. If you witness one partner constantly putting down the other or making humiliating comments, or constantly coercing his or her partner to do things the other doesn't want to do, you could be seeing psychological abuse. Let the person know that you are concerned and willing to help. If you notice that one partner must account for every penny spent, or that one partner withholds cash or uses money to threaten or force behavior, then you are seeing economic abuse. If you see one person controlling another by using sacred texts to manipulate their behavior and require complete obedience, this could be textual or spiritual abuse. This kind of abuse is particularly difficult for in-laws to recognize since they may be uncertain about what is acceptable behavior in another culture, although people know the difference in their own culture. If you suspect such abuse, read the texts to understand misinterpretations, contact several leaders and members of the group, or ask professionals in your community how to best approach your loved one. Again, the family member who was abused needs to know there is someone he or she can talk to and go to for help.[8]

Sexual abuse can occur both inside and outside of marriage. In the United States, marriage is not a license to rape another person.[9] Any coercive sex is abuse.

Men can engage in any of these abusive acts, but so can women. I repeat, when you suspect any kind of abuse, you must address it. If you cannot address abuse directly, you must get a surrogate—another family member, a friend, or a professional—to do so. Offer refuge and emotional support. Because abusers can appear to be perfectly nice, charming, and insightful people when they are not abusing, their abused partners may find it difficult to leave the situation. They are tied emotionally to the abuser, or they may feel that they are trapped with no other options because they have no money or skills and have children to support. It is often very difficult to leave an abusive relationship. Thus, instead of suggesting that the person leave the marriage, ask what is working in the relationship and what is not. If you are uncertain what to do or say—most of us are—you can anonymously contact hotlines, halfway houses, and support groups to get advice and assistance. Many communities now have these resources. You can look on the Internet to find resources to help you sort out how to help. In this way, you can help the victim figure out why he or she is staying in the relationship.

> *Jody married Rob, who seemed to be a really nice guy. But as the years went on, we noticed he constantly criticized her. We did not want to interfere, but the put-downs grew in frequency. I felt we needed to talk to both him and her. My husband felt strongly that we should stay out of their business. I just did not know what to do. Finally, I went to a lecture on domestic violence, and I understood that I had to speak to my child. My husband was not happy, and neither was I. After all, over the years I had grown fond of Rob. He was a good provider and seemed to love his children. I did not want to break up my daughter's marriage, but I saw her becoming quieter and quieter and a nervous wreck. I feared that this son-in-law whom I had grown to love was hurting my daughter.*

Confronting an abuser or suggesting that one partner should look closely at the relationship can feel like a betrayal to the other person. Few of us want to destroy marriages by pointing out the difficulties. When our own relative is the abuser, we feel shame. We also feel disloyal when we acknowledge the symptoms we see. Sometimes we wonder whether it is our business to intervene. We worry about causing disagreements with our own partners when we raise the issue of abuse. However, we do both partners a favor if we help them see the cycle of violence they are experiencing. One way is to share our observations without casting aspirations on either party. Another is to ask our children how they are feeling in their life. Our job when we sense abuse is to let our children and in-law children, parents, or siblings know that they can always talk to us and that we will help them out. Just as Mothers Against Drunk Driving has taught us that "friends don't let friends drive drunk," advocates for abused women and men have shown us that intervening can save a life. It takes courage to recognize the problem and even more courage to address it. When intervening in intimate relationships, both blood relatives and in-laws often feel uncertain of their role. In cases of suspected abuse—however uncertain—we must offer, at least, a sympathetic ear.

WHEN NOTHING WORKS

Not every in-law problem can be solved despite our best intentions. No relationship is trouble-free except in the movies. Even when we make a good-faith effort, sometimes we cannot succeed by talking or reaching out. It is then that we need to find a way to relate that is tolerable and does not rub the other family members the wrong way. Maybe you choose to focus on one aspect of the relationship that you can improve and repair in order to get some satisfaction. Maybe you just accept that not all problems can be solved and that acceptance alone takes pressure off. Maybe you find appreciation and caring from those outside your family circle. Focus on what you can do, but with the realization that improvement in relationships takes time and effort and does not always work. Sometimes all we can do is set the goal of improving our own behavior without the expectation that others will improve theirs. Then the dislike and annoyance of an in-law is less likely to taint what is good in our own life.

QUESTIONS

Note to parents: Please respond as both an in-law child *and* an in-law parent to explore how your own experience as an in-law child can inform your behavior as an in-law parent.

- What obligations do you feel you have to your in-laws?
- What obligations do you think your in-laws have that you do not wish to fulfill?
- What did you dream your relationship with your in-laws would be?
- How did it actually turn out?

- How do historical views of in-law relationships play out in your own life?
- What gendered patterns constrain your in-law relationships?
- What gendered patterns enhance your in-law relationships?
- When do you feel your in-laws have overstepped their boundaries?
- When do you think your in-laws feel you have overstepped their boundaries?
- Do you find it easier to relate to some of your in-laws than to others? If so, why?
- What aspects of your in-law relationships are ambiguous?

CHAPTER 2

Where Do I Fit In? The In-Law Parents Speak

INSTRUCTIONS NOT INCLUDED

All over the world, parents experience a kaleidoscope of hopes, joy, pain, and insecurity when their children marry. Even individuals in long-standing marriages have conflicting dreams. Some parents hope to incorporate the new in-law within their nuclear family, and others are content to let him or her remain on the periphery. Some parents react with pain and disappointment: "*I was hoping for a new daughter/ son, but we have nothing in common.*" Others express uncertainty: "*My son's wife thinks we treat our son like a child, but we are just trying to stay connected*" or "*I don't know—should I treat her/him like my other children? How do I actively bring her/him into our family circle?*" Still other parents feel cast aside: "*My daughter-in-law has taken my son from me. She won't let us visit. They rarely come to us*" or "*My son-in-law is always busy. When we visit, he's at the office, or working in his study or on his car.*" They may not like their child's chosen mate, or they may not want any disruptions to their own family. Some parents are leery of investing too much energy into the new partner, fearing future divorce. Others worry about being disconnected from their children and future grandchildren. Just like lions, tigers, and elephants on the nature channel, a child leaves his or her parents to create a new unit, ending one stage of life and beginning another. For the parents, this can feel like a loss.

All stages of parenthood can be understood as losses and gains, or exchanges. Sure, we lose the deliciousness of snuggling an infant, but we gain a curious toddler. We lose the toddler to school and gain time to focus on other aspects of our lives. As our children grow, we lose a playful young person but hopefully gain an interesting adult. At marriage, we do lose the primary loyalty of our now-adult child, but we gain some freedom and, potentially, another caring and loving family member.

NESTING AND EMPTY NESTING

The generations are not in sync, nor are they static. As the parental generation moves from first-stage parenting to the empty nest and then ideally to productive aging, the children typically move from separating to coupling, working hard, and parenting or feathering their nests. Of course, not all adult children couple, nor do all have children, but most will separate and join with another person for long periods. There will be periods of closeness and periods of distance between generations. There will be times when the children are so busy with their career and kids that they can't even answer phone calls or e-mails. Other times, the older generation is so stressed with caring for their other children and their own parents or dealing with an illness or focusing on their career that they drop the ball on communication.[1]

The needs and desires of one generation may be quite different from those of another generation, as exemplified in this Thanksgiving conversation.

> MOTHER-IN-LAW: *I am just so grateful to be 60 years old and have my health, two wonderful children, two in-law children I adore, and one grandchild and another on the way. I wish I could freeze this moment and just be surrounded by all of you forever.*
>
> DAUGHTER-IN-LAW: *I don't want to freeze this moment. I am eight months pregnant. I want to meet this baby. I want to get on with my life and family.*

SON-IN-LAW: *I don't want to freeze this moment. I am a low man on the totem pole at work. I get the worst shifts. I have to do miserable repetitive work. I want time to fly so I can begin my family and get to some interesting work.*

Even in the most loving families, life stages lead to different perspectives. Either generation might be caught in the middle with caretaking responsibilities of both younger and older family members.[2] The early years of marriage often occur while the younger couple is striving to build careers. They have little time for one another, much less either of their nuclear families. By contrast, the relative freedom and opportunity of the empty-nest years may leave parents more open to extended-family ties. They may have time and energy to give to those who may not have the time or energy to receive it.

To incorporate new members into the family, the parents must open the family circle. This can feel difficult for parents who enter the in-law relationship deeply embedded in the earlier stages of parenting their other children. These parents have their rules and regulations and may not want to expose their children to conflicting ideals.

Susan and David have three children: Catherine, 20, a college junior; Devin, 16, a high-school junior; and Tracy, 12 (going on 15), an eighth-grade girl. Catherine is engaged to Tom, 25, who works in information technology. They both live in his apartment. Their work and class schedules mean that there is great flexibility in their schedules; meals and sleep are at odd hours. Susan and David know about this living arrangement, though they do not openly acknowledge it. They live an orderly life, in which meals are at specific times, laundry is done on Monday, and bedtimes are well-prescribed. When the couple visits, the parents insist that they sleep in separate rooms. Susan and David do not discuss their reasoning with Catherine and Tom, as they believe parents rule their own roost and do not need to give explanations for their behavior. Besides, they are not comfortable talking about sex, particularly with a young man who is not yet a member of their family. They worry that the young couple's lifestyle will disrupt the order of their family life. Tom thinks his future in-laws are hypocrites and worries that they do not approve of him.

Susan and David need their routine to cope with their own two careers and their community and family responsibilities. They cannot afford to waste a minute if they are to keep order, support their children, and build their work lives. They also are trying to instill their social and religious values into their two younger children. They do not want either of their younger children to think that premarital sex is permissible. They are upset that Catherine is engaging in behavior counter to their beliefs but realize that, outside their home, they cannot control what she does. Susan and David can explain their reasoning to Tom and Catherine. It might mitigate Tom's disdain and reassure him that they like him. However, to do so would mean confronting the complexity of their own feelings, their affection for Tom, their disapproval of their daughter's lifestyle, and their worries about their other children, all of which take precious time and energy. Susan and David could agree to disagree openly with the couple but stand firm in their decision to set rules in their own home. In this way, they could share their concerns as parents and begin building an open relationship with their future son-in-law.

* * *

For other parents, as their family grows older, they could experience increased financial pressure from having to pay other children's expenses and health-care costs for their own aging parents.

When Gloria and Harold's son married, times were challenging. Their daughter still had two years of college remaining at a school where tuition was a financial stretch, even though she was a work-study student. Harold's parents both had health problems requiring financial, as well as physical and emotional, support. As much as Gloria and Harold wanted to include their daughter-in-law, their energy available for doing so was minimal. They hoped she would understand.

However, since their daughter-in-law may not really understand the family's obligations and financial situation, she might assume that Gloria and Harold dislike her. Unless they explain some of their circumstances to her, she may feel hurt or neglected. They do not need to share their bank account with her, but they can share their situation in broad terms. In this way, she will feel included.

Still others find that the nest may be emptying. It may be a time of less financial pressure as college bills and mortgages are paid—a time when the parents are free to roam.

> *Barbara and Henry see a new life ahead with the end of tuition and mortgage payments. They have enough set aside for a comfortable life in retirement. They had always wanted to get an RV and travel the country. Their only daughter, Laura, earned her master's degree and is teaching. She marries Eric, the man of her dreams. Sooner than planned, Laura gets pregnant, and Eric loses his job. The young couple needs to move into Laura's parents' house. Barbara and Henry are happy to let them use their home while they travel but do not want the kids and grandchild on a permanent basis.*

Hopefully by the time they return from their travels, Eric will have another job. However, he may not. Barbara and Henry will need to figure out for themselves whether they want to change their priorities. They may decide that as long as Eric is truly making a good effort to find work, the couple can remain. However, if so, they must clarify with both themselves and the young couple the tasks they are willing to share and those they are not. They may decide to charge the couple in-kind rent—that is, require housekeeping tasks in exchange for their housing. When the baby arrives, all may feel differently, so they will all need to reevaluate.

* * *

It is not always easy to be perfectly frank with either our children or our in-law children. However, unless we are honest about our aims, dreams, and requirements, we cannot honestly negotiate differences. Surviving difficult discussions is actually fortifying for families. It assures family members that they can differ and still be a part of the family unit.

The older generation may hope to fill their lives with more or less contact with their children, and during the first years of marriage, the new couple's primary focus may be on each other, not the extended family. Later, the adult children concentrate on their responsibilities to their own children. For the parents, this can feel dismissive, when, in fact, it's the natural course of development. The new couple is building its own nest. Their parents are not in the center. Some in-laws blame the new family member for pushing them aside. The conflict between the perspectives of two generations shows itself in attitudes toward vacation.

> *Anwar and Jackie had a two-week vacation in which they planned a second honeymoon. They had worked hard all year and looked forward to renewing the vibrancy of their courtship by hiking, schmoozing, and making time for loving. Anwar's parents were deeply hurt that they were not interested in using their vacation time to join the family on their annual trip, a tradition that had been taking place for 20 years. They made it clear that in their minds, Jackie was ruining their family's fun and cohesion. Jackie railed at her in-laws' demanding ways. Anwar was torn. He loved his nuclear family time but also knew he and Jackie needed time alone together.*

Most likely, when adult children go off on a romantic vacation, they are not trying to hurt or dismiss the older generation. They just want to enjoy each other. It is not easy for either generation to understand or figure out exactly what the new member's role is in the family. Because of this, it is easy to blame in-laws. Regardless of the particular issues, the task for the older generation is to incorporate the new family member into an existing family structure. This requires incorporating new ideas, new customs, and new ways of doing things.

LIFE KEEPS CHANGING

From the parents' viewpoint, it is difficult as well as exciting to absorb a new person into the family. Just as the arrival of child number two was complicated by conflicting emotions of joy, resentment, rivalry, curiosity, love, hatred, disillusionment, jealousy, and caring, so, too, is the entry of any other new member into the family.

The marriage of a child is like a new baby, a divorce, or a death—it involves reconfiguring the family.[3] Parents are unsure of how to rear-range their lives to include another person. In some families, there is no question that the newcomer deserves the family's loyalty. In others, the parents are uncertain, and in still others, the parents are unwilling to make any accommodations.

> *When Julie, a social worker, became pregnant, she married wan-nabe rock star Justin. Her mother, Myra, with some justification, was horrified that this pot-smoking waiter with musical ambitions was going to be the father of her grandchild, husband to her daugh-ter, and her son-in-law. She came to help after the birth. Justin would arrive home late at night with beer on his breath and one in his hand. When he'd finish the bottle, he'd throw it in the trash, not the recycle bin. Then, even though money was scarce, the "rock star" threw out leftover food, bought plastic bags instead of using recycled ones, and refused to repair anything in the house. A battle royal ensued. Myra did recycle at home, though when she was stressed for a big party, she jumbled all the garbage. Her unwillingness to bend the recycling rules, even when she did so herself, was a readily avail-able way for her to display her displeasure. However, her misplaced concerns prevented her from focusing on the core issue of Justin's irresponsibility.*

Myra could not change her daughter's decision. Like so many of us, she focused on a behavior rather than on the real problem, which was that she worried about the welfare of her daughter and grandchild and therefore disliked Justin. Also, it was painful for Myra to admit her sense of failure and disappointment in her daughter's choice of spouse. Moreover, by focusing on the environmental issue, she was unable to describe her frustrations to her friends without sharing with them her daughter's personal life and what she viewed as her own failure.

There is no Dr. Spock parents' guide to help Myra here. There are few guidelines anywhere. Like so many of us, Myra was unwilling to discuss matters regarding her adult children with friends who were a source of support when her children were young. She was embarrassed by what she perceived as her daughter's failure. She felt it reflected badly on her, and she did not want to denigrate her daughter's reputation by airing Julie's dirty laundry. She knew she was making a big deal out of garbage, but she did not know how to overcome her feelings of dislike and worry. What she could have done was help Justin feel comfortable with the baby by including him in the bathing or by teaching him to diaper the child. She could have shown interest in his music by asking him about it. Somehow, she needed to find a positive way to interact with him since the future would not change the fact that he was the father of her grandchild.

* * *

Incorporating new family members requires new behaviors, new methods of communication, and new narratives. Newness lacks the comfort of familiar and satisfying routine, but not all changes are due to the new person in the family, as change also happens when both we and the circumstances surrounding us change.

> Renee repeatedly called her daughter-in-law, Lucy, who did not pick up the phone and instead responded by text. At first Renee was hurt and worried that her daughter-in-law did not want to talk to her. To Renee, real communication meant talking, but to Lucy, communication took many forms. Upon reflection, Renee realized her daughter-in-law was responsive and had communicated with her. However, she still found electronic communication unsatisfying. She was uncertain whether to discuss this with Lucy. Renee was in new territory.

Despite knowing that communication modes have changed, Renee was taken aback by Lucy's response because of her own wish to communicate the old-fashioned way. She was surprised by the speed with which the younger generation communicates and a bit shocked that "acceptable" responses seemed universally to be so telegraphic, so curt, so seemingly uncaring. Renee's disappointment was due to societal or technological change in communication rather than to different needs or different definitions of closeness. Even those of us who text and use technology in our work lives are sometimes annoyed by the way technology has changed our personal interactions.

FAMILY MEMBER OR INDIVIDUAL?

As new parents, we went from being independent adults to intimate, 24/7 caretakers of our babies. We spent years figuring out how to make good lives for our children and still have some life of our own. Sometimes we railed at the burden of being responsible for others, and at other times we reveled in our children's companionship and accomplishments. Now, once again, we must revisit the process. We must build our own life without daily child-care responsibility. To maintain close ties with our own children, we need to open our family circle to include, if not embrace, new in-laws.

Figuring out how to sustain family bonds yet remain a fully functioning, independent adult is tricky. In the Western world, we put more emphasis on autonomy than some other cultures do. Individuals can, and often do, differ on the importance they place on autonomy or affiliation, and each person may shift over a lifetime. On a daily basis, the tension between independence and connection plays out in deciding how much time to spend together, how near one another to live, and what finances—if any—should or could be comingled. Each person, as well as each generation, is likely to have dissimilar and sometimes conflicting thoughts in each one of these areas. Most of us assume that our own ideas are the correct ones, that we know how close each generation should be and how much time each should spend with the other.

Parents may say, "*My kids are dutiful, but I have no place in their lives. I am not sure they care one way or the other. You would think the least they could do is to pretend to be interested.*" When the children and in-law children make decisions about everything from where to go for the holidays to what, how, and whether to practice a religion, parents feel pushed aside. For the older generation, the feeling of being discounted is particularly acute if one is single and has not created alternative groups with whom to celebrate holidays.

Parents not only want good relationships with their children and in-law children, but they also actually need these relationships to thrive.[4] Bad relationships with children and in-law children can add enormous strain to parents' lives. For each of us, small issues are magnified when we are already feeling vulnerable.

> *Debby's son and his wife visit a couple of times a year. They come to the house, mess up the rooms, and have breakfast and then leave to visit the son's friends. Debby dreads their visits. "They treat me like a hotel. I feel abused and taken for granted much of the time. I want to scream, 'If you're going to treat me like a hotel, then stay in a hotel!'" Debby remembers fondly enjoying coffee with her son before he married.*

Debby's son may assume that her house is still his home, and that his mother is thrilled that he is remaining connected to his local ties. Debby has forgotten how often she felt ignored when he lived at home. Debby blames the couple's fast exits on her daughter-in-law. But her daughter-in-law is merely taking signals from her husband. After all, it's his family. Debby is lonely and wants, if not expects, the young couple to spend every minute with her. She is sure to be disappointed. Realistic expectations are the foundation on which we build a supportive home. However, if Debby has a specific expectation, she might be pleasantly surprised that her son and daughter-in-law are willing to comply if she verbalizes it. Debby could say without anger, before the kids come, that she would like very much to spend some time with them—maybe a meal, maybe a walk. She could explain that she's flexible. When parents can state their needs and limit them in both time and scope, they allow their adult children to have their own agenda as well as spend some time with their families.

PEOPLE ARE ANNOYING

Individual personalities also play a part in enhancing or disrupting the development of the new relationship. One story told to me in many versions is illustrative:

> On my birthday [substitute Mother's Day, anniversary, etc.], my children and grandchildren took me out to McDonald's [substitute any low-end food chain, Wendy's, Taco Bell, etc.] for dinner at 4:30. The little ones were so proud to be celebrating me and my special day. It was so adorable!

But I also heard these same stories in a very different version:

> Can you imagine how insulting it was? On my birthday, my daughter and son-in-law took me and their kids to McDonald's [Wendy's, Taco Bell, etc.] for dinner at 4:30. They chose a restaurant I don't like and a time that was convenient only for them. My son-in-law is so cheap. He didn't consider me at all!

I think all readers would agree that we would rather be around the person who interprets our efforts positively than the person who interprets them negatively. It may, in fact, be that the children and grandchildren were thinking of their own convenience. Or it may be that one grandparent chose to view this as a positive inclusive event, and the other chose to see it as an insult and an opportunity to blame the in-law child.

Pessimism, condemnation, minimization, and judgment are all behaviors that we can change by first noticing them and then practicing alternatives. We can ask a friend to observe and help us see our own actions or even join a group of other concerned in-laws to learn new behaviors. Mutual help groups enable us to learn what aspects of our relationships are normal and which are unusual, as well as how others respond to difficult situations.[5] The Internet, too, gives us a chance to peek in on the lives of others. We can look at both parenting blogs and in-law blogs to hear other perspectives and to learn how others feel.

Parental personalities are not the only factors in facilitating or hindering relationships. It is easier to deal with the more optimistic in-law children. One person put it succinctly: *"Maybe it's the individual. I have two daughters-in-law. One I get along with. The other seems to want to keep me at a distance. I do try to treat them the same. But somehow one thinks I am great and the other thinks I am a pain in the neck."*

We have all dealt with difficult people in our families and elsewhere. Some of our own children qualify, and even some of us. Sometimes we ignore these difficult types. We recognize their annoying ways were apparent before we entered the picture. Their complaints or insults are not really about us. While we can't change the other person, we can figure out how to respectfully deal with him or her.

Sometimes we are so focused on ourselves that there is no room for anyone else. We need to make that room. We don't have to approve of every decision our in-law makes. We can acknowledge that people differ or we can continue to believe that our ways are the right ways. It may feel great to assure yourself that you are right, but it does little good. We all need to see both our own perspective and that of our children and in-laws in order to get along.

My father-in-law was fond of a cautionary poem with little literary merit but much wisdom:

> Here lies Mortimer Grey.
> He died defending his right of way.
> He was right, dead right
> As he sped along,
> But he's just as dead,
> As if he were wrong.

In-law parents can be right—dead right—in feeling that their children should spend more time with them but dead wrong about how they handle the relationships if they don't consider the others' view.[6] Before parents blame their in-law children, self-reflection is in order, which means confronting their own attitudes, their desires, and even their own aging.

RECIPE FOR SUCCESS

Parents are no longer center stage in their children's lives. The parental years of calling the shots are over. Parents are no longer the decision makers. They stand in the wings, on the periphery of their children's family drama. If our children regularly choose us over their spouse, there is probably a divorce in the future. A married child's loyalties need to lie elsewhere.

To maintain good relationships with our adult children, we need to try to love our children's spouses and welcome them into our family, regardless of our immediate reaction to them. If our offers of help are rebuffed, we can ask how we could be helpful. If, even after trying, we do not like our in-law children, we need to be the ones to find some redeeming feature or some common interest. It doesn't serve the parents' needs, or their children's, to engender animosity. Parents cannot just pretend to put up with an in-law. They need to work diligently to create situations or neutral topics that avoid confrontation.

Knowing when to confront someone or when to avoid an argument is an art, not a science. Experimenting, by commenting on small matters and asking for forgiveness when they are not well received, can help in deciding which actions are wiser. If, upon reflection, parents realize they cannot change the situation, they need to do their best to understand it. Otherwise, the likely result is unproductive resentment and anger, which could force children into a choice between their spouse and their parents.

When children marry, it is time for parents to act like the adults they are. Adults know they can't always get their own way. They know life is imperfect. They know they need to be disciplined and thoughtful in what they say and do. Gone are the days when they could disregard the feelings of others and think only of themselves and their own perspectives, if there ever really were such days.

Parents taught their children to share. Now it is their turn to remember those lessons. They have to share their children with their spouses, their siblings, their grandchildren, and the other in-law parents. This is not a time to measure; instead, it's a time to give what we can and hope it will be appreciated.

Only by listening with curiosity and understanding without trying to change the other person do we have a chance to connect. When we are willing to show ourselves as whole human beings, vulnerabilities and all, are we then able to expect our in-laws—and everyone else—to see us as such.

I encourage in-law parents—and indeed the children—to think of good motives for behavior before they think of bad ones. When you visit your kids and your son-in-law is away at work past midnight, assume he is building a career, not hiding from you. Or when your daughter-in-law doesn't tell you about a lunch she had with a mutual friend, do not assume she is trying to keep secrets from you. Instead assume she has been too busy or it slipped her mind.

In so many aspects of life, our head and our heart tell us different stories. We will never completely resolve this dissonance, but we can learn to live with it. If we focus on our children's happiness and satisfaction, instead of focusing on our disappointment, we have a key to greater joy. Of course, our children, just like us, do make compromises, and we can either dwell on them or bask in their flexibility. We can applaud their efforts at making the best of challenging situations. We can encourage them to become part of their new families even as they continue to be a part of ours. We find other ways to be proactive. One mother-in-law wrote the following to me:

> I have three sons. When they married, I wrote my daughters-in-law a letter telling them what kind of mother-in-law I wanted to be. I told them if I didn't follow this, all they needed to do was wave this letter in front of me. One time, one of my daughters-in-law did wave it at me, and I knew I had overstepped my bounds. I stopped. It worked.

It would be wonderful if we all could be flexible and understand ourselves. Even those of us who can do this most of the time will have lapses into rigidity and blindness. The best we can do is stay our own hand, wait until the anger subsides, and in lieu of that apologize when we do fly off the handle.

Otherwise, we are likely to damage either our relationship with our child or in-law or their marriage. Parents can inadvertently wreck a child's union without even realizing it by insisting their own ways are the only ways.

QUESTIONS

- How did each of your in-law relationships change for better or worse over time and through many stages?
- How did you and your in-laws negotiate these changes?
- What sorts of tensions arose?
- How did you deal with them?
- In what situations do you thrive?
- In what situations do you feel they thrive?
- In what situations do you feel minimized?
- In what situations do they feel minimized?
- How did you incorporate the new family member into your world without infringing on the newlyweds?

CHAPTER 3

How Many People Did I Marry? The Adult Children Speak

MORE THAN I BARGAINED FOR

Many Westerners marry a person and only later realize that they actually married a family. Today, with many couples living together before any ceremony, they may make this discovery prior to any formalities. Sometimes the lesson comes early on when the dating couple's plans to go hiking are trumped by a request to repair a father's screen door. For others the insight comes right before the wedding, when some "strangers" (i.e., the future in-laws) have the audacity to think they have a right to insist on the time and place of the wedding and the guest list. Still others make this discovery soon after the wedding, when weekend plans to plant a garden are replaced by a request to shop for a new dress with one of their moms. Sometimes, it's the siblings who make demands: they need money or help with the kids. For other couples this discovery comes only when a parent or sibling becomes ill. Suddenly, the spouse is putting the family of origin first. Romantic notions of love and even the routines of daily life are rudely interrupted when family members claim time, effort, or money from a spouse. The whole family seems to be more than they bargained for when they agreed to tie the knot.[1]

YOURS OR MINE

When a couple gets together, each partner has a different definition of the "usual and customary" family obligations. One person thinks once they have grown and flown the coop, they have no obligations to anyone in their birth or adopted family. Another person may feel closely bonded to his or her parents and want to sustain that relationship. For one member of the couple, the nuclear family—Mom, Dad, and sibs—is all that requires obligatory attention. For the other member, the whole extended clan—aunts, uncles, and first and second cousins—has claim to the younger person's considerations. Or one partner accepts social obligations but absolutely rejects monetary ones.

Suddenly, the couple sees that its shared but limited resources of time, energy, and money are stretched in ways that one partner accepts and the other sees as inappropriate or unfair. The conflict that arises between the couple has ramifications through the generations, since giving money to parents may preclude giving money to children.

> *Patel and his mother are very close. She divorced when he was young. She remarried a man whom she thought owned his own business, when in fact his creditors owned it. When Patel started earning money, his stepfather frequently turned to him for loans. Patel saw granting these as part of a son's obligation to his mother. Now that Patel is married, his wife, Kendra, sees these requests as part of an unending chain that will ensure that they can never afford children. Patel is torn between two loyalties: his mother and his wife. He makes a good salary, yet he knows his wife's concerns are valid. They cannot afford to continue to lose money on his stepfather's poor deals. Clearly, this dispute is causing tension between the couple and can create a rift with his mother.*

As a good Indian son, Patel is obliged to support his mother. If Patel neglects his commitments to his mother, he will surely lose respect in both his own eyes and hers. Kendra feels differently. She would certainly help parents in a crisis, but she sees these requests for money as an unending cycle. Moreover, she does not believe parents are her first responsibility. She also does not want to give money to a man who has proven himself incapable of staying out of debt. The two need to resolve their differences but also figure out a way that they can help his mother without allowing her husband to squander the money. In the long run, Patel will be more protective of his mother if he sequesters the money from his stepfather. Patel could buy his mother what she needs instead of giving her cash. On the other hand, he and his wife will need to reconcile their different senses of obligation. Otherwise, they will find themselves constantly arguing, and Kendra will be sure to have a contentious relationship with her mother-in-law. Every culture and every family negotiates a whole array of responsibilities. While the difference in cultural prescriptions is obvious here, it exists in many families.

The young couple may not understand the importance of in-laws until they themselves become ill or lose a job and the in-laws come to the rescue. The siblings may offer help when no one else comes forward. Family members are a social safety net for each other since most of us would not leave relatives destitute. Most of us hope a family member would help us out in our tough times (and all lives have tough times). New in-laws can be a source of great joy or enormous aggravation. No matter what the definition of family may be, being a member brings with it both obligatory and voluntary expectations. Some are pleasurable and some are not. One's tolerance for unpleasant interactions is based on past experience, a sense of duty, and the ratio of current benefits to perceived costs. Sadly, we don't gain the benefits of family support without some unpleasant obligations.

The in-law tie, like the step relationship, is formed neither by blood nor by personal consent. One is stuck or blessed with what comes along with one's spouse and with only a dim idea of how this new family is part of his or her life. It leads the in-law children to declare, "*That woman [or man] knows no boundaries,*" "*She is interfering,*" or "*My father-in-law is so controlling.*" In-law blogs are filled with negative comments like this one: "*My in-laws expect us to spend every moment with them. I feel like screaming, 'If you want grandchildren so badly, give us some time to make them!'*" Bad feelings lead many in-law kids to shun their spouse's parents.

WARRING PARTNERS

Sometimes interactions with the older generation cause arguments between the young spouses. The new husband wants to spend time with his family while the young wife wants to spend time with hers. She resents that their money goes to help his dad and not hers. He is tired of spending holidays with her family. Each one is resentful of claims of superiority of the other's family values or skills in any arena. *"I'm tired of hearing how accomplished your family is. Mine are good people, too!"*

Demands, or what are perceived as demands, from the older generation evoke pain, anger, and hurt in the younger generation. It can seem easier to avoid the older generation than deal with the inevitable tension created. *"You always take your parents' side. You never listen to me."* Conflicting loyalties lead to unhappiness. Spouses want affirmation from their partners that they are right. But the partner makes his or her own judgment, feels no need to take one side or the other, and lets the chips fall where they may. Each partner's perspective is modeled on birth-family patterns. Many misunderstandings arise because in-laws do not understand subtle differences in family culture and family politics, and if they do, they do not agree.

Eric and Sheila have been married for three years. Eric's father buys a new car and wants to give the young couple his two-year-old Honda. Eric jumps at the chance for new wheels. But Sheila grew up in a family, though not poor, in which the children were expected to work for any purchase. If she were given a reward, it was because she had achieved something or had earned the money for it. She cannot imagine that her in-laws do not have ulterior motives. She is uncertain why or in what way they want a return, but she is positive that this car comes with strings attached. In Eric's family, by contrast, there is nothing exceptional about this offer. His parents help him and their other children without expecting any quid pro quo. Sheila just cannot believe that his parents would be generous for no reason at all. In her view of the world, only hard work pays off. Any other type of gain is suspect. Sheila is angry that Eric will not even entertain the notion that his parents are trying to weasel their way into their life. Eric is hurt that Sheila suspects his parents' intentions and angry that she refuses to accept his view. Everyone is upset.

While we would hope that we could each see others' perspectives, we all see the world primarily through the lenses with which we have been raised. We use our own pasts to interpret the present. How we make a place for ourselves in our spouse's family and how we learn and come to accept their ways of doing things while remaining a loyal member of our own family are serious challenges. Sheila may actually feel bad that her own family would never have made such an offer. For her to accept the car, she would need to acknowledge that her parents were correct in encouraging their children to work hard yet also agree that gifting the car is an act of generosity and not manipulation. Sheila wants Eric to agree with her thinking, but he cannot because he grew up having completely different experiences. Neither yet understands that their families each had encouraged worthwhile but different values.

* * *

Doing things the way the other family does them can feel disloyal to one's family of origin. While the individuals in the new couple are finding a place in their new family, they are picking and choosing what aspects of their old families they want to incorporate into their own nest. Trying new approaches can feel traitorous as well as exciting. If they reject a sentiment from their old family, that family may be hurt. However, if they resist the other parents' values, the new family may be insulted. Every new couple's life is a series of negotiations as they find their own unique paths and blend new and old ways.

Some decisions do pose difficult dilemmas for young couples. They learn quickly that they cannot always please everyone—even themselves.

Ibrahim and Betsy have three kids under the age of six and live near her parents who help Betsy out every day with the brood. Ibrahim is then offered a better job in another state, close to where his parents live. He welcomes the move, as his parents are becoming frail. They fight about whose parents are putting more pressure on them concerning the move. Neither realizes that this disagreement is only part of the problem. They have different desires and needs. Each of them wants to be near his/her parents. Betsy may need or want help with the children since Ibrahim is always working. Ibrahim feels that he must care for his parents, and living so far away from them makes it difficult. Rather than confront their own problems of sharing the workload and fulfilling filial duties, they pass the blame to their parents and do not confront each other. Their avoidance of the cracks in their young marriage will not make the imperfections go away and is likely to disturb both sets of in-law parents.

Blaming in-laws for problems between the couple is a common means of avoiding internal family difficulties.

*   *   *

Shortly after Carol and Wei-Lu decided to marry, they realized that they would need to be very sensitive to their cultural differences. He exclaimed with delight, "Now that we have decided, we must go and ask my parents," to which she responded, "Yes—we must go tell my parents." They laughed but knew they had challenges ahead. From that point on, whenever they had a disagreement, they assumed that they had cultural differences that would require either compromise or a way to honor both traditions. Of course, some of the time, the problems were plain old personality quirks that every couple must deal with.

Because Carol and Wei-Lu were cognizant of the enormous differences in their upbringings, they approached every disagreement as a problem to be solved rather than as evidence of character flaws. This helped calm their anger when difficulties arose. They were, at least initially, able to blame that amorphous category of cultural differences rather than each other or their parents.

LET ME DO IT MY WAY

Every man is a king in his own castle, and every woman is a queen—that is, until the in-laws come, and then the troubles begin. One friend I have complains of headaches that come on three weeks before her in-laws arrive. She knows that criticism is coming. For the parents-in-law, it is all very ambiguous. If they are family, they may feel that they can come in and rearrange the books, take over the food preparation, and comment on the decor. If, however, they are outsiders, they have none of these privileges. The fact is, they are both family and outsiders—it is all very murky. While in-law parents tell me how helpful they are when they visit, in-law children complain, "*They come and take over. He does the lawn, she does the laundry. She tells me I don't fold right. He tells us we should edge the flower beds. I wish they would just leave us alone. Thank you very much—we will do our things our own way!*" Others say, "*There is no pleasing them. We just aren't as capable and aren't as fit as they were as parents or as housekeepers. In short, we can do nothing right.*"

Indeed, in-law parents may be critical, and many are. But it is also possible that in-law children are insecure. Comments intended to be helpful are taken as criticisms. Who among us is not insecure when we are learning? And isn't much of life learning to tackle new situations? There is plenty of room for taking comments as criticism and plenty of room to be seen as meddling and nagging. With every decision, the young couple is defining their self-concept to themselves and to the world. A big wedding or a small one? A French provincial couch or a modern one? Recycled or new? When young couples choose among multiple ways of doing any task, they are choosing how to live their lives. Some will value cleanliness and order more than others. Some will value a beautiful home, while others prefer travel. Embedded in each of these decisions is a whole complexity of thought. When the older generation questions the choice, it feels like disapproval and like an attack on the couple's taste and lifestyle. Questioning their choices feels like a personal insult.

A friend recently reminded me that when I was newly married, my mother-in-law brought her fabulous home-baked goods to my home. I was annoyed. I thought she believed I could not be a good wife to her son. Thirteen years later, when I had three children and was commuting an hour for my doctoral studies, I was grateful and thrilled when she filled my freezer.

Nothing changed in my mother-in-law's behavior. Instead, a lot changed in me and in the environment. The women's movement had encouraged me to define my wifely role in new ways. I felt proud and secure in my new definition, which did not include cooking well but did include providing adequate meals and loving my family. I no longer saw my mother-in-law's cooking as a threat. I now understood how complex bringing up children is and was ready to admit I needed all the help I could get. I now saw her cooking as a gift and a confirmation of my life choices. Over the years, my mother-in-law and I had come to respect each other for the very different attributes and skills we each had.

Sometimes we are afraid that when others get to "really" know us, they will find us unworthy. Thus, we hide our vulnerabilities or even our true selves. New parents, for example, hold fast to the advice of experts since their own experience is limited. Some read all of the books they can and talk endlessly with friends before making any of the numerous decisions surrounding a new baby: Nursing or bottle-feeding? Cloth diapers or disposable? A nanny or child care? They are aware of the awesome responsibility they have in raising a child. Once they decide, they may be unwilling to hear opposing views or suggestions for modifications; doing so will only increase their underlying uncertainty and sense of inadequacy.

Issues run from the trivial to the more consequential. A young new cook puts pot holders on hooks in her pantry and does not want to hear her father-in-law's suggestion that the pot holders would be handier in a drawer near the stove. A young couple opts to live downtown to be close to their work and hears the father-in-law's suggestions about double locks because they are on the edge of a dangerous neighborhood as bigotry rather than an idea worth considering. One way we all deal with the uncertainty of our choices is by holding fast to our decisions and discounting the opinions of others.

When parents-in-law give suggestions, it can seem like an intrusion or an uninvited assumption of a parental role. When the advice begins to annoy, one young man uses humor and, without anger, says, "*I can only take one father at a time.*" He recognizes the lack of clarity in the new family roles but also signals that he cannot tolerate the notion that his in-laws assume that they can intervene in his life. Sometimes in-law children are happy to include their spouse's parents as friends, colleagues, or fellow travelers but not as parents. Respectful humor works well to make it clear that advice is not always welcome.

TOO MUCH TIME, TOO MUCH ENERGY

It takes time and energy to figure out how close you want to be to your in-law family. And it takes time and energy to figure out their family code of conduct. It even takes time and energy to agree to disagree. So much newness can be exhausting. For those who are happy with their own families or those who have never had much use for their own, it hardly seems worth the effort—that is, until one needs financial, physical, or emotional support from the extended family. However, if the couple and the in-laws do not come to some mutual understanding of these extended-family obligations, decades of negative feelings, or even hatred, can ensue.

Sometimes the in-law kids just don't like the in-law parents. Perhaps they are unlikable, or perhaps they are just different in an uncomfortable way.

Bill's father-in-law, Randall, has more conservative views than Bill does on just about every subject. Randall tries endlessly to engage Bill in discussions of politics or religion or race. Bill knows his father-in-law's definition of a discussion is for him to pontificate and for Bill to listen. Bill also knows that if he contradicts his father-in-law, the discussion will degenerate into a yelling match. He could listen and not react or banter with his father-in-law, but that is not his style. He would rather leave the room, and he usually does. Randall is frustrated. For Bill, Randall is doubly a time sucker. His persistent efforts to engage Bill are one problem, but the fact that he takes Bill away from his wife is another. What's worse is that these encounters make

his wife upset with both him and her dad, and he is the one who has
to mop up her tears.

Randall continually reaches out to Bill in a manner that doesn't work. Both men know that they are miles apart politically. If Randall would try to connect with Bill on less contentious topics, they might do better. Bill is trying to be a good son-in-law. He wants to avoid conflict yet not avoid his father-in-law, since Randall is indeed the father of his wife. However, there are some people who enjoy themselves by provoking arguments. When no common ground can be found in discussion, pleasantries and sports talk serve to lower the temperature. They won't create intimacy, but they can hold controversy at bay.

NOT SUCH A BIG GENERATIONAL DIVIDE

As is becoming evident, many in-law complaints are similar on both sides of the generational divide. Like in-law parents, in-law children have different personalities. Some are restrained, and some are welcoming. Some are optimistic, and some are pessimistic. Some avoid contact with their in-laws because that contact offers little more than stress and discomfort. Many would rather have a good relationship with their in-laws or, at least, a cordial one, but they do not like the sense that they are always under scrutiny, always being judged. They want some contact but fear that if they let the in-laws in, it will be like giving them an inch while they take a mile. Some miss that safe haven of unconditional love that they found in their own nuclear family. Some are concerned with being disloyal to that family of origin. All are trying to figure out what the role of these in-laws is in their lives.

Even when in-laws have good relationships and delineated roles, misunderstandings and hurts arise.

Mildred's mother-in-law, Sheryl, frequently babysits for her grand-
son. Mildred is grateful for her help, as her consulting job makes it

difficult to find child care for all of the irregular hours she works. She arrives home one day to discover that Sheryl had taken her son to buy his first Halloween costume. She is disappointed and a bit annoyed as she realizes that this task had special meaning to her as a mother.

Sheryl thinks that she is being helpful, while Mildred feels that she is taking over her maternal role. However, Mildred understands that she cannot criticize her mother-in-law because she is indebted to her and because she has never told her that she was looking forward to buying the costume with her son. All this insight, however, does not stop her feelings or the miffed look she gives her mother-in-law. Sheryl does not understand why Mildred gives her this annoyed look. Being aware of every eventuality or the complexity of another person's feelings is virtually impossible. However, we can be aware that there will be misinterpretations of our good intentions.

The problems of both generations are similar. Both generations are ambivalent. Both generations feel misunderstood. Neither generation knows *how* to bridge the divide. Parents try to help and it is taken as criticism. Children try to build their own strong marital bonds and it is taken as a rejection of the parents. Both generations are afraid to give up the habits with which they are secure. Both are afraid of making mistakes and afraid of the unknown.

We can learn from those who made positive comments about their in-law parents: "*My mother-in-law is fabulous. Although she doesn't babysit regularly, I can count on her in a crisis*" or "*My father-in-law is a great cheerleader.*" These in-law children have chosen to focus on the good attributes of their in-laws. They give credit to the in-laws for those qualities they love in their spouse. They understand that their loved one is a composite of many influences and therefore do not blame the in-laws for the flaws they see in their spouse (and we all see flaws in everyone except, of course, ourselves). Any amount of warmth and support is accepted and appreciated. Focusing on the positives tips the scales toward seeing one's in-laws as a blessing rather than a curse.

Good relationships with in-laws are earned, not assumed. Those who blame receive blame in return. Those who accept are more likely to be accepted. Curiosity and a willingness to entertain suggestions instead of rolling your eyes in disdain help avoid troubles.

* * *

Many parental in-laws do invest emotional energy, time, and even money into their in-law children. They weave them into the fabric of their lives, and when a couple splits, the whole family unravels and has to mend. Like it or not, one becomes part of an extended family. One's own attitudes play a large part in making the new family comfortable or uncomfortable.[2] I recently attended the funeral of Jeffrey Stamps, a brilliant systems theorist and a good friend. Jeff was a wonderful human being. His son-in-law, Jay Albany, gave the eulogy we would all hope to receive—one that was well deserved in this case.[3]

> *My father died when I was 14, and I have always felt so blessed that Jeff has been a second father to me....*
>
> *Jeff was always showing me how to do things. He had a scientific approach to even what would seem like ordinary tasks: a system for everything. The perfect way to start a fire in a crosswind. When and how to use a bowline knot. But most memorable of all, at least to me, someone who made very regular trips schlepping back and forth from New York, was how to pack the car....*
>
> *For Jeff there was an absolute science to packing a car, and that man could fit any number of bags and irregular shaped objects into a vehicle. He would lay all the bags out in a staging area, and carefully formulate a plan for the most efficient use of space, even allowing—in advance—for that one last bag of food Jessica, my mother-in-law, was sure to race out of the house with seconds before we pulled out of the driveway....*
>
> *I remember one time Miranda, my wife, thought it would be a good idea for me to shadow Jeff packing so I could pick up a few pointers. I went out to the car, and I wanted to be helpful, so I promptly grabbed the heaviest bag and tossed it in the middle of the trunk. "Not so fast young man," he said. "You have much to learn about car packing."*

I am happy to report that a few months ago, Jeff gave me a ceremo-nial badge for having achieved a Better Than Average merit badge in car packing. Unfortunately, I am not cut out to be an Olympian in this event.[4]

Jay could easily have been insulted by his father-in-law's pedantic way, but instead Jay chose to focus on the love and affection that pro-pelled Jeff to counsel Jay in trunk packing. He knew what mattered most. In his words, *"The topic that united us most was our shared love for his daughter Miranda. It was a great topic."*[5] Jay took an active part in mak-ing the wonderful relationship he had with his father-in-law. He took Jeff's tutelage as an expression of love and a chance to learn. He chose not to see it as criticism. He found common interests and expanded his own interests to increase those commonalities. I have heard many sons-in-law complain that their father-in-law is a "control freak," that every-thing has to be done his way, and that he is rigid and not open to new ideas. Jay did not do this. Jay had the confidence in himself to realize that he could learn and that his father-in-law had love to give. He was not in competition with his father-in-law. Instead, he took advantage of a second chance to relate to an older man, an opportunity that had been cut short earlier in his life when his own father had died.

It really is quite simple to create working relationships with one's in-law parents. As one 47-year-old daughter-in-law quipped, *"Just invite them, include them, and be nice to them."* However, like everything else in life worth doing, it takes discipline. You may need to complain to a friend to let off steam, but then regain your perspective. What follows are some helpful hints.

Focus on the Positive

Begin by assuming that your in-laws have good—not bad—motives and that they are not "out to get you" or your spouse. Make a list of all the good qualities they have. Forget the ones you don't like. This takes restraint. But you can get into a good habit by noticing and focusing on the positives. Assume the in-laws are merely trying to find a place for themselves in the lives of the people they care about. Remember that your definition of what is socially appropriate, or what boundaries are necessary, may be different from that of your in-laws. Differences are not the same as malevolent acts.

Fake It Until You Make It—Maybe the Good Feelings Will Follow

Do the right thing. Send those birthday wishes. Be polite. You will never, ever regret having been civil, though you may regret having been rude. The momentary pleasure of feeling self-righteously justified in yelling at someone rarely serves to grease communication. As my mother used to say, "*You* be the big one; *you* show you can get above the anger and act with graciousness." At least you get to feel like a hero.

Be Generous in What You Accept as an Apology

People apologize in many ways. They don't always use the words *I am sorry*. Sometimes they just move on and act as if nothing happened. This may be their way of saying, "*You are worthwhile enough to me that I don't want to damage the relationship*." Other times people say they are sorry and don't mean it. Don't look for the perfect apology. Perfection can freeze us from enjoying the adequate or from seeing even the tiniest olive branch.

Criticize Your Own Family, but Let Others Criticize Theirs

Since each family has a whole web of relationships and experiences known only to the participants, it is best to avoid putting down your in-law family. Of course, a corollary to this advice is to never gossip about family members—yours or theirs. Be the repository of information, not the spreader of bad deeds.

QUESTIONS

- What would my ideal relationship with my in-laws be?
- Who do I think should be treated as family?
- What do my in-laws think should be the ideal relationship with me?

- What would my spouse like my relationship to be with her or his parents? Siblings? Extended family?
- When do I get upset with my in-laws?
- When does anger at my in-laws spill over into fights with my spouse?
- When do I feel criticized by my in-laws?

CHAPTER 4

Have I Been
Displaced? The
Siblings Speak

BEFORE THE COUPLING

In the beginning, there are the siblings. They love each other, they hate each other. They play together, they fight together. The issues are great and miniscule. The intensity of the feelings underlying these childish loves, spats, and jealousies never completely disappears. It rears up in the 20s, 30s, and even beyond the 40s.[1] As life progresses, the subjects of the spats evolve into disagreements about lifestyle, money, and disciplining of children. The siblings may have been very close and shared every detail of their lives, or they may have been constantly at odds, showing each other up at every turn. Some may be from big sibling groups who know each other so well that they interrupt to complete each other's sentences.

When a sibling marries, the spouse of the sibling-in-law may become frozen in the family pecking order by association. That is, he or she may take on the status of the spouse becoming the success or the failure of the family, the good one or the bad one. Siblings-in-law marry into an existing situation filled with the baggage of years of competition and/or caring of which they may know little or only one side.

Once there is an engagement, subtle changes begin to occur. Even the in-law-to-be who has been around for years now has a new status—one the wedding will confirm. Siblings sense it, as does the rest of the family. The process is interactive. The range of reactions can vary widely. One sibling may welcome this newcomer into the family with openness: "*I always wanted a brother and now I have one!*" Another may find it hard to do so and claim, "*He's different from us.*" Some declare derisively, "*I'm glad I am not married to him*" or "*He likes her, I don't have to.*" Some feel competitive with the newcomer whom they see as richer, prettier, or smarter. Others may feel the newcomer isn't up to the family's standards. He or she may seem less trustworthy, less well-off, or less well-connected than "*our family.*" Some will resent the attention and time this newcomer gets from friends and family, and young siblings—those under the ages of 10 or 11, for example—may not even understand the significance of the whole relationship.

The in-law's own family experience will color his or her role in the interaction. Some new in-laws may consider any attention to birth siblings on either side to be completely optional. For others, sibs are part of familial bonds with all sorts of implied obligations. An only child on either side of the new pairing is unlikely to understand either the intimacy or the aggravation of the sibling relationship.

The new person who enters brings subtle changes to the whole culture of the family. The in-law notices the grating habits that the rest of the family has come to overlook or just live with. He or she may even escalate them.

Jane, an only child, marries Robert, who is one of four siblings, each of whom has three children ranging in age from 17 to 7. Jane had grown accustomed to having the whole holiday plan revolve around her and her needs. Robert's family has to accommodate the plans of many family members. In order to do this, the family does not sit down for a family meal; rather, they graze when it fits into their schedules. Jane complains that the holidays do not seem like family times. Robert relates this to his mother and father. His father immediately says he, too, is bothered by this informality and suggests to his wife that she consider changing this practice. She becomes livid and says to her son, "How dare your wife question the way our family lives." Jane has no understanding of the complexities of bringing a large family together. In addition, she has unwittingly touched on a sore spot in her in-laws' marriage. She has wandered into a minefield of a long-standing disagreement.

Jane assumes her form of family celebrations is the best one. As an only child, she has not had to negotiate with the needs of her siblings. Her family holiday celebrations are far less complicated to plan since they involve fewer schedules. Instead of enjoying her new family's fluid gatherings, she only longs for what she knows. Jane's mother-in-law has had long experience in trying to meet the needs of all family members. She knows that each parent and each teenager has multiple obligations and desires beyond the immediate family. She does not want to pit their schedules against each other. Thus, she has decided that even more important than sitting down together is the opportunity for the family to *be* together informally. Her husband, who does not take an active part in planning family events, has longed for the Norman Rockwell version of holidays. Jane does not know her husband agrees with his father and for that reason related her comment to his mother. She also does not realize her mother-in-law resents her husband's criticisms since he does not help with holiday preparations. Jane's comments now put her in the middle of a family disagreement. Sometimes when the newcomer takes cues from his or her partner, he or she risks being held responsible for revealing or escalating already-existing family tensions. Families are complex political organizations, and until one is well versed in its norms and intricacies, one can easily become unsuspectingly embroiled in controversies.

* * *

If there is no love lost between the new in-law and the sibs, even sibs who were once best friends and playmates can fall further and further away. The in-law may be reluctant to spend time or cooperate with someone he or she does not like. Gradually, small snubs grow without either person knowing it, resulting in both parties losing a potential source of support. For the newcomer, the ways he or she is welcomed into the family are unlikely to be forgotten.

> *Lucien did not like his brother's fiancée, Briana. He couldn't say why. He just did not like her. Because he did not come to the engagement party, Briana felt she did not need to reach out to him. His toast at the wedding was mostly about his closeness with his brother—he barely mentioned the bride. Briana was hurt. She was reluctant to attend any family functions at which Lucien would be present. She was unable to overlook his behavior.*

Even though Lucien did not like Briana, there may have been other factors, such as cost or work commitments, that prevented him from attending the engagement party. Lucien may have seen the function of his toast as a chance to laud his brother. It is also possible that his dislike of Briana was actually fear of losing his brother. Briana's interpretation of all his behaviors was that he intentionally slighted her. This assumption justified her anger and her decision to give up trying to befriend him. Their relationship will remain frozen unless Briana is willing to be generous and understanding of Lucien's slights. Hopefully, over time, Lucien will be willing to apologize and change his view of Briana. If unaddressed, these small slights can lead to a lifetime of distance.

TA-DA! THE WEDDING

Though the "bridal industrial complex" and our consumer culture will have you think that the napkin colors, flowers, favors, and other wedding paraphernalia are the most important decisions in planning a wedding, they are not. Family relationships are. The choices you make about these relationships will have the most enduring consequences. Bridezilla and Groomzilla may get their way for the wedding day, but those willing to think beyond the big day will earn a much better start in their new family.

The excitement of the wedding simultaneously brings out the best and worst in everyone in the family. The sibs are not immune. Sibs may watch the wedding planning with a careful, comparative eye. They want to be sure that this couple is treated just as they were. They may be very sensitive to any consideration from the newcomer and feel no reluctance about creating a scene.

> *Doris did not want any bridesmaids when she married Milton because she thought the whole idea was silly. Her sister was the only attendant. Milton, like so many grooms, left the details of the wedding to the bride. He neglected to mention that his unmarried, older sister, Renate, was upset, and she never voiced to Doris how important being a bridesmaid was to her. At the wedding, Renate blamed Doris for all that seemed wrong. She did not like her table. She commented that the service was too slow and that her food was cold. For Renate, Doris could do nothing right after overlooking her as a bridesmaid. Five years later, Doris had two children under the age of two and broke her leg. Renate had just been laid off and could have helped out, but she still held on to her anger and hurt from the wedding and refused to do so.*

Early slights, no matter how unintentional, can lead to long-term ill will. Doris thought the wedding was hers to design, and she never thought to consider how important this day might be for her sister-in-law who idolized her brother. Milton did not realize that he should act as communicator of his sister's position. Doris did not think about the pressure Renate might feel about her own social life since she had no marriage prospects and was older than her brother. She took Renate's insults about the wedding as personal disapproval rather than as a sign of Renate's hurt. Doris did send her birthday gifts but tended to only invite Renate over when she and Milton had other dinner guests. Renate tended to escalate every minor comment into an insult, and her resentment grew from an annoyance to justification for feeling no obligation, whatsoever, toward her sister-in-law.

The wedding is more than the couple's big moment. It is also an opportunity to get off on the right foot with the new expanded family. It is an opportunity for the couple and all the in-laws to find common ground in a shared experience. Giving all of the sibs wedding roles, no matter how small, helps. They can pass out programs or welcome guests. They can wear corsages and boutonnieres to identify them as part of the bridal party. They can give a toast at the reception. After all, this day also marks a change in their lives. Their sibling's primary loyalty is no longer to the original family circle. Including siblings brings them into the new circle. Even before the nuptials, including your sibs-in-law of all ages in an activity of any sort, whether it be a board game, a walk, or simply watching TV together, will help smooth the path. Include them in the bachelor and bachelorette parties or in shopping for the dresses. Any activity will create some common memories.

AFTER THE HONEYMOON

Even if the sibling and the in-law were best friends before the coupling, the marriage signifies a change, and jealousies can arise. Siblings of a newly coupled person may feel that they are losing their best friend or a playmate. They resent this new person who is co-opting all the time and energy of their brother or sister and begrudge sharing resources with an intruder, even if that intruder had been around a good while. Those resources may be material, or they may be the time and attention of their sibling or their parents. The siblings feel resentful and displaced.

Sahila and I were best friends before she married my brother. Once they started dating, Sahila monopolized his time, and things only got worse after the marriage. My mother adored her, and somehow the two of us became very competitive—more like estranged sisters than friends. I was single and wanted to continue partying with her. She seemed to want no part of me. I was hurt and could not get past that hurt to even like her anymore.

It was not until I married that I understood why she preferred spending evenings with my brother rather than with me and why my mother used compliments to make her a part of the family. I liked it when Mom praised my husband. It still took Sahila and me years to rebuild our friendship.

In the throes of new love, Sahila made the mistake of thinking she no longer needed close women friends when she married. She ignored her friends, including the one who would soon be her sister-in-law. She did not recognize that sibling rivalry was part and parcel of why her friend was so upset with her for spending less time with her. Jaya was hurt and jealous that Sahila had replaced Jaya in her brother's heart and in her mother's. Since Jaya did not yet have a serious boyfriend, she was not able to fully comprehend the needs of the new couple. Fortunately, as Jaya gained insight in the relationships of couples, she forgave Sahila and came to understand her mother's actions. She called Sahila and tried to renew their old friendship by sharing some of their mutual interests.

* * *

After the wedding and the honeymoon, the new couple is often still involved in forming their own unit. They make choices about how to spend their time and their money and where they want to live without even asking their siblings' views. A sibling may have married well and suddenly has affluence that was unimaginable before, while the other sibling may have married someone still in school or with huge debt. One sibling may opt for outdoor activities, the other for indoor. One couple may eat only local and organic foods, and the other is a fast-food fan. One sib has kids immediately, the other waits five or ten years or opts not to have them at all. The sibs' lifestyles and life stages don't mix well. As time wears on and each becomes settled in a new life, the siblings find themselves with little in common. They drift apart, with consequences beyond themselves, as seen in this story about Esther and her brother.

Before Esther met Maury, she spent almost every weekend with her brother and his wife, sitting around schmoozing and watching TV. Maury opened her eyes to the outdoors. Now she spends the weekends kayaking and hiking. For a while after their marriage, Esther and Maury tried to be cordial and spend time with her siblings, but after two unsatisfactory visits where they felt bored, they decided enough was enough. The outdoor life was for them. Esther's parents kept asking her if she had seen her brother recently. She was reluctant to tell her folks that she and Maury now have little in common with her brother and his wife. She knew a lecture on family loyalty would ensue. As a result of her drifting apart from her brother, walls developed between her and her parents.

Maury and Esther did not mean to hurt any of their family members. Their free time was limited, and they wanted to use as much of their weekends as possible to enjoy life and time together. Because Esther's family had come to expect weekend togetherness, Esther and Maury's absence was noticed. Esther knew she was breaking a family norm, so she felt uncomfortable and therefore further distanced herself from her siblings and her parents.

Different backgrounds, different values, and different definitions of hospitality can lead in-law sibs to resent each other. New opportunities for animosity arise.

* * *

Katherine marries her high school sweetheart, a fireman named George. Beer and potato chips are his idea of hosting a big gathering. Her sister marries a successful Wall Street banker, and George comes to dread the invitations to their house. While he loves his sister-in-law, he hates wearing a tie and a jacket and coping with too much silverware. He also hates feeling inadequate and insecure because his brother-in-law makes so much more money. As a result, he disparages his brother-in-law, calling him a show-off and the people who attend these gatherings snobs. George also does not want his children exposed to what he perceives as their materialistic values. Eventually, he tells Katherine that she can see her sister without him, leaving Katherine torn between her husband and her sister.

Neither couple meant to cause a rift, but George's discomfort led to a loss of sibling closeness. Equally disappointing, his attitude led to fewer and fewer opportunities for the next generations of cousins to share time together. George chose to vilify his in-law siblings rather than look at his own discomfort. Perhaps if Katherine could level with her sister about George's discomfort, her brother-in-law might be perfectly comfortable if George didn't wear a tie. He might also enjoy sharing a beer with him and his friends. He might even brag to his friends that his brother-in-law is a firefighter. George could decide to learn the purpose of each piece of silverware. It is not very complicated, but to do so he would have to give up his thoughts that learning these social skills is somehow an infringement on his identity. Or George could decide to just be himself and not worry if he is using the right silverware. Or, as a last resort, they could avoid the discussions altogether and decide to meet in less formal settings.

Like so many of us, George would rather not spend time with his in-laws. However, the sacrifice of a few hours, if he were willing to give them, could lead to a lifetime of connection for his children and his wife. Perhaps, one day, even he might benefit from one of these connections in an emotional or financial way. Being a part of most families requires enduring some uncomfortable and boring moments, but for many, the rewards of closeness and comfort are worth the trouble.

* * *

Each family participant has a unique idea of what hospitality means, but these ideas don't always overlap. Some want to spend every minute together, and others want to eat and run. Some consider the preparations part of the family ritual, and others expect a prepared, formal dinner.

Corinne invites her brother's whole family to come to Vermont for the holidays. To her, everyone making all the preparations together defines a family holiday. She welcomes her brother and his family to her home, saying, "Welcome! My fridge is your fridge. My living room is your living room. Just take anything you need. Sheets are in the linen closet." She believes, quite proudly, that this sharing of her home defines graciousness and creates camaraderie. She views her casual ways as making everyone comfortable. Her brother's wife, Marisa, sees it differently. She and Corinne's brother have traveled eight hours by car to be with his sister for the holidays. The unmade beds and general absence of preparation make her feel unwelcome and quite insulted.

Neither sibling prepared the newcomer for the differences in lifestyle that she was about to encounter. Corinne's definition of thoughtfulness and concern is her sister-in-law's definition of laziness or rudeness. Marisa, who is the housekeeper, shopper, and chef in her own home, would never treat people so casually. Corinne has inflicted a major blow to her relationship with her brother's wife. Unless they discuss how each family likes to entertain or choose to recognize and respect that being a guest is as difficult as being a host, neither Corinne nor Marisa will recover from this holiday visit and its inadvertent slight.

When Marisa returns home, she writes—what seems to her—a hilarious description of the weekend on her Facebook page. Without much imagination, it is easy to read her humorous posting as insulting to her siblings-in-law and not particularly flattering to the rest of the family.

This misunderstanding is now posted on the Internet. Her sister-in-law, Corinne, sees it, and the whole family now weighs in about the miserable weekend. Suddenly, what was a difference in lifestyle between the two in-law couples turns into a family conflagration with various members taking one side or the other. If you want peace in a family, do not post family business on the Internet!

THE NEXT GENERATION ARRIVES

The passion all parents put into decisions about how to bring up their children escalates the chances for trouble. Individual families develop a way of living and raising their children, which can alienate siblings from each other. Their routines and methods of bringing up a baby may be quite different. Some families keep their children on a tight schedule, and others let their children decide when to eat and when to sleep. One family doesn't allow hitting, while the other brushes it off as "just a stage." One sibling-in-law believes in discussion or "time-outs," while another believes a good swat is what a child needs. One sibling gives advice to an in-law on how she and his brother should live their lives, and the in-law finds this condescending. Spending time together becomes hard. Fights arise, disagreements are rampant, and too many arguments and not enough real conversation result from little respect for the other's choices. It is easy to say that one no longer needs his or her old family because it's simply too stressful.

Karen and Gordon have three kids who are quiet and calm. The two older children like to play house while their baby sister sits beside them and watches. Karen's brother, Kevin, has two boisterous boys. They love to play "catch me" and run around like crazy. During one of their tours around the house on a rainy day, Karen's eldest nephew trips and falls on her baby. Gordon, with the instinct of a protective parent, picks up his screaming baby. He yells at his nephew and sends him to his room. Kevin and his wife are horrified that someone other than themselves would discipline their child. They tell Gordon in no uncertain terms that he is never to do so again: "In our family, we talk with our children; we don't send them to their rooms, and no one else has the right to discipline them."

Each in-law is simply protecting his own child. Both sets of parents are confused. Is the uncle, as a member of the family, entitled to discipline his nephew or should he wait and report the incident to the parents? They attack each other for their actions, rather than understand that parental protective instincts are strong and that any discipline distant from the event can be ineffective. Both parents and children may need to learn to take reprimands from others. Had Kevin been sensitive to Gordon's fears that his baby was hurt, he might have postponed his anger and later discussed how the two should interact with each other's children. Or Gordon could have apologized later for punishing Kevin's child, and the two could have had a discussion about the role of uncle. Unless they talk about this situation, they will remain uncomfortable, with each person defending his own methods of discipline. They will avoid getting together with the children and dread the times they are forced to be together.

WHEN SIBLINGS HAVE IRRECONCILABLY
DIFFERENT PHILOSOPHIES

Sometimes siblings, who once spent hours on end together, develop such different views that they cannot see a way to even come together. In becoming individuals, they choose very different paths. One or the other may become an expert or a fanatic on a particular subject. One of the spouses may be unbending in his or her commitment to a philosophy or lifestyle. Sometimes the differences in views involve risks.

> *Like their siblings, Victoria and Max are well educated, but they have come to very different conclusions about the scientific evidence on vaccinating children. They do not believe in vaccinating their kids and have not done so. When Max's brother, Joel, has a baby girl, he refuses to allow his niece and nephew to visit. He and his wife accept the scientific evidence that Max and Victoria reject and refuse to expose their daughter, who is too young to be vaccinated, to the risks of illness and possible death from the diseases that her cousins might carry. Victoria and Max are deeply insulted.*

Joel cannot risk the health of his newborn baby. Nothing trumps health and safety. He could have spoken with his brother before the baby was born. It might have eased the pain, but until his daughter was born, he had no idea about his need to protect his baby. Max and Victoria could decide to visit the baby without their children.

Sometimes families hold so tight to principles that the ideas take priority over relationships. This and other strong ideas—whether religious, political, or philosophical—can drive families apart. Only if families prioritize relationships over ideological positions can they modify their behavior and find a way to keep both their principles and their loved ones. For those who hold their beliefs strongly and rigidly, there may be no compromise. Unfortunately, the price to pay in such a case often is a loss of closeness with their family members.

A brother-in-law who has become very observant religiously might not attend his sister-in-law's bat mitzvah because the men and women sit together. The religious person feels that he is principled, while the less religious family feels that his failure to attend his sister's important ceremony is rude and insulting. The familial obligation and the religious tenets are in opposition. Sometimes the sibling or parents can intervene to get the more observant individual to compromise and attend the party, if not the ceremony. However, it takes great understanding on the part of all family members for one to accommodate to ideas that seem harsh to others in the family. Other times families adopt a "live and let live" philosophy and enjoy whatever activities do not put them in conflict.

Often the real issues are the same old ones among the siblings. Who is boss? Who decides what should happen? Who am I? Struggles have always been a part of sibling life, and they will continue to be so. Siblings-in-law sometimes are recruited by their spouse to complain and do the dirty work of causing problems within the family.

*   *   *

Another way that siblings differentiate themselves and their families is with food.

Rhona and Herb are fanatics, or so his brother-in-law thinks, about having their family eat only organic and healthy foods. Casper, Herb's brother-in-law, is sure that organic labeling is a fraud. He is unwilling to spend his limited income on foods that cost more with no benefit he can see. When his brother-in-law and family visit, Casper is also unwilling to forgo his Saturday ritual of taking his own kids for ice cream, which Herb thinks is unhealthy. The two sets of children find each other's eating habits "strange," and the teasing that begins about their different habits all too often gets out of hand. Rhona would be

willing to allow her children to have the occasional ice cream, but she
rather enjoys seeing her brother Casper so annoyed since he teases her
about her organic ways.

As outsiders, we see how their problems could easily be avoided. Casper could take the children to the zoo rather than for ice cream. Herb could decide that an occasional ice cream will not lead to poor health, but neither wants to give in to the other. Rhona recruits her husband to annoy her brother. If the parents want the cousins to care about each other, the parents need to nip the teasing in the bud. In this case, the siblings are playing out their old annoyances with each other and have no desire to compromise.

TEASING AND CASUAL COMMENTS

Teasing can be affectionate, a way of sharing a common knowledge, or it can be a tool of derision. Siblings often reconnect by mocking each other when they have not seen each other for a while. The in-law sibs may or may not be "in" on the jokes. Their newer position in the family makes them sensitive. As children, any of life's arenas were fodder for comments. Now that the siblings are also members of separate families, some topics become off-limits. The mocking and teasing that initially created intimacy become stale. Life may have changed since the sibs last met. One sibling-in-law who was very successful has lost a job. Another may be grieved because he or she has no children. Teasing the siblings or siblings-in-law about their successes and failures is remembered in stereo. When one is unhappy, casual comments, too, are heard louder than intended and can hurt.

Adina and Jason desperately want to have a child. Adina's brother
and his wife, Wendy, have a two-year-old and are expecting another.
It all seems so easy for them. In a passing comment, Wendy mentions
that she has a friend who adopted a child. Adina and Jason see her as

pressuring them to abandon their hopes for a pregnancy, and they are deeply hurt by her comment.

Wendy means no harm. She doesn't understand how sensitive any pregnancy- or adoption-related comment might be to her sister- and brother-in-law. Adina and Jason dread family reunions because they fear similar pressures and comments from Wendy and others. Wendy can apologize even if she thinks she has done nothing wrong. However, some issues are so raw that only time and acceptance can mitigate the wounds. Wendy can just understand the upset and allow herself to be the brunt of Adina and Jason's unhappiness and take comfort in knowing that she is not the real cause. The whole issue might melt away when Adina and Jason form a family by birth or by adoption.

In each of our lives, there are major disappointments. Family members will hurt each other unintentionally. Hurt is part of being in a family, but hopefully the family's love and support is well worth the pain. Keeping a family together takes tolerance and understanding.

TOGETHERNESS AS A FIRETRAP

Holidays create the perfect stage for troubles to arise. For the sibling who cannot have children or who has decided not to have them, holidays with sibs and sibs-in-law can be painful or just annoying. While some choose to focus on being great uncles and aunts, others choose to be miserable.

Geographic distance also adds to the potential problems, particularly if one sibling's family is local and another lives far away. The distant family may feel that when they are in town, they deserve all of the parents' attention, while the local sibs fault the distant in-laws for the invasion and disruption of routine. The familiar family gathering is no longer the same in both substantive and trivial ways. The local couple may be familiar with Mom and Dad's house, while the travelers may not know where the serving platters are. Their well-intentioned assistance in cleaning up becomes a nuisance of endless questions, leaving everyone annoyed, not loved.

One couple may live so far away that they never come to holiday celebrations and develop their own rituals with friends in their new community. Though they are technically still members of the family, their new customs and new memories do not include the other siblings. As a result, time and geography make the sibs and their spouses virtual strangers. In other cases, one sibling celebrates every holiday with his or her in-laws and the original siblings drift apart.

Gift giving can easily become a battle in which sibs and sibs-in-law vie for status and praise. One sib's generosity becomes another sib's "put-down."

Joseph gives an expensive motorized car to his four-year-old nephew, while his sister can only afford a $10 board game. Accusations fly: "Joseph is trying to lord his success over us. He wants to show us up."

Many families stop these troubles before they start by setting rules ahead of time. They limit the price of the gifts, each family member pulls a name from a hat, or they decide not to exchange gifts. It is indeed a challenge for families to show affection and caring without hurting each other.

Vacationing together can reinforce childhood bonds or can tear rip them apart. One sibling family may resent the cost and style of the trip or the location, while another may resent the obligation of togetherness. Or one of the sibling families may be excluded altogether. Only advance planning in each one of these areas can help siblings and siblings-in-law avoid the pitfalls.

*   *   *

Many siblings consider themselves open and flexible people and are surprised to find themselves judgmental and unable to get along with their new in-law sibs. They know that they are disappointing their parents who had hoped their children would remain close forever. They are also disappointing themselves. Some do not want to accommodate or incorporate new lifestyles into their circle, while others enjoy the self-righteousness of believing that they do things the "right" way and their married sibs-in-law do it wrong. These thoughts typically remain unchanged until someone loses a job or gets sick and comes to the other for help. Only then do they realize that putting up with annoying behavior or "crazy" ideas can be important in order to keep family bonds strong.

> *Jordan was constantly peeved by his brother-in-law, Isaac, who tried to convert him to his brand of Christianity. He had no patience for people who believed that they knew the word of the Lord. He resented his parents for trying to retain their role as peacekeepers by urging him to ignore Isaac's preaching. When he was diagnosed with cancer, though Jordan did not agree with Isaac's interpretations of God's laws, he saw the worth of Isaac's beliefs because Isaac helped him financially and with all the tasks that Jordan's illness required.*

Ignoring half of the picture is a useful skill.

THE LONG HAUL: ISSUES THAT DON'T GO AWAY

Long-Term Disability

Marrying into a family with a sibling unable to earn a living can mean financial and caretaking responsibilities for in-laws. Although the newly married sibling may feel responsible for his or her brother or sister, the new spouse might not and, thus, may resent the time and money spent on the sibling. The long-term consequences of disabilities are significant in caretaking, cost, and family relations. Wheelchair accommodations and day care or medical care cost money. Explaining to your child why his or her uncle who has Tourette's syndrome is allowed to swear or why his or her autistic cousin sits alone in the corner requires emotional energy. Siblings-in-law may not want to give financial or emotional support. While support groups at local hospitals and community centers are helpful, not everyone wants to attend.

> *Ryan's sweet and loving older brother, Frank, has been developmentally disabled since birth. Ryan has been involved in his care for as long as he can remember. He visits his brother weekly and takes him out. He fills in when his parents take a rare overnight getaway. His parents have discussed their hope that he would become his brother's guardian when they die. Ever since Ryan was in his late teens, his parents have included him in all the legal and financial preparations for his brother's future. Later, Ryan marries Theadora, and when he introduces her to his brother, she seems to like him. However, as time goes on, Theadora realizes how much of Ryan's time his brother takes, and she becomes resentful.*

Ryan and his parents have established routines over the years. Ryan's life has now changed. Both generations would benefit from including Theadora in their family discussions. She might be able to make suggestions on how both she and Frank could share Ryan's time. She might be willing to contribute to hiring help so that his parents could have respite, and she could have her husband's attention. If she has a role in deciding how she and Ryan might participate in Frank's care, she is more likely to enjoy her time with him and be willing to share her husband with him.

* * *

If in-laws are expected to be involved now or in the future in the supervision of a disabled family member, it stands to reason they should be involved in discussions about both care and finances.

When a sibling is working and living a typical life but is mentally challenged, the family may give the sibling more responsibility than the in-law child feels is appropriate.

> *Janice marries Michael, whose younger brother, Steven, has mild mental challenges. Michael wants to treat his brother as if he were*

normal. He feels that Steven can babysit for their sleeping toddler and sees this as a benefit for all of them. He and Janice get a night out, and Steven feels useful and proud for being able to help. Janice disagrees. Although she likes Steven, she is uneasy about leaving him alone with her child, thinking he might not be able to handle an emergency.

Those who have lived with a person with disabilities may see them differently from those who have not. Over time, either Janice or Michael might change their opinion of Steven's capabilities, but for now, arguing will not help. Janice and Michael may find it productive to explore openly and creatively how to include Steven in ways that will be comfortable for both of them.

With diminished government programs, much is expected of families. Many parents have planned for how to provide for their disabled children once they are no longer capable of caring for them. However, some have not done so. Having ongoing conversations that involve the children and their spouses or partners will keep an open, productive dialogue and give the children who will ultimately inherit this responsibility a say in what approaches might be best for everyone involved.

Addiction

Even harder than dealing with unequal financial or quality-of-life resources in sibling groups is dealing with a sibling who just doesn't want to work, feels entitled, or just can't seem to "get it together." Maybe the cause is addiction of some sort, or maybe the "laziness" is due to learning disabilities. Whatever the source, the in-law may think that the family is enabling the sibling to be dependent, while the family thinks they are facilitating growth by giving the unlucky child one more chance. When it comes to a sibling who is not "getting it together," the in-law's role may be limited to sharing concerns and frustrations but also listening to the ideas of the family. No in-law can change the family dynamic, especially not in the short term. But they can express views, with great delicacy, about what is appropriate for the couple's energy, time, and money, and possibly offer insights for the wider family. They can also set limits on what behaviors are acceptable in their own homes.

> *Richard knows his wife's sister, Emily, has had a drug problem. One day he notices things out of place in both their bedroom and their bathroom. He worries that Emily has been searching there for money and drugs. He knows his wife does not want him acting as the policeman or detective over her sister. He also knows that he is unwilling to allow Emily to meander around his house alone again, and he is unwilling to help Emily feed her drug habit. Additionally, he knows Emily needs help and that he must have a frank talk with his wife about his suspicions, though doing so will be unpleasant because his wife wants to believe that Emily is no longer using drugs.*

As much as families hate to admit it, addiction affects the whole family. Emily's addiction is also opening the family to the potential of becoming victims of violent behavior if, for example, her drug-addicted friends learn that she has access to money and drugs. Richard in no way blames his wife, but he does know that he must set limits to survive his sister-in-law's visits. He can talk lovingly with his wife and explain what he observed. He does not need to require her to police the sister, but he does need to let her know what he finds acceptable in their home. Richard might suggest ways that they can include Emily in their lives but limit her access to their home, thus declaring his willingness to help but not to facilitate Emily's self-destructive behavior.

Together they may decide to get help from an addiction counselor, or if his wife is unwilling, he can go himself. The couple might be able to convince the rest of the family to join them. If they do, they may all grow closer. However, not all families are willing to face addiction. Richard and his wife, however, must confront the problem if they are to continue seeing Emily.

Many siblings-in-law are angered that they must spend their time dealing with addiction when they themselves are not addicted. The silver lining is that what we learn from another's addiction will help us with our own children or perhaps with some colleagues.

Transgenderism

Some families face challenges they never expected. Social norms change. What was completely taboo years ago is now out in the open. As norms change, so do families, but it takes time. I often hear the oldest child declare, "*In my day, my parents never allowed me out after midnight*" or "*In my day, my parents never allowed girls to sleep in my bedroom.*" Families evolve and adjust to new circumstances and to new social mores. A new person entering the family has not had time to adjust and understand new circumstances and may react badly initially.

> *Mallory's brother, Keith, used to be her sister, Cora. Cora, who is transgendered, has become Keith through a physically and psychologically arduous process—one that has been difficult for his whole family. Mallory marries Reed, whom she knew in high school. He refuses to call the former Cora, Keith. He refers to him as a she. Mallory herself finds the whole matter uncomfortable, but she realizes that Keith seems happier as a male, and she still loves her sibling. She knows the hell Cora went through to become Keith: the hormones, doctors' appointments, surgeries, and social challenges. Reed is embarrassed by the whole issue. He does not want his sister-/brother-in-law at any social gatherings. He keeps asking, "How will we explain this to our children? They will see pictures of Cora when she was a young girl and not understand how she changed." He also worries that one of their children will be transgendered, and he is not certain society will ever accept transgendered people.*

Reed needs time and education. The family, and even Keith, took a while to figure out how to understand the changes in Cora. Human variation is vast. Some variations are well understood, others are not. Patience, understanding, and education will go a long way in helping the newcomer understand.

In some ways, this situation is like that faced by any family living with one member with physical or mental challenges. Consider a family with a child who is autistic or who has cystic fibrosis. Consider a family having to deal with a member who has been in a horrendous accident and needs several years just for physical recovery. Consider a family with a son or daughter who tests HIV positive. Some siblings are proud that their family has grown from coping with such challenges, while others feel jealous of siblings whose conditions require time, energy, and money. Still others feel tainted or embarrassed by their siblings. And many feel all of these emotions from time to time. Regardless of the nature of the challenge—physical or mental, long term or short—all family members go through periods of acceptance and rejection. Those newer to the situation, such as those marrying in, face the additional challenges of suddenly being part of a conversation that may have gone on for years and about which they know only a little.

EVERYTHING YOU NEED TO KNOW YOU LEARNED ON AN ELEMENTARY SCHOOL TEAM

Since elementary school, we have all been on one team or another. We did not always like our teammates, but the price of admission was worth "putting up" with those members we didn't particularly like. Maybe they were the athletes who were essential to winning, or maybe they were the coach's kid. We invited the whole team, including the obnoxious ones, to the victory party. We even hugged the unpleasant kid when he or she made the winning goal or caught the third out. At work, we encounter all sorts of individuals—some of whom we like, some we abhor—but we must interact with all of them if we want to keep our jobs. We try to ignore the flaws. We focus on the task. Whatever you do to work with people you don't particularly like will help you in dealing with siblings-in-law. Your job is not to make trouble in the family, but rather to get along. You have done that in other settings to keep harmony. Now it is really important to draw on the skills you learned from your outside experiences to enjoy the benefits of support that come with good family relationships.

SOME SIBLINGS-IN-LAW WORK IT OUT

We can learn from those who have good relationships with their siblings-in-law.

> *My sister-in-law and I are a great team. From the beginning, she wasn't my type. She was more Prada and I was more Birkenstock. But we worked well together. I think we just knew we had many years ahead and many holidays to share, so we decided to figure out a way to make things work. When our kids were little, we just divided the holiday meals. She brought some items and I brought others. When our mother-in-law was ailing and the kids were bigger, we went to our mother-in-law's house and cooked together. She did most of the cooking and I did the cleanup.*

These two sisters-in-law set priorities early on. They agreed that, come what may, they just had to get along because they would be the ones left when the parents died, thus giving them a lifetime together. They focused on that big goal of keeping their husbands' family connected and worked hard not to judge each other's style. They were flexible. Neither changed, but both accommodated. Not a bad recipe for a family meal!

* * *

The second story is from a woman who was having great difficulty with her own in-laws until she observed her sister-in-law.

> *I used to get angry when my father-in-law gave me advice, but when my sister-in-law came into the family, I observed her. She has a wonderful way of taking unsolicited advice. She says something to the effect of, "Oh, thanks for suggesting that. I will add that to the considerations. I appreciate your thoughts." She does what she is going to do, but one has the sense that she takes in what others have to say and doesn't get angry. If someone in the family does it better, she does not*

take offense. I have tried to learn from her how to do this. My sister-in-law uses the useful bits of someone's advice and disregards the rest. She is the better for it.

Although these stories may seem trivial in comparison with some of the dilemmas families face, the methods of shared problem solving and learning from each other are useful in any situation. All over the world, siblings can and do help each other.

GOOD THINGS DON'T ALWAYS STAY IN SMALL PACKAGES—NOR DO THE BAD

Financial, social, and philosophical differences often start out as small annoyances, but they can grow into very big problems. Whether the disagreements are in gift giving, hospitality, or discipline, each tiff can morph into what seems like World War III. Don't let that happen. You and your sibs have been fighting since the sandbox, but the family bond has kept you, if not liking each other, at least recognizing some unique connection. Step back; consider. Don't make a big deal about every slight! For many of us, siblings and siblings-in-law are like chronic diseases: we just have to learn to live with them. For others, they are people who add color and flavor to our lives. Creating good experiences and limiting the bad can help you and your siblings-in-law improve your interactions.

You may not love your in-law sibs, but you can try to enjoy at least one thing about them. You don't have to be best friends, but everyone involved will benefit from being good enough acquaintances.

QUESTIONS

- Under what conditions do you and your siblings-in-law get along well?
- Under what conditions do you and your siblings-in-law get along badly?

- Does anything distinguish the two?
- What do you think your relationship with your in-law sibs should be?
- What does your spouse think?
- If you have multiple in-law sibs, are the relationships different? If so, how? Why?
- What issues are most contentious for you and your in-law sibs?
- What things can you talk about?
- What can you not talk about?
- How do you and your in-law sibs celebrate holidays and other family events? Are you happy with the occasions? If not, what would you like to change?
- How do you like the gift-giving practices of your in-law sibs? What would you like to change?
- Are there other areas that cause problems between you and your in-law sibs? Child rearing? Issues with your parents/parents-in-law? Vacations?
- Are there any ways in which you disapprove of how your parents/parents-in-law treat their various children? Are there ways that you approve?
- What kind of help would/could you give to a disabled sibling/sibling-in-law? Would you feel differently if he or she were your sib rather than your spouse's?

CHAPTER 5

Dueling and Other In-Law Games: The Two (or More) Sets of In-Laws

For some parents, being an in-law is a competitive sport. The weapons of choice are time, money, and grandchildren. They keep score. Who gives more materially? Who can buy the kids' loyalty with the nicer vacation? Who spends more time with the kids or the grandkids? Who do the grandkids love more? These matters loom large in their analysis of closeness. These folks are out to win, but being an in-law is a game of sharing!

No formal or informal rules govern the interactions between two or more sets of in-laws. Each pair or group of in-laws must resolve their relationships for themselves. Some assume that after the couple's marriage, they are family. Others assume that they will meet around the wedding and not see each other again until the grandchildren's high school graduations. Like the children, the parents often do not know what their expectations are until they are not met. Some in-laws expect attendance at all their marvelous celebrations and terribly sad events. They may view these events as opportunities to connect and share the texture of life, and they may even be insulted when the other in-laws don't attend an important family event. Others see them as private matters from which the in-laws are excluded. Between these two ends of the continuum, there is a myriad of anticipations and endless possibilities for misunderstandings.

FAMILY-VALUES WARS

If the two in-law parents do not like or respect one another, their meet-ings are burdensome. Being with the kids' in-laws takes time away from activities they enjoy far more. It takes years to sort out obligations to each other. Some families never come to an agreement. If they continue to feel hurt without understanding the other family's views, they are in for a rocky road. Almost all areas of life are affected by parental attitudes and perspectives. They often clash.

> *Marcel and Beatrice believe that children should not marry until they can support themselves, both financially and emotionally. They have told their son and daughter-in-law that they love and respect them but do not believe it is healthy for married children to take money from their parents. The other in-laws feel it is important to share when their children need money for tuition or mortgage payments; besides, there are tax advantages to doing so. Each year, they give the kids as much as the gift tax law allows. Marcel and Beatrice are certainly affluent enough to do the same, but they see the other in-laws as infantilizing the young married couple.*

Judging the values of others leads us into trouble. Both sets of in-laws have good reasons for doing what they do. All either parent couple can do is accept their differences and work to refrain from demeaning the other. The number of children, the health of their parents, as well as their attitudes toward all of their obligations affect a parent's willingness to give time or money to a particular couple.

Neither set of in-laws really knows the other's financial situa-tion. Appearances can belie reality. Sometimes those with the trap-pings of affluence have little disposable income. It is easy to make assumptions about financial status without knowing the total picture of the family's financial obligations. The couple may be supporting a disabled sibling or two parents in different nursing homes. They may have huge financial debt from business or education. Too often in-laws berate the values of the other family simply because they spend money differently.

* * *

Drew and Amy have one child. While they are not wealthy, they are comfortable and are willing and wanting to share disposable income with their daughter Louise. Louise is married to Lewis, a young man from a more affluent family. His parents, however, have four other children and believe that anything they do for one child they must do for all, either now or in their wills. Thus, they hold back on helping the children. Drew and Amy see his parents' unwillingness to share as stingy, and they resent it. But they do not consider Drew's parents' perspective.

The structure of the family also can influence the attitude of one set of in-laws toward the other. Some find it difficult to deal with the sadness of a newly widowed or divorced person. Likewise, they may not approve of the lifestyle of the other parents who have never legally married. In-laws become bewildered when they are confronted with new traditions and new lifestyles.

* * *

Hilary's in-laws have always included her mother, Celia, in all the holiday celebrations. Celia assumes that she will be invited again this year. Hilary casually mentions how excited she is that her in-laws are taking her and her husband to visit their other child in New Mexico. Celia has been widowed for years, and Hilary is her only child. She is hurt that she was not invited to the usual in-home celebration and annoyed that her child's in-laws did not tell her directly. Celia sees the generosity of the other in-laws as an obligation.

The blurry distinctions between who is family and who is not cause this misunderstanding. As family, Celia would expect to be notified of this year's holiday plans. However, as a guest, she does not need to be notified since the invitation is purely optional. The ambiguity of the relationship causes misunderstanding.

* * *

Remarriage can create delicate situations as well.

> *Five years after the marriage of Isabelle, their oldest child, the parents, Maureen and Theodore, divorce. Theodore marries Lee and appears blissfully happy. Maureen is bitter and miserable. Isabelle's in-laws feel it is important to include their child's in-laws any time their mutual children visit since the adult children come to town infrequently. They are willing to have Lee, but Maureen won't come if she is in attendance. They are now torn. They hope to foster relationships with their children and grandchildren and all the in-laws. They like both Maureen and Theodore, but they do not want their time with the grandchildren and children to be ruined by the divorced couple's animosity; nor do they wish to choose between them. They wish the two of them could just grow up and get along.*

Sometimes in-laws are dragged into the other's squabbles. Family politics are impossible to understand—do your best to not become enmeshed in them.

CULTURE WARS

Sometimes the culture wars begin before the marriage: one set of parents disapproves of the other's child because the intended is not educated enough, is not sophisticated enough, or is from the "wrong" race or religion. It's tough to forgive anyone who finds your child unworthy.

> *Warren has an acute case of type 1 diabetes and by age 30 has had a kidney transplant. Despite his medical problems, he completed school, holds an excellent job, and founded a buddy program for inner-city kids with diabetes. He and Illona fall in love. Her parents warn her against marrying him. "A lifetime of illness awaits you," they say. "You will be a*

nursemaid and a young widow." Warren's parents are deeply hurt. Their son is a real catch. He has faced adversity and turned it into triumph.

On the one hand, Warren's parents are right to be hurt. Illona's parents are seeing the disease and not the person. Warren's family knows firsthand that poor health can strike at any moment. They know how hard Warren has worked to remain positive and to continue learning and working. They know they are blessing some young woman with a good man. Illona's folks, on the other hand, have some justification for concern. Illness takes time and money and much emotional energy. They like and respect Warren but fear for their daughter's well-being.

Unless both sets of parents do what Warren has learned and focus on the joys of the present, they will be locked in a duel, each feeling that they have contributed the better half to the marriage. Worry about the future can consume the present.

The TV series *Dharma and Greg* used class conflict as a source of humor. A hippie family and an upper-class family struggle to come to terms with each other. One likes spontaneity and the other likes predictability. The differences go beyond wealth and class. At times, contempt for another's lifestyle not only prevents in-law couples from connecting, but escalates into a moral battle. Although Dharma and Greg get along well, the in-laws create problems ranging anywhere from what to wear to what is family.

Some parents do not approve of their children's in-laws.

"My son's in-laws ride motorcycles, and he has taken it up. We are not only appalled, but worried! Our kid could be killed."

* * *

"They're such stiffs. The country club, the green slacks with little turtles. They never have any fun."

* * *

"It's disgusting—my daughter's father-in-law comes to the table in an undershirt with his belly hanging out. I can't bear to look at him, let alone eat with him."

Although many of the complaints are based on variances in attitudes and tastes, one side looks down on the lifestyle choices of the other. Many parents escalate their differences into grievances. They roll their eyes. Rather than trying to understand each other and learn new ideas from their differences, they argue. We nurture grievances against others because it makes us feel morally superior. It gives a sense of power in a situation in which we feel powerless. We then can enjoy and justify our role as the long-suffering aggrieved party. The self-righteousness that "our way is the best way" has many theaters of battle. One set of parents swears by alternative medicine, and the other discounts exercise and herbal remedies. Other families are able to sit down and look hard to find something in common.

> We couldn't believe it when we met my son's future in-laws. They were motorcycle hippies—the husband with long hair pulled back in a ponytail and the not-so-slim wife with a tight top. They did not like what I said no matter what. I tried everything! Eventually, we discovered we both loved the Beatles.

Any small thread can be a beginning. In this case, the Beatles led to a tour of each other's CD collections, then to an exchange of good music websites. Eventually they enjoyed a concert together, and, lo and behold, they had a common experience on which to build. Pretty soon they were enjoying the pursuits of their mutual children together.

FINANCIAL SKIRMISHES

Weddings are famous for bringing out family conflicts. The in-laws' first negotiation is often a financial one—who will pay for what? Sometimes, in-laws expect the other side to give resources that they may not have. Or one side wants a bigger wedding than the other can afford. Negotiating with strangers about matters with high emotional content is a recipe for disaster. It is better to be clear about what you can afford to contribute.

Even paying in restaurants can become a source of conflict. The in-law who always grabs for the bill may either be making a lovely gesture or "one-upping." Although the giver may mean it as a gracious gesture, the receiver may view it as an insult. Interpretation of an event is just as important as the happening itself.

Some in-laws offer the couple family vacations in an effort to continue a long-standing family tradition. Their counterparts may view this as an effort to bribe the couple to spend more time with them. Some grandparents can afford to give lavish gifts. Those who cannot may see the other in-laws as indulgent and become jealous and concerned that their children will turn from them. However, we all can afford to give of ourselves, which is a gift that can build stronger bonds than any material contribution.

One set of in-laws might suggest that their child's betrothed sign a prenuptial agreement in which the intended in-law agrees to make no claims on the future spouse's current assets in case of divorce. The other set perceives the request as a lack of trust or disapproval of the match. They are incensed that a parent would even suggest that divorce is in the offing. It is difficult to forgive other in-laws who may imply that your child is unworthy. The in-laws with the financial means are trying to protect their child. Those without excess capital think such a request is rude, unnecessary, and an aspersion on their child's character. Remnants of marriage as a business contract govern one family. Romantic notions dominate the other.

When a prenuptial agreement is suggested in a parental second marriage, the intended and the children become the potential beneficiaries of a well-constructed plan. They could also become potential adversaries. The intended spouse may be hurt that he or she is not trusted. The children, if they are old enough to understand, may worry about their future educations or hoped-for inheritances. One generation thinks that they are talking about money and the other thinks that they are talking about approval or trust. In truth, they are doing both.

PILLOW FIGHTS

Competition for the grandchildren's love gets confused with disciplinary attitudes. Just as the siblings and their spouses may dispute child-rearing matters, so may the pairs of in-law parents. Some grandparents believe children should have a set bedtime; others let them stay up until they tire. Each set of dueling in-laws thinks their method of caring for the grandchildren is the right one and, therefore, sees alternative methods as bribery, insensitivity, or rigidity.

They may differ more broadly on how to handle the "rules" the parents set for their little ones. One set believes the parents are in charge and follow the rules precisely. The others believe that grandparents are supposed to spoil the children and ignore parental rules. Still others make exceptions around the edges. They let the grandchildren stay up ten minutes extra or agree to read them a second bedtime story.

Dueling in-laws complain to their children. They complain to their friends and to anyone who will listen about what horrible people the other in-laws are and about their terrible influence on the grandchildren. However, children can benefit from many influences and usually are clever enough to know which ones are more beneficial than others.

LOSING WITHOUT A WAR

The most common complaint of in-law parents is not, however, a result of warfare. It is more a loss by attrition. The kids, whether because of geographical closeness or preference, are closer, spending more time with one side of the family than the other. More commonly, it tends to be the wife's family who remains closer in the young couple's circle. Whichever side is closer, the more distant set of in-laws feels left out. They miss intimacy and connection with their own child and with his family.

> There is a particular issue that my wife and I have experienced—and we have found that several other people we know have similar situations. It is one in which our son, after marrying, has cut off virtually all contact with our family. He and his wife spend a lot of time with his in-laws, but they are virtually non-communicative with us. The

more that we've shared this info with friends, the more we discover
that this is not a particularly unusual situation.

My wife quotes an old saying, "A daughter is a daughter for all of
her life, but a son is a son until he takes a wife." I think that's cute,
but it doesn't soothe my heart. When he married, I fantasized gaining
a daughter-in-law, but it seems instead that I've lost a son.[1]

Parental feelings of loss and jealousy are not only real but also common. The minister who sent me this message has many options for communicating with his son. However, even professionals who know the options can find using them to be difficult, especially when they feel bereft and undervalued. Feeling unappreciated often leads in-laws to interpret their kids' obligation to the other in-laws as a snub.

It is painful when our children are absent for even one holiday, let alone every vacation. Of course, we can try to focus on our children's happiness and success. Still, many parents feel deserted. Certainly there are moments when we are jealous of the other in-laws. We may think the kids or grandkids like their in-laws better or that they can give more. These are natural feelings. We can recognize them and maybe share them with a spouse or a friend, but we are unwise to act as if the other in-laws are taking our children from us. No one ever teaches us how to share our children. We write the instruction manual as we go along.

It is indeed wonderful that we love our children so much that we want them by our side always, but obviously it can't be so. Most children and grandchildren thrive with multiple inputs. You can find ways to stay connected to your children and grandchildren that give more pleasure than pain. If you try something and it doesn't work, try something else. Forget the competition. Build your own relationships and let the other in-laws build theirs. Run your own race at your own pace.

Lost connections can be repaired. Complications such as distance can be fixed by meeting halfway or by taking turns driving to each other's houses. Technology like Skype, e-mail, and texting, while not perfect substitutes for direct contact, can facilitate interaction. Several grandparents told me about Skypeing with their children and using the computer to not only talk, but to show their new projects and purchases—even their new abodes. Many read stories to their grandchildren, each having a copy of a book as they read aloud. Learning new ways to use technology can enable us to stay connected. Sometimes we must settle for imperfect solutions in the hope that, over time, more satisfying outcomes will result.

FOOD FIGHTS

Different families eat differently. One person's healthy eating is another person's definition of orthorexia, "an obsessive-compulsive disorder that creates severe phobias about eating impure, unhealthy food."[2] Rather than having an indulgence now and then, people with this disorder stop eating entire food groups and are horrified if the other in-laws dare to give these taboo foods to the grandchildren. As we saw with the siblings, food can become a battlefront. In-laws obsessed with healthy eating disdain in-laws who even occasionally chomp down fast food. Some foods are seen as good, and others are seen as bad. Dueling in-laws conflate the foods with the person—the other in-laws become good or bad. For them, food symbolizes "virtuous" behavior.

Some in-laws are so obsessed with eating only pure foods that they won't eat at each other's homes. While food can become quite the battleground, what to eat may just be the beginning, as this disagreement can lead to entirely new ones. Different customs and cultures can clash and cause arguments. Some families prefer to sit down together to eat, while in other families, each person chooses his or her meal from the fridge. Particular families follow Emily Post's etiquette instructions; others follow their own culture's rules. None of these behaviors is bad. They just conflict. What is bad is a supercilious attitude toward manners, customs, and ideas different from your own. In-laws who judge the other in-laws for making different decisions in the realm of manners lose respect for each other.

Along with food come libations and the question of whether to drink alcohol. That's only the beginning of the question. How much to drink, when it is appropriate, and in what context it should be done are all queries that soon follow. Alcohol can be a social nicety or part of the meal, but it can also be a demon ready to envelop a life.

> *Harold and Carmen are invited to dinner by their son's future in-laws, Shirley and Johannes. The dinner begins with hors d'oeuvres and drinks. Harold, who has been sober for ten years and still attends Alcoholics Anonymous (AA) meetings, orders a glass of water. Thinking that Harold is being polite, Johannes presses for something more "satisfying." Harold overly firmly says, "Water will be fine!" Johannes knows he has made some sort of error but does not know why everyone is uncomfortable. When the four parents proceed to discuss the wedding plans, Johannes insists on an open bar. Harold is firm—no liquor can be served at his son's wedding. He does not mention that he has met many of his friends through AA. The in-laws think that he is cheap and offer to pay, since drinking is an important part of socializing for them.*

In both of these cases, Harold would have spared the other in-laws angst and confusion by telling them why he does not drink alcohol and why he wants none at the wedding. However, Harold fears the future in-laws might think less of him because he once had a drinking problem. In other situations, people are uncomfortable around alcohol or follow religious taboos against alcoholic drinking. Others have relatives who drink too much, and the in-laws want to ensure that the wedding proceeds smoothly.

PEACE AT ANY PRICE

No matter what the in-laws think of each other, trying to get along is worth the effort. Life happens—a sickly newborn, a chronic disease, an accident. Nothing in life is predictable, and events can force more interactions with the other in-laws than either generation may have ever wanted or predicted. Should a baby be born prematurely or twins arrive or some medical disaster occur, the parents-in-law may even find themselves sharing a two-bedroom apartment with the other parents.

Philip and Aisha knew their families did not particularly like each other,
even though everyone behaved themselves well at the wedding. Because
negative feelings were in the air, the subsequent holiday meetings were
a bit tense, but nonetheless cordial. However, their first child was born
with severe problems, which required close monitoring. Aisha had to
remain in the hospital due to her own medical complications. The two
sets of in-laws were forced to rally for the common good. They put their
dislike aside and took turns checking on the baby and feeding him.

Anticipated or not, in-law parents are forced together in emergencies.
Getting along with the other in-law parents involves deciding that the
commitment to your children in itself provides a basis for a relationship.
The arrival of any grandchildren only enlarges that base of commonality.
You do not have to be best friends, but you do need to get along enough to
avoid creating problems for the adult children and grandchildren. As one
mother put it, "I would do anything I can to help my kids have peace at
home and a peaceful marriage, and it takes being nice and being flexible."

We can provoke problems for our children, or we can prevent problems by encouraging our children to be present in the lives of the other
in-laws, as well as in our own lives. We can share holidays together or
merely exchange greeting cards. When all parents feel appreciated and
honored, fewer problems arise.

In-laws cannot change each other. They can, however, make sure that
they themselves are reaching out and continuously searching for new and
interesting ways to connect. For some families, this is an opportunity to
build a broader, more inclusive relationship, even if in-laws see each other
infrequently. They can bond over disagreeing with their children, loving
the grandchildren, or sharing the workload of grandparenting. They can
even bond over having mutual worries. For others, they must work hard
to see what the other family has to give their children and grandchildren.

A COMPLETELY DIFFERENT BATTLEFRONT

Sometimes the other in-laws are forgiving, but the adult children are
embarrassed by their parents.

Dean asked his mother-in-law if his newly widowed mother, Trudy, could come to Thanksgiving dinner since he did not want her to be alone for the holiday. His mother-in-law immediately agreed. She even apologized that she had not mentioned the idea first. Although Trudy knew no one other than her children at her in-laws' home, she listened politely during the hors d'oeuvres, but halfway through the meal, she started texting and did not stop until dessert. Dean was horrified. He felt he had gone out of his way to include his mother and she was behaving rudely.

This story was told to me with several different particulars. The in-law parent was invited to the other in-laws' home and drank too much, fell asleep on the couch, dominated the conversation, or argued vociferously. The details do not matter. The in-laws decided to ignore the behavior. However, the adult child was embarrassed and subsequently reluctant to include his own parent again.

Respect and formal discourse and polite manners are the backbone of any effective social interaction. We may chafe at social conventions, but polite behavior can reduces stress. If nothing else, social niceties reduce the reasons for anger. Politeness gives each of us something specific to do to avoid collisions. Sometimes a simple birthday e-mail or a thank-you note will suffice to make someone feel cared for and included. These acts of politeness give in-laws reasons to thank each other, communicate over something with little emotional baggage, and establish an ongoing relationship.

Politeness may be window dressing, but it is only a first step. Deep divides are often subtle. For some, the route to fulfillment is individual achievement and independence. Others value harmony and accommodation.[3] Some like excitement, and others like predictability. In any case, most of us mean to be reasonably affable. None of us knows how to act in all situations and with all people. The other in-laws give us opportunities to increase our repertoire of behaviors and to learn about new worlds, new ideas, and new ways of living—but only if we are open to them.

FIND A STRATEGY

Some in-laws just like each other. They are the lucky ones. Others must work at it. In-law relationships are not war, contests, or battles. These relationships provide a chance to use all the cooperative and innovative insights you have to solve problems. Look at your disdain, your anger, your hurt. Go the extra mile to figure out why you are so troubled by the actions of the other family. You certainly cannot change their ways of doing things, but you can work at changing your attitude. You can look at the derogatory motives you have ascribed to them and reframe them in a more positive light. You can be curious about their lives. Everyone has an interesting interpretation of his or her own life.

Try seeing the establishment of a working relationship with the other in-laws as a puzzle to be solved or an important challenge to be met. Figure out how you can meet it. Find some space where you can connect, even if the person is not "your type." The other in-laws may well be an asset you can draw on when times are tough. Whether that proves true, together you all can help your mutual children and grandchildren.

Those who successfully negotiate in-law relationships do so by ignoring differences, finding commonality, and not judging. They focus on the positives and rip up the scorecard. They run their own race. They do not try to be what they are not, but they do try to expand who they are.

The job of in-law parents is not to cause problems or make their children's lives more difficult. Everyone's job is to keep the big picture in mind. Forget the small slights. We are all moving targets. We are growing and changing. Some are traveling and retiring. Some are developing new careers and new interests. We are all on different learning curves. We can change our perception of ourselves and of others. We don't want to assume we can't change, nor should we assume others can't change. The tincture of time cures many discomforts. When there are real conflicts—such as one set of in-laws insisting all the holidays take place at their house or never allowing the other in-laws a chance to be with the grandchildren alone, or our own children preferring to be with the other in-laws—then we have to work around the situation. We can create new moments for congregating with our children and grandchildren. We can develop new interests. Some would call it being mature while others would call it giving up and giving in, but ultimately we gain little by putting our children in conflict with their in-law families. The relationship between the in-laws, like everything in life, is a work in progress.

We facilitate that progress by being willing to adapt to change, by being creative in finding new ways to be a part of our children's lives, and by finding satisfaction in our own lives.

QUESTIONS

- What is your biggest fear about your child's in-laws?
- List all of the ways you think your child's in-laws helped raise a nice child.
- How do you and the other in-laws agree about spending money?
- How do you disagree?
- Does this suggest any activities that would best be avoided?
- List the foods that both you and your child's in-laws enjoy.
- Do you and the other in-laws agree on child discipline? If so, how? If not, how?
- What have been your most successful interactions with your child's in-laws?

CHAPTER 6

In Love, but Not in Law: Unrelated "In-Laws"

When does someone become "family"? Neither our language nor our social conventions have caught up with the changes in our society in which many of our loved ones live as if they were married but are not, and in which they see each other frequently and exclusively but are not married. When I was young, if one brought a date to a family event, it was practically an announcement of an engagement. Now, family members bring casual acquaintances as well as significant others. The other family members are uncertain whether the guest is really meant to be included in the family circle. They wonder how much energy they should invest in a particular relationship. Will this informally connected potential in-law be around for a while? It is often difficult to determine. Asking can sometimes help. At other times, we just need to be gracious and act "as if" the person is family.

Either generation may include couples in long-term relationships that are not sanctioned by marriage. Laws, rules, regulations, and customs have a great impact on what a family looks like in terms of its legal status, but the law alone does not define relationships, nor does social convention. Divorce, death, remarriage, and any version of a two-person partnered unit are puzzling to all of the folks who are part of the partner's family. Traditionally, in-laws were the parents of one's spouse or the spouse of one's child. Extended in-laws included siblings, aunts, uncles, and cousins of one's spouse. In some cultures, one's child's in-laws became part of the extended family and the adult child became part of a spouse's clan. Now the very definition of in-law is in question. Is one still an in-law if one is divorced? Is one an in-law if one is in a long-term partnership? Are in-law relationships defined by love or by law?

Many couples may have bought a home together and had children together, and they may be as committed as any legally married couple. Between the two, their relationship may be clear, but for other family members, it is often less so.

Both generations find great ambiguity around their roles vis-à-vis these partners of family members. All involved are uncertain how much to invest emotionally in these "in-laws by love." Yet some of these relationships are effectively permanent. Are these unmarried long-term partners in-laws? Does either generation want to invest time and energy into relationships that might not last?[1] There is precious little advice, much less a term, on how to relate to those persons who are family by love but not by law. Sometimes those "in-laws by love" do indeed take on the role of in-law.

> *We really like Dave, and it is a joy to see our daughter happy again after her divorce. I hate to make trouble, but I feel that I must address an issue. My quasi son-in-law (they have been living together for two years) drives fast. I'm petrified for my grandchildren. My grandchildren are terrified to drive with their acting stepdad. My kids live four hours away, so our custom has been to meet halfway whenever we take the kids for a weekend. Recently, the grandkids have been confiding to me that they don't like to ride in the car when Dave is driving. "He goes too fast, Grandpa!"*

When young children spontaneously bring up fears of speeding drivers, they should be taken seriously. The quasi father-in-law wants to say something, but he is afraid that he will ruin a good relationship for his daughter and that he will not be able to see his grandchildren if he alienates Dave. However, he certainly will not see his grandchildren if they die in a car crash, and he could never live with the guilt of not having raised the issue. Since safety is the concern, he must not bite his tongue. He must think about how to say it, what to say, and when to say it. Dave could become very angry, so he probably does not want to broach the subject of speed just before Dave is about to get on the road—there's no need for road rage to exacerbate the problem. He also must be careful not to implicate the children so that Dave does not take out his anger on them.

He could speak with his daughter, though the relationship may be so important to her that she may not mention the speedy driving to Dave. Or he could talk directly to Dave without anger, but with real concern. The grandfather must give Dave a chance to explain. He must also express his concern and his own fears. The discussion might degenerate, but unpleasant conversations and angry feelings are often part of any family relationship. Dave may rethink after the conversation, or he may not. There are risks to speaking up, but the risks of remaining silent in this case are greater. It's all new and very complicated. Both generations will cross invisible lines. Expect it, forgive it, and try to do it better next time.

QUASI IN-LAWS COME IN MANY PACKAGES

Changing reproductive modes may or may not bring people we don't even know to the family circle. What is the extended families' relationship to the surrogate mother who is also the aunt of a grandchild, or to the sperm donor of your grandchild, or to the mother who gave the child to your children in an open adoption?[2] The old roles and definitions do not cover these connections. We must figure out new ones. Each family is crafting a new social order as it goes along.

Marilyn and Risa have a baby boy with the sperm of a gay friend from a large Turkish family. Risa's mother is a big presence in the little boy's life. Marilyn's mother is dead. Marilyn and Risa want to use the same donor for a second child so that the children will be genetically siblings and because they are so delighted with their first child. The sperm donor is in and out of their lives—he's not really a steady presence and is instead more like a distant uncle. When they contact him, he says he is happy to be a sperm donor again, but his mother wants to meet her grandson and wants to be more involved with her grandchildren if he should ever donate his sperm again. After all, these are the only grandchildren she is likely to have.

The couple is ambivalent. They are not sure that they want this new person in their life. They are not sure what it will mean, and they are unsure whether they want to introduce a whole new culture and new religion into their own family. They worry that once they let the grandmother in, the whole clan will want to be involved as well.

Some people view family connections as burdens: the more people there are, the more complications there will be. Others view these new additions as enhancements to their lives. Marilyn and Risa can decide how they want to interact with the sperm donor's family. They could add support, or they could be a burden. Of course, they cannot know in advance. They can meet the grandmother and slowly begin to develop the rules of engagement. The other grandmother can see the sperm donor's mother as a competitor or a helper or yet another person to truly love her grandchildren. The choice is theirs.

*   *   *

Sally, a pregnant teenager, decides that she will put her child up for adoption when it is born. She finds a family that is willing to have an "open adoption." She picks what she considers to be an ideal family for her child. When she meets them, she loves them, and she thinks, "If only I had a family like this." She is young and immature, still partying and far from settling down. When she has the baby, the new family is supportive, stable, and loving, unlike her own family, who isn't thrilled that she is having a baby out of wedlock. She is happy that her child will go to this great family. She stays in touch, and they exchange photographs and even meet a few times as the child grows up. The issues are not (as would be expected) her role as a mother, but her role as a daughter. She calls for advice, she wants to visit—not so much to be with her daughter, but to be with this family, who she wishes would adopt her and be her mother and father. How does the family integrate this young person into their lives? They are indebted to her for this wonderful child, but they are not sure they need another child to care for. This isn't what they expected.

Having a baby and giving it up for adoption are enormous events in a young woman's life. Often the young woman does not understand what the emotional consequences of her decision will be. In this case, the parents can continue treating Sally as the biological mother of their child and not as a daughter by focusing their conversations only on the baby. When she asks for their advice on personal matters, they might suggest others with whom she might talk. This may hurt her, but it also might be helpful to her and give her the boost she needs to create her own life.

IT'S NOT YOUR DIVORCE

When divorce happens, the parents are often torn between loyalty to their own child and a desire to maintain good relationships with a person who was once a loving member of their family. If parents want to see their grandchildren, they better have established a good relationship with the person who spends the most time with the children.

My son was married and had a drug addiction, so his wife divorced him. I was upset at his wife. It took me years to admit that my son was no angel. After all, he was never drunk or high in front of me. He was a good earner and seemed to be a model dad. He bought the kids clothing and cooked dinner. Thank goodness, I was smart enough not to berate her. In time, it became obvious that he was dysfunctional. He forgot to pick up car pools and stopped showing up for work. I felt very torn. I wanted to support my son, but I also wanted to see my grandchildren. I decided to help my daughter-in-law out by inviting the kids to come for vacation. I thought I was doing a nice thing. She agreed to send them on the condition that I follow a court order that stated my son needed to take a test for traces of drugs before every visit, and that he would not be allowed in the house if he failed. How was I to comply? It felt terrible not allowing my son in his own house! I just didn't understand how this could help his addiction. On the other hand, I wanted to see my grandchildren. Reluctantly, I agreed to her conditions. But I was not happy. In addition, I did not squeal on my son to my daughter-in-law, nor did I tell him what I knew about her.

With divorce, there is always his story, her story, and the truth. It took this mother a while to realize the truth. She was wise to offer assistance to her daughter-in-law. It wasn't easy to face the reality of her son's problems. If she had merely remained loyal to her son, believing her daughter-in-law to be the villain, she would have lost her grandchildren.

When one person in the relationship has an addiction problem, one cannot expect things to work out. Addictions happen in both generations.

* * *

Elissa's mom was divorced for 14 years and was very lonely. Finally she met Dennis. It was such a relief to Elissa to see her mom happy again. "Dennis was charming. They went dancing and hiking. She was whole again. Gradually, I came to understand Dennis was also a drinker. He had a chaser in the morning and continued drinking throughout the day. He was morose by evening. Mom wanted to take the grandkids, but I did not want them exposed to Dennis's habits. I encouraged Mom to divorce him, but she said he was a good man and she was enjoying life so much more than when she was married to my Dad or when she was single."

One never knows what goes on in another person's marriage—not even the parents or the children. Elissa can continue to keep her children from her mother, she can suggest that her mother come to her house without Dennis, or she can put limits on what her mother can do with them and explain her worries about Dennis vis-à-vis the children.

* * *

Taking sides is not productive. You can let your child or parent know that you love them. The decision to divorce is not yours. As an adult, you have the right to choose with whom you or your young children will associate. A former in-law may or may not be a person you can choose.

> My son was a wonderful boy. OK, so he had his tantrums some-times, but what kid doesn't? He was a wonderful father. He took his preschool-aged children every weekend on a different adventure: the zoo, the park, the library. He seemed to be a good provider. Well, he and his wife did not get along; I had the good wisdom to stay out of it. After they divorced, to my horror, my son never visited his kids! He went off with some floozy. Well, I guess she wasn't such a floozy. He devoted all his energies to her kids and neglected his own. We stepped in and paid his child support since he wasn't giving his ex-wife anything! She had no skills and had been a stay-at-home mom. She was (and is) a good mother. We felt it was important that our grandchildren have every opportunity. While we are not wealthy, we are comfortable. Many of my friends thought that we were just bribing our daughter-in-law to let us see the kids. But we felt we were fulfilling our son's obligation. I told her that I hadn't divorced her—my son had.

These parents found a way to be involved with the mother of their grand-children, their former daughter-in-law, after the divorce. They main-tained their ties. They found a niche for themselves after the divorce. In both this case and the case of the mother with the son addicted to drugs, despite their feelings of love for their son, the mothers did not demon-ize their former daughters-in-law. Instead, they offered assistance. They set rules about not being the go-between. In both cases, the parents modeled cooperative and kind behavior. While their feelings were not neutral, they did not take sides, but instead helped their daughters-in-law in the difficult times of reconfiguring a family.

Often in a divorce, it would be easy to get involved as each spouse justifies his or her rancor. The feelings around the divorce itself are often temporary; people are in turmoil at that time and may be angry. It is impossible to take back what we say in times when others are divorcing. This is a time for listening. We are all capable of being mean. We all want others to forget what we said in our most unhappy and angry moments. Forgetting the transitory moment can help heal the wounds for all family members. The time and energy devoted to a now ex-relative for some can feel wasted; others recalibrate their relationship and decide that maintaining old ties is worth the trouble. They can continue the bond, but in a new way—the bond is no longer sanctioned by marriage, but is one built on affection and the warmth of former affiliation.

When your child divorces, you don't have to. You can decide that the person who was married to your child still has your affection. You can include that person in holidays. You can help that person out. You can jointly figure out visiting schedules for the grandchildren. If you are an adult child who does not want to divorce from your in-law parents, let them know, *"Your child and I are divorcing, but I want you in the family."* Then act accordingly, just as you would if they were still legally related.

*   *   *

Sometimes "divorce" happens even without a marriage. Strong quasi in-law bonds can survive even these breakups.

When Penny's mother first learned that her daughter and I were in love, she ran screaming out of the house. She cried for days. She was distraught that her daughter was a lesbian. For seven months, Penny's father would screen my calls and not let me talk to Penny. Finally, they both realized that they could not stop us, but they were not happy. Penny and I were both from good Catholic families. We had 24 years of Catholic education between us, so we understood how difficult our coupling was for our parents. We talked about their disappointment in us and agreed that we would just try to be understanding of these parents who had been good to us.

In the end, I developed a really good relationship with Penny's parents. Penny and her mom would go shopping for the day, and her dad and I would run errands and cook dinner. Later, when I had more money and they didn't, I bought them a used car. When her dad's Parkinson's disease advanced, I got him one of those chairs that had a clicker you could press to lift you out of it. He really loved that and needed it. He is dead now.

When, to my deep sadness, Penny and I split after 27 years and two children, Penny's mother maintained contact with me. She invited me to her seventy-fifth birthday party and told me, "You'll always be in my family and in my heart." I gave them a lot over the 27 years that Penny and I were together, and they gave love to me and to our children—and Penny's mother still does. I am grateful. Though I was hurt by Penny's folks' initial reaction to her "coming out" as a lesbian, I also understood it.

This young woman showed great maturity in understanding Penny's parents' shock and disappointment even though she and Penny were proud of themselves. They made a deliberate decision not to fault them for a lack of understanding. Penny's parents later showed great love as they adjusted to their daughter's homosexuality. They understood that both women were more than just their sexual orientation and appreciated their good qualities. Although these women were never married by law, they were married by love, and they embraced each other's families and were, in turn, embraced by them. Thus, the "in-law" relationship continued long after the demise of the couple's all-but-legal marriage.

For the parental generation, ambiguity surrounds divorce and remarriage. There is a first daughter-in-law and a second daughter-in-law, as well as their parents, siblings, and so forth. Perhaps the second daughter-in-law resents that you are still friendly with the first daughter-in-law, who happens to be the mother of your grandchildren, and you certainly want to stay on good terms with both. Then there are the existing children of the second daughter-in-law. What exactly is their relationship with you? Should you treat them like grandchildren? Do your own grandchildren resent that? And how do you interact with their own two or more sets of biological grandparents? It goes on and on. These are real contemporary issues happening all the time. You can find solace in the numbers of others dealing with the same issues you face, but there are few prescriptions.

FAMILIES RECONFIGURED AFTER A DEATH

Sometimes families are split by death and reconfigure later. What is the role of the trailing in-laws—that is, the in-laws of the late spouse?

> *Recently my son-in-law visited with his new wife and her three children from her previous marriage. My daughter died after lingering with cancer. We love her husband and remained close after her death. We often took the grandkids to give him some respite. I noticed during their last visit that the stepmother of my grandchildren paid a lot of attention to her biological kids, but gave much less to her husband's children. My grandkids have suffered so much with the loss of their mother. It pains me to see how she favors her own children.*

Although these in-laws were happy that their former son-in-law was building a new life for the kids and himself, they could not help but be sad for themselves and for what might have been had their daughter lived. They tried to be welcoming to the new wife, but the scene was clearly painful to observe. Like in-law relationships, step relationships take time to build. Maybe the new wife felt that her biological children needed extra attention during the visit, as they were uncomfortable visiting these strangers who were not officially their grandparents. Or maybe the wife really does always show favoritism to her own children. It will take time to really know whether her favoritism is a problem. In the meantime, the grandparents can model inclusive behavior by including all of the children in projects and excursions. They can also keep developing the relationship with the new wife. Sometimes we just have to keep doing the right thing. The grandparents can offer to take all of the children so that the new couple could have a day of freedom together without responsibilities. We don't have to act on every inkling. If the problem goes on for a long while, the in-laws can share their observations with their former son-in-law or with the new wife. She may be unaware of her actions. But parents-in-law cannot fix every problem. Like parenting, in-lawing is an art, not a science. We can only do the best we can.

* * *

Sometimes permanent bonds are forged even with extended family members.

> *My father married Hester two years after my mother died. In attendance at the wedding were my sister and her husband, my husband and me, and Hester's brother and sister-in-law. We particularly took to the new sister-in-law and the brother and began to think of them fondly as an aunt and an uncle. It seemed like we all got married that day. We spent the holidays together and shared each other's accomplishments, however small. When my dad and Hester died, we all remained connected. I think we just liked each other. I know both my sister and I go to this step-aunt-in-law for advice, for the wisdom that comes from living, and we treasure the way this step-aunt-in-law and step-uncle-in-law have stepped in as substitute grandparents, applauding our children as they go through life.*

We are lucky when our in-laws are nice people who are easy to love. However, even if our in-laws are not easy to love, we do have some control over the qualities we focus on, and that can make all the difference. None of us is perfect, but most of us have something worthwhile to offer each other.

Intergenerational in-law relationships are hard for both the parents and the adult kids. Is the stepfather-in-law who raised your husband from age 14 the grandparent of your children? And when it is the parents who remarry, the children may feel abandoned, despite the fact that they have families of their own. They are accustomed to being the primary focus of their parents' lives. Children of any age can become jealous of a new love interest.

* * *

Sharing a parent's love is not the only concern for the children. They may be concerned that the monetary assets that they expected to receive, regardless of whether they were ever discussed, may now be spent on a new spouse or even worse: a new family created by the new unit. Children are also concerned about saving their deceased parent's memory.

> *I moved in with Tony about a year after his first wife died. My husband had died 13 years earlier. I figured his girls would be upset, so I left the painting of their mother on the wall. My feeling was that it wouldn't hurt me to have her smiling down. However, I hate clutter, so I took her snapshot off the refrigerator. The girls were upset. That taught me to go very slowly about changing things. This house was their mother's house. I tried to be respectful of the first spouse. I did not try to be the girls' mother, but I created a space where they were welcome and where they could all come and gather. I babysat for their children. I cooked meals for them. On the anniversary of their mother's death, they all went to the cemetery and did not include me. I would have gone but was not upset that they did not include me. I was not part of their mother's life.*

This quasi step-in-law knew that she could not replace the adult children's deceased mother. She honored their feelings and understood that the picture of their mother was exactly that—a picture of the girls' mother, not a competitor of hers. She carved out another relationship with her stepdaughters and with her husband. She became a counselor, an advisor, and a trusted friend.

Sometimes the competitive feelings are not between the new and the former spouse, but between the generations. When a parent marries a contemporary of his or her child, or when a child couples with a contemporary of his or her parents, then the complexities multiply. Is my contemporary really my stepmom? Is my contemporary really an in-law child? Did I get replaced in my role as child or parent? Tread carefully and carry a big basket of forgiveness. There may be many gaffs as you cross lines in which age, role, and affection—or a lack of it—converge. Hidden in those gaffs may be some gifts. After all, each situation brings difficulties and opportunities, though sometimes we can't tell one from the other until time helps us sort the whole thing out.

PLENTY OF LOVE TO GO AROUND

With all the people who come along as significant others, there is no need to hold back on your affection. If the new person remains in the partnership, you will have shared some good times and have a nice foundation for further developments. If not, well, you had a chance to see your relative happy for a short while at least.

All of the various and sundry new family connections that result from more than the old-fashioned methods of reproduction offer in-laws a chance to be creative, to write their own rules, and to find out what works. But beware: ask any artist—getting it right takes much trial and error. Forgive mistakes and keep on trying.

QUESTIONS

- Who in your family is not related but is, or should be, treated like an in-law?
- What keeps you from including a new person in your family?
- How do you feel about ex-members of your family? How can you include them?
- How do you raise difficult topics with nonrelated quasi family members?
- How do you raise questions with family members about nonrelated but long-term companions?

CHAPTER 7

Diversity Comes Home: Intermarriage

BLESSING OR CURSE

Every marriage is an intermarriage. Two people mean two backgrounds, two upbringings, and two family cultures—or maybe more. Some differences are glaring and others are subtle. Race, national background, religion, and class may seem obvious. But within each one of these categories, there are many different subgroups. We merge these into big umbrella classifications, which hide some differences. The classification of African American, for example, includes descendants of former American slaves, as well as immigrants from the Caribbean islands, South America, and Africa. Some would argue that white folks from Africa belong in this category, too. The classification of Catholic includes those who practice and those who have not been in church since their christening. It also includes people from many nations. The term Native American includes former enemies from many Indian nations, for example, the Hopis, the Iroquois, the Navahos, and the Cherokee. Many of us are intermarried by one definition and inmarried by another. Two evangelical Protestants marry—one a black person, the other white. A Native American and a Latina marry. They are both "persons of color" but come from different nations. A straight man comes from a gay family. We are all patchworks of categories. These classifications both unite and divide us.

Each one of these groupings has history, culture, and maybe even God on its side, justifying why its practices are worthy of preservation. These forces work against compromise. Our national and religious ideals often conflict with our desire to preserve our families. Accepting an outsider may involve rejection by one's community or at least going against the accepted norms. Despite what we would want to think when confronted with an in-law different from our own family, we may find ourselves having thoughts and judgments we had not expected.

RACE[1]

As much as we hate to admit it, race and skin color and shapes of noses or eyes have status overtones in many societies, and some races have more privilege than others. Parents may be sophisticated and have friends of all stripes, or they may be downright prejudiced against a particular race. Their displeasure may be founded on bigotry, or it might be based on the knowledge that societies do advantage one characteristic over another. Future in-laws find themselves worrying that their mixed-race grandchildren will not be accepted by either group. They worry that the children's skin will be too dark or too light or that their eyes will be too round or too slanted. They worry for their grandchildren's future. They may think the food and social customs of the other racial group are less prestigious than theirs. They may fear the newcomers will have different views from their own, forgetting that even those from the same race may have dissimilar values and looks. Parents fear their history will be lost, and with that loss will go their own connection to their own parents.

Alicia, a light-skinned African American, meets Cleave, a white man, in a park while walking her dogs. One thing leads to another, and a romance buds into a marriage. Cleave's family welcomes her into theirs. They like her looks, her humor, and the fact that she had worked her way through college. But they worry that their own community will look askance at the marriage. While they are proud that they have brought their son up without prejudice, they fear for their unborn grandchildren. They worry they will be arrested as teenagers, since they read in the newspaper about the dangers of "driving while black." Cleave's parents expect to absorb Alicia into their circle but have no desire to be part of hers. They do not invite Alicia's family to their home and politely refused Alicia's parents' invitation. They are afraid to visit her family and dislike the loud music they expect to hear in Alicia's home. The couple of times that the in-laws met before the wedding were awkward.

Alicia loves her family and thinks that even though Cleave's parents are nice to her, they should welcome her whole clan. She does not want or need to be tolerated, nor does she like seeing her family overlooked or prejudged. She resents her in-laws' attitude that she needs to be rescued from what they see as her "unfortunate background," even though they don't really know anything about her.

Cleave's parents haven't socialized with black people before, and despite their education, they assume all of black culture is ghetto. They fear the potential loss of status that their grandchildren and son might experience as part of this minority group. They risk losing the affections of their daughter-in-law and future grandchildren if they continue to assume their superiority. Alicia's family does not enjoy their phony friendliness to their daughter. They resent the unspoken message that Alicia would be better off if she left her birth family and became part of theirs. Both families may be cognizant of the power differentials within the society, but if they are to enjoy their children and grandchildren, they will need to learn more about each other as individuals and focus on their mutual interests in their children. Couples marry in the context of societal stereotypes, but those stereotypes do not always confirm reality—nor do they need to define their relationships. We all perform best when we are respected. These two families can only reconcile if they each have the curiosity to learn each other's stories. Alicia's family knows that society does not always appreciate their race, therefore, they can acknowledge Cleave's folks' concern. However, they are also justifiably angered by Cleave's parents' attitude. Cleave's folks fail to appreciate that Alicia's parents risk the same disapproval in their community. Just as Cleave's parents, in some corner of their heart, think it would be socially easier if their son married a white girl, so may the black family harbor the same thoughts. Both sets of parents could be on a journey of acceptance and appreciation of each other's struggles if they choose to. Categories can blind us to what we have in common.

* * *

Even within races there are concerns about skin color.

> *Radha met Raj at medical school. Her parents were both physicians in the United States and had sent her to the finest private schools. She had jet-black skin and was quite beautiful. Raj had lighter coffee-colored skin. His parents were engineers but had been laid off several times. He came to medical school after working his way through state college. Both parents were thrilled that their children had chosen to marry Indians, even though her family was from South India and spoke Tamil at home and his family was from North India and spoke Hindi at home. They had feared that their children would marry Americans. At the wedding, Radha's mother overheard Raj's mother saying to her close friend, "They are such a wonderful couple; too bad she's dark."*

Radha's parents are upset that their bright, beautiful, and financially well-off daughter was criticized for being dark. Paradoxically, her mother secretly had been pleased that she married a man with lighter skin. Skin color, in many cultures, confers or withholds status—thus, ambivalence may mix with pride. Both sets of parents long ago realized that their decision to move to America might eventually mean their children would choose their own spouses. While Raj was from a different part of India, a different linguistic group, and a different caste, both parents were pleased that because their children had chosen Indian mates, there was a chance they might keep some of their ancient customs. Humans are complex and often hold conflicting views. Much of our learning is making distinctions, fitting people and things into categories. Race, in general, and its subtleties within groups—as with Radha and Raj—are far from neutral, whether within society or within the family. These societal issues are well documented academically and in the daily news. Within the family, everyone needs to readjust their attitudes and prejudices. When a person of a different religion (or sect within the same religion) or a different race (or tone or culture within that race) marries into the family, the adjustments are complex. Some in the family may be shocked. Their disapproval may be open and loud, or it may be whispered behind the backs of the bride and groom. Others, hopefully, will react more positively and supportively, their acceptance modeling the sort of understanding that can build the family, not tear it down. In-laws are influenced by the imperfections in the societies around them. In-laws can berate each other for their ambivalence or accept that society is imperfect and, therefore, their own feelings are often imperfect. These imperfect feelings can and do change and do not have to be accompanied by dislike or fear.

RELIGION

Religions are both universal and particular. Universally, they are about the human quest to understand our place in the universe. They explore how to relate to other humans. Most preach kindness and justice, feeding the poor, and healing the sick. If we all followed the basic principles of our own religion, we would do justice and love mercy and walk humbly together. Often we confuse religious observance with moral character and moral sensibility. Intermarried families tend to do best when they focus more on the universal themes and less on ideology. The ways of expressing these universal hopes and the symbols surrounding them create the tensions. The search for God does not separate humans, but finding him does. Our certainty of our own rightness might help us get through life's troubles, but it will not help us with our in-law children from another religion.

Those couples from different religions have the advantage of knowing that sensitivity and compromise will be necessary if they are to live peacefully together and with their in-laws. Their differences are hard to avoid. Either the couple or the in-laws may not be interested in making compromises. What holidays should they celebrate? Ramadan or Passover? Christmas or Chanukah or both? Diwali or Nowruz? And are these religious holidays or merely family get-togethers? Can each family member decide his or her own meaning for the holiday or must one believe its religious tenets?[2]

When Steve and Nasreen married, Steve agreed to raise the children as Muslims. He is from a completely secularized Christian family, and he realized that religion was central to Nasreen's life. His family did, however, make a huge deal about Christmas. Usually they celebrated at Steve's sister's home. One year, she was unable to host. The family asked Nasreen and Steve to hold the festivities at their home. Nasreen knew how important Christmas celebrations were to her in-law family and wanted to be respectful. However, she did not feel comfortable celebrating it at her own home. For her, it was one thing to celebrate Christmas in her in-laws' home and quite another for her to have a Christmas tree in her home. After much discussion with her husband, she agreed to hold the party but not have Christmas decorations or a tree. To her, displaying the symbols of a group that had persecuted her people during the Crusades felt disrespectful to her heritage. Besides, she did not want her four-year-old to think that Christmas was his holiday. The family was disappointed when they arrived to find no tree and told her so.

Nasreen and Steve came to a compromise that worked for both of them. He had his family party, and she did not have to create a holiday that was not her own or her son's. The extended family, however, had not been informed of their reasoning. Many discussions, many experiments, and several Christmases later, they came to accommodations that worked for all family members. When Christmas was held at Steve's sister's home, all of the decorations were acceptable, but in Nasreen's home, only greens were used. Their affection for each other trumped their disappointment. Unfortunately, however, this is not always the case.

* * *

Symbols of peace and joy to some are the reminders of persecution for others. One's perspective grows out of the history one is taught. When children arrive, unfamiliar customs and symbols can disquiet family members. Centuries of forced conversions can make christenings and baptisms repugnant to Jews and Muslims. Yet those who believe in the divinity of Christ worry that their unbaptized grandchildren will not find a place in heaven. To Jews and Muslims, the ritual circumcision of males is very important for both religious continuity and health reasons. Others may find it unnecessary and even revolting. There is no denying either the depth of feelings or the potential for tension, but understanding and knowledge can mitigate disrespect. As tourists, many of us visit the shrines of others and admire their beauty or listen with awe to their music. We do the same for our friends who practice religions different from ours. We are all tourists in the religions of others—be they friends, in-laws, or other family members.

> Daniel's parents were not pleased when he married Rosalie, a Christian, but they tried to welcome her into the family and help her pay her college loans. However, they did not go to their grandson's christening when he was two months old. It was just too painful. The baby's great-grandfather had been a Holocaust survivor. Rosalie was furious. She had been willing to have a ritual circumcision for her son on the eighth day, which her in-laws attended with great joy, but Rosalie also wanted a christening to honor her faith and her parents. She told Daniel, "We had the circumcision for you, and they should have come to the christening for me."

Neither the parents nor the children had shared the plan in advance. Rosalie thought she was compromising. When Daniel's parents saw how hurt their daughter-in-law was, they were even more distraught. They knew they did not want to lose their connection with their son and his family, but they could not change what they felt. Finally, they talked with other people whose children had intermarried. They decided to just continually reach out to the daughter-in-law in other ways. At first, she continued to resist. It took many years, but over time, they healed the rift and eventually were able to talk openly about why the christening had been so painful to them.

Religious observances can both exult and compromise our moral character. Sadly, religions have left many of us with bitter feelings for historical wrongs. Focusing on the commonalities will not erase differences, but it will create a neutral turf for families to come together. Most religions suggest accepting the imperfection of life, of ourselves, and of others. Those who only focus on the differences miss a chance to enhance their own religious understanding by exploring the universals of their own religions.

Both parents and in-law children can only benefit from learning about each other's customs and ceremonies. Perhaps they will discover which ones they can enjoy together and how. They may not even realize how important their traditions are to them until a birth or a death occurs and they realize that there seems to be no common way to mark the experience. If both generations explore what aspects of their heritages they want to pass on, there is room for much discussion. Knowing how others have handled religious differences can help, too. All of us are limited in imagining possibilities. When we share our experiences with others, we gain new perspectives.

Same Label, Different Practices

In terms of family adjustments, intermarriage rough spots can emerge even when both families have the same religion. The more religious are appalled by the lack of observance by the less religious, and the less religious find the more observant rigid and anachronistic. Whether the in-laws are Protestants, Catholics, Jews, Muslims, or Hindus, differences in religious observance can strike at the very core of family customs, values, and habits.

Integral to any religious practice are often local customs. Catholics in Mexico, unlike those in Ireland or Boston, celebrate Our Lady of

Guadalupe. Jews from Arabic countries pray with sounds found in Arabic music, while the Jews from Eastern Europe pray with melodies similar to European folk music. Hindus in North India celebrate holidays different from those in South India. Standards of modesty for Muslim women vary by country as well as by religious conviction. Examples abound:

Aafreen marries Mustafa. Both are Muslim and observe all the holidays. Aafreen wears Western clothes and a kerchief over her hair. Mustafa's family wants her to dress more modestly with a cloak over her jeans.

*   *   *

Leah is an observant Jew; she belongs to a congregation with mixed seating. Her husband, Maurice, and his family are also observant but only pray in synagogues with separate seating for men and women.

*   *   *

Maureen goes to church every Sunday and takes Communion. Bill, who also was brought up Catholic, goes only on Easter and Christmas.

*   *   *

For Ann, the church is the center of her life. For Tom, although he, too, is Protestant, the church is a place to visit for weddings and funerals.

*   *   *

Mona Lal is a devout Hindu and vegetarian. His wife, from another part of India, eats meat, but not beef.

Those from the same religious background are often surprised to find how much negotiation is necessary between the couple and their families if they are to find some religious common ground. Expecting to think like another person, let alone another family, is unrealistic. Of course there will be differences.[3] Even in families from the same religion, different members must still accommodate.

> *When Marie died, her family held a mass in her honor. Frances, the oldest daughter, insisted that all of the siblings and siblings-in-law take Communion; she was certain that their mother would have liked it. Frances told the others in no uncertain terms that they would humiliate the memory of their mother if they did not comply. The others balked. There were many religious differences, even in this completely Catholic family. One couple was living "in sin," though they no longer saw it that way. Another was divorced and, therefore, could not take the sacrament. Several others were no longer believers. A huge argument erupted.*

Fortunately, the priest intervened and suggested that each child could honor the deceased by following his or her own conscience. Forcing others to pray the way we do can only lead to animosity. There are always solutions, but the willingness of the family members to find and accommodate to these solutions may differ.

In-laws are wise to respond with something deeper, something roomier, than the usual admonitions. Families need something that addresses the new complexities of religious identity emerging before their eyes—more "both/and" than "either/or." The family does not have to retreat from its own beliefs to welcome others. A willingness to make small compromises may be enough. Curiosity about differences and humility about the "rightness" of one's own ways will be helpful to all as in-laws incorporate each other into their families. An appreciation for variety and for the right of adults to choose their own values can enhance connection and understanding.

*   *   *

Some families literally don't speak the same language. Despite such an enormous challenge, however, families manage to communicate nonetheless.

> *Elvira and her mother-in-law had no common language. Elvira became an expert at reading body language. She and her mother-in-law smiled*

a lot, baked together, and tried desperately to find common interests. With no real conversation, the days felt rather long when the in-laws visited, so they tried to do activities they both enjoyed. Their conflicts arose not about language, but about social class. Her mother-in-law was from an upper-class family in Malaysia, and Elvira was from a working-class family in Newark, New Jersey. One day she served the dinner and put the pots directly on the table. By reading her mother-in-law's face, she knew she had done something wrong. Although Elvira was concerned about serving the food piping hot, she decided to acquiesce to her mother-in-law's gestures. Accommodating was more important to her than doing things her own way in her kitchen.

Even without words, people can communicate, and they can fight. The will to understand each other is a most powerful tool.

CORE VALUES

Some humans have raised the basic human bodily functions of eating, sleeping, and drinking to an art form, while others stay with the basics. Five-star restaurants or porridge, $6,000 mattresses or rope cots, champagne or beer, marble bathrooms or the fields all serve basic human needs. Class and taste dictate what in the spectrum of solutions for dealing with biological needs each of us will choose. On the one hand, the choices are trivial since they all get the job done. On the other, they differentiate, they connote status, and they provide comfort. Eating foods we know and being served them in the manner in which we are accustomed are familiar routines. Their absence, as we have seen in other chapters, can cause plenty of trouble.

Imagine how much more trouble can be caused when families differ on what they perceive as core values. When this occurs, both families are challenged to reconsider their positions and may find themselves in conflict with their communities.

Our son is marrying Janine. We like her a lot. Her parents divorced when she was four, and her father married a woman soon after.

Her mother also married a woman. We don't hold this against our daughter-in-law-to-be. However, she wants them all to walk down the aisle at the wedding. Our community believes that marriage is only between a man and a woman. It will embarrass us to have those two women walk down together. For us, "Don't Ask, Don't Tell" is a good policy; their walking down the aisle will flaunt their homosexuality. Besides, we doubt our church would allow it.

The clash is big here. The groom's family believes that the core value is love solely between a man and a woman, and the bride's family believes that the core value is love of any type. If these in-laws want a good relationship with their daughter-in-law, they will have no choice but to accept her parents. After all, all four of her parents brought her up to be the lovely woman their son loves. Accepting that may embarrass the groom's parents within their community. Of course, the couple could hold a small informal wedding in another venue. However, his parents would not only lose their dream of their son marrying in their own church, but also risk alienating the other family. The bride's parents do not care if the wedding is in a church, but walking down the aisle is extremely important to them. One side must compromise. Each family must decide what it is willing to give up without dictating what the other family can or should do. In-laws cannot choreograph the relationships and values of another family.

Whenever intermarriage occurs, all involved must face their own prejudices. Sometimes we must educate our communities and choose between them and our parents or our children. Each person must decide the kind of accommodations he or she wants and is able to make. As with religion, focusing on the universal helps, but ultimately all of us must make peace with strangers who are related to people we love if we are all to get along.

TRADITION

Within the good, there is always some bad. Patriotism helps our country remain strong and unites very disparate groups with a common history, common hopes, common stories, and common goals. However, patriotism gone awry can lead to dismissing the national aspirations of others. Believing that our way is the only just and right way can lead to war both within and outside families. People who see the world in this manner risk alienating newcomers to their families. For example, in-laws from patriarchal societies can interpret independence as rude and disobedient. And in-laws from societies that value independence can view patriarchal actions as controlling.

> *Krista met Fareed at work. He was handsome, dashing, and very wealthy. Fareed was struck by the strength of Krista's personality, her ability to make decisions, and her ability to support herself. She met his family and liked them. She admired their story. They had come penniless from the Middle East and had worked hard, all pulling together to achieve the American dream. She noticed that the father dominated the conversation but thought little of it. However, after the marriage, Fareed's father expected her to acquiesce to his every request, including being present every Sunday for a four-hour dinner and giving her salary to the family whenever someone was in need. She was horrified. She asked Fareed to explain to his father that she was brought up differently and that she needed to work or play on her own on Sunday and keep her own money. Fareed, however, knew his place in the family. He had to honor his father. He would not support her in her bid for independence.*

Neither Fareed nor Krista discussed these issues in advance, as it never occurred to them that they were making different assumptions about their place in the family. Many of us are unaware of hidden norms in relationships. Fareed's father believed, as head of the family, that he had the right and responsibility to protect and care for all in his family. Krista thought she had the right and responsibility to care for herself. The father was holding too tight. He could not release his son from obligations that might no longer be considered mandatory by the younger generation and by a wife from a different culture. Krista was perhaps not sensitive enough to the demands of her husband's family's culture. Both held rigidly to their notions of what was proper. Neither would compromise.

Fareed was caught between the two, and Krista felt unsupported. Neither parent nor in-law child could bend, and, as a result, this marriage eventually dissolved. The pull of different family expectations was too strong for the couple to withstand. We ask a very big price when we force our spouse or our children to choose between us and their families. None of us can serve all of the needs of another person on our own.

*   *   *

One set of in-laws may insist that their culture dominate the young family. Some families feel so strongly about their national heritage that they insist that all of the children go to school to learn its language and customs. The person who married into this family may not want the children to attend that school, drive car pools to that school, or attend national events and ceremonies.

> *Betty Ann was from Wisconsin and of a Swedish heritage. She was brought up as a Lutheran, but church meant little to her. She was married to Constantine, who came to the United States from Greece when he was ten. Their marriage lasted nine years, during which time they had two children—a boy and a girl. Her in-laws insisted on speaking only Greek to their grandchildren and that they go to church school twice a week to learn to read and write Greek. While Betty Ann had no problem with her children learning a second language, she resented her in-laws for not speaking English when she was around. She also celebrated her Christmas and Easter, as well as theirs. Eventually, she and Constantine divorced. Religion and language were not the problem. They just could not seem to get along. In the divorce agreement, Betty Ann agreed to continue the children's Greek education. She kept this commitment. Her in-laws neither offered to drive the children nor did they thank her for doing so.*

In-law parents may forget or ignore the sacrifice that their in-law children make in agreeing to educate their children in another heritage.

Obviously, appreciation goes a long way. Acknowledging an in-law who comes into a family with a culture worthy of preservation, too, can go a long way to building bridges. Sometimes in-laws forget that even those who seem like mainstream Americans also have backgrounds and traditions they think are worth preserving. In-laws give a gift to each other when they honor both their own traditions and some of those of the family into which they marry.

While there are no easy answers to getting along with those from different backgrounds, insight, thinking ahead to the consequences of one's actions, and discussing with children and in-law children how they might like to interact are all important tools in mitigating problems. It may take years to come to comfortable ways of getting along, but unless common ground is found, either the parents or the couple will become alienated.

THE MIX MASTER

No matter our age or cultural traditions, we can learn from those who have worked things out, even if it took several years.

> *Jane's parents are avowed atheists; they live a day's drive away from their children and grandchildren. Norton's parents live five minutes away and see the kids and grandkids all the time. When Jane's parents visit, Norton's parents want everyone to go to church together on Sunday, although the younger generation practices no specific religion. Jane's folks are not pleased. They would rather that their children and grandchildren had no religion, but even more so, they would really like time alone with their grandchildren. The four in-laws do get along, largely because they all make the effort and because Jane's parents reason that going to church will not hurt the children. After several years of this, only recently did Norton—on his own— turn down his parents' invitation for church and Sunday mid-day meal, saying that Jane's parents deserved some special time with the*

children. Jane's parents really appreciated their son-in-law's gesture and told him so.

Jane's parents had been polite and patient despite their disappointment about getting their own time with their grandchildren. They coped with a less than perfect situation to keep family peace. In the end, however, thanks to their son-in-law, they got the time with their grandchildren that they had wanted, and the children did not have to go to a church that was not meaningful to them. The time alone with their grandchildren gave Jane's parents a chance, if they wanted to use the time that way, to share their own spiritual ideas with the grandchildren or just to play and enjoy one another. Norton's parents still had the opportunity to share their religion with their grandchildren—just not every week. Norton's willingness to speak to his parents created a much more satisfactory situation. Sometimes one generation can help the other.

EYES ON THE PRIZE

Expect that it will take a long time to learn and understand each other's comfort level. Reserve judgment and avoid objectification, trivialization, and degradation. The underlying assumption of assimilation is that ethnic groups should conform to the norms and values of the surrounding society while also maintaining their own customs. No matter who we are, we struggle with walking the line between our collective national identity and our individual religious and cultural identities. Anger, rage, and blame are not productive. Adaptive family responses require care, concern, and mutual support. We often assume that if only our family were alike in terms of religion or race or culture, everything would be fine. But in truth, our families change because they are expanding and the environments around them are expanding, too. We cannot freeze the past. If our goal is to keep parents, siblings, and grandchildren all caring about each other, we have no choice but to modify some of our ways of thinking and doing. We need to deemphasize "them" and create an "us."

QUESTIONS

- What aspects of your heritage do you want to pass on to your children and grandchildren?
- How do you explain your own traditions and your feelings about them to your grandchildren and to their other grandparents?
- How do/did you explain your own in-laws' different cultural practices or religious beliefs to your children?
- How do you react when your in-laws discuss their heritage, culture, or religion?
- Are there cultural or religious practices you have that make your in-laws uncomfortable? How do you deal with that?
- Are there rites that your in-laws celebrate that you do not? Why? How do you explain your feelings to them and to your children or grandchildren?
- Are there religious events that your in-laws attend that you do not? Why? How do you explain your feelings to your children or grandchildren?
- How might you pass on your traditions without trampling on the beliefs of your children?
- What can you do to make your in-laws more comfortable?

Chapter 8

Whose Child Is This? Grandparents, Parents, and Grandchildren

At the end of the day, many of us get along for the kids. Whether we are parents dealing with difficult in-laws or grandparents who don't particularly like our in-law child or even someone who was not expecting a grandchild to enter our lives at all, most of us come to love, or at least tolerate, the babies. They are the best incentive for accommodating in-laws we may not like.

NEW ROLES

The arrival of a new generation not only transforms the couple into parents and their parents into grandparents, but it also can magnify tensions between the generations. Grandchildren create new territory for all. The couple must ensure that their own nest is secure enough to take care of the child. Their time is consumed by the new offspring. Their emotional life is filled with the insecurities of preparing their child for a future they do not know. They may not have time or energy for the grandparents and certainly not for any in-law grandparents, with whom they may still be establishing a relationship and with whom they may not be entirely comfortable. While parents and children have renegotiated their roles many times as they grew together over the years, adult in-law children and their in-law parents are new to this task, at least in this configuration. There are no established means of dealing with any disagreements. Neither generation knows its role.

With the baby's arrival, tensions may arise between parents and grandparents since all are taking on new roles while building in-law relationships. No one really understands what he or she wants until the baby is born. Of course, what everyone wants keeps changing. Some grandparents may be busy with their other children when the first grandchild arrives and retired when the subsequent ones are born. Some parents want the grandparents' wisdom, experience, and time. Others want no interference at all. Parents may need help with their first child but feel competent with number two, or vice versa. Many grandparents are judgmental about the way their children and children-in-law raise their grandchildren. They may not approve of the parents' choices due to cultural, religious, or age differences. Grandparents who judge are likely to be judged themselves. Judgment leads both generations to defend their ways and to aggrandize their own methods of bringing up baby. Each generation assumes it knows what is best and can find the other lacking.

To compound the situation, we may be surprised to discover that we play our new roles better or worse than we'd expected. We may have fantasized that we would be ever patient and loving yet are surprised to find that we can be too short-tempered. Figuring out what each of us wants takes a lot of self-knowledge and experimentation.

For grandparents, this self-awareness must extend to facing and accommodating their own physical limits. Parenting and grandparenting are hard physical work. It is difficult to acknowledge our infirmities, especially to our own children.

Nicole and Richard were both pleased when a work promotion required that they move very near Richard's parents, Donna and Alan, who were in their 70s and in good health. They previously lived near Nicole's parents, who were more than a decade younger and more active and energetic. Moving around with two toddlers proved a challenge for all. Nicole had relied on her parents, and they felt the loss of the nearby grandkids. Nicole had hoped to rely on Donna and Alan as babysitters, as she had done with her own parents, since she preferred family care to hired care. Donna had rearranged her schedule so that she could be as supportive as possible. She discovered, however, that as much as she adored the grandkids and as much as she didn't want to think about it, an 18-month-old and a 3-year-old were more than she—or she and Alan—could handle on their own. Every time she attempted to raise the issue, she thought her daughter-in-law evaded it. Nicole actually sensed something was amiss but didn't know Donna well enough to read her signals. Both Nicole and Donna knew something wasn't working, but neither felt comfortable discussing her doubts.

Our in-law children often do not know us well. They may misinterpret what we see as honesty for complaining or for unwillingness to be supportive. Or in-laws may be reluctant or feel that it's "not their place" to confront us with possibilities we may not be ready to face. Here, your own child can play a mediating role, if you are careful not to force your child to take sides. The adult child can be a translator between the parents and the in-law child. In this case, had his parents told them of their inability to keep up with the little ones, Richard could have told Nicole that his parents were not the type to complain or slack. She had no way of knowing this. He might have suggested they get some part-time help to assist in the afternoons. The key is to not cast aspersion but focus on solving the problem.

No matter how much love parents and grandparents have for the grandchildren, both generations can easily get bogged down in the details of daily life or annoyed because the other generation does things (in their eyes) in a totally unacceptable manner. Everyone involved benefits when their goal is to relate to one another in a manner that enables the grandchildren to thrive. Without such a goal in mind, grandchildren can become pawns in a low-grade war in which the battlefronts are discipline, food, gifts, and even lifestyle.

Young children may have no idea what an in-law is, but they can see, hear, and sense when there is tension in the family. The following comment by a grandchild was overheard in a nursery school car pool: "*My mommy doesn't want my grandpa to visit unless he calls because he watches her like a cop. Daddy says his dad can come any time. Mommy and Daddy were fighting. I don't think Mommy likes Grandpa.*" Our children mimic our tone or words. They do what we model. If they see us behaving with tolerance and kindness, forgiving slights, they learn from what we do. There may be many awkward moments as all players try to figure out what they want and what they have to contribute to the grandchild and to each other. Not surprisingly, the difficulties multiply when the grandparents relate badly to their own child's spouse or partner. They may find that their own children, if they have good relationships with them, may be highly effective mediators, advocating for their partners while representing their parents' point of view in conversations.

IN-LAWS CAN BE HELPFUL OR HURTFUL

In-law parents as well as one's own parents can serve not only to give respite but also to pass on beneficial information to the younger generation. Having grandparents as a constant can give children a sense of stability and comfort, making them aware that they are well loved and cared for. Grandparents can help nurture a child. If anything tragic were to happen to the parents, grandparents can be guardians. There is abundant evidence that keeping children's grandparents in their lives is highly advantageous. If parents want as much support as possible for their children, they will need to foster good relationships with their in-laws as well as with their own parents.[1]

In-law children often complain that their in-laws are too critical, too interfering, and too overwhelming: "*They are my kids, and I don't think your folks should be criticizing how I raise them,*" "*Let us make our mistakes; goodness knows your parents made theirs,*" and "*It is so difficult meeting everyone's needs; I feel pulled apart when they visit.*"

Many parenting lessons are those learned at our own parents' knees. Others come from what we've observed among family and friends. However, those very lessons set up a venue for in-law complications, as experiences can be very different, thus creating many discrepancies for the couple to work out in child rearing and family interactions. Every conversation involves a speaker, a listener, and all the noise in between. That noise consists, in part, of past interpretations and present anxieties that color and distort perceptions. What one person associates with warmth and love, the other may see as controlling. What the grandparents' own child finds familiar, the in-law child might find threatening, discourteous, or confusing.[2] What is said with love or concern from the speaker's perspective may be heard as criticism. Each hears through filters created by his or her own past experiences and by the discomforts in his or her present situation. Generational differences can further complicate things. The younger generation may feel misunderstood, judged, or unheard. A suggestion by an in-law that parents should enjoy the present because childhood is fleeting can annoy the parents, who may be completely exhausted and overwhelmed by days that seem interminably long. To them, the grandparents "just don't get it!"[3]

It may never have occurred to parents to ask what role the grandparents want in their lives and the lives of their children. Think back to your own life when your children were really little. What did you discuss with your own parents? With your in-laws? Some parents may never have had grandparents of their own to know what role they might play. Neither parenthood nor grandparenthood comes with an instruction manual. Each must write his or her own. Of course, once each player has figured out a relationship with one person, that relationship will need to be figured out again with another parent or another child. Sadly, no secret recipes work for all of us or work all the time.

Many grandparents unexpectedly become the full-time caretakers of their grandchildren as a result of death, prison, drug abuse, or military service, to name a few.[4] When the grandparents have formal custody of their grandchildren, the lines of command are clear. When they do not, or when they gain custody only temporarily, the situation is far more complicated for everyone involved. All over the country, grandparents are tending to children whose parents are deployed around the world in military service. Many provide services for months at a time and then are pushed aside until the next deployment months later.[5] When circumstances force parents in and out of their children's lives and surrogates must step in, it is confusing for all—parents, grandparents, and children.

> *Courtney joined the National Guard after her divorce to help pay the bills. Her husband's irresponsible and philandering ways were just too much for her. His parents helped out on the weekends when she needed to work. When she was deployed to Iraq, she had to leave her four-year-old son with her ex-husband's parents because her own parents still worked full time. Nine months later, she returned to a son who clung to her but refused her discipline. As far as she was concerned, the son she returned to was out of control. While she did not want to deprive the son of his grandparents, she was really angry that they had not followed her wishes about keeping him on a schedule with a cleanup time, a bedtime, and a personal responsibility time to brush his teeth and take a bath. Courtney was so peeved that she could barely talk with her in-laws. Moreover, reentry was difficult in other ways. She was jumpy and afraid of sudden loud noises. Because she had to work outside the home as well as parent, she needed her in-laws' help but had no idea how to get past her anger. Yet she knew it was necessary to maintain the relationship with her in-laws for her son's sake, as well as for her own. She also knew she might be deployed again.*

This family should seek whatever help is available from the military counseling service. Courtney needs support from people who have some understanding of the difficulty of her transition. Her in-laws, too, would benefit from knowing why tensions have grown between them and Courtney. Perhaps the in-laws felt that because the boy's mother was gone they needed to show more coddling and less discipline. Their motives may have been good ones. Courtney can explain her current difficulties with her son. This discussion will give her a chance to look at her own parenting style. Since both she and her in-laws have the same hopes and dreams that the child will grow up to be healthy and happy, they can start from this point to empathize with each other and come to some accommodation of each other's parenting rules, if not to a perfect resolution of their differences. Since another deployment might be in the future, Courtney has few choices but to work things out with her in-laws so that her son does not feel like his mom and grandparents are divided. Hopefully she and her in-laws can create a shared vision for the young boy. However, this is not always the case. If they cannot come to a consensus using all of the community resources available to them, the boy is likely to suffer.

IN-LAWS AS GRANDPARENTS

Everyone says how wonderful it is to have children and grandchildren, but when the newborn is screaming, the toddler is leaving food droppings around the house, and the teenager is sleeping until noon and ruining the schedule, it is hard for both parents and grandparents to believe it. When grandparents and children-in-law disagree about how to care for the newest generation, grandparenting hardly seems so wonderful.

Jennifer loved her own children. She had been a devoted mom and an elegant mother-of-the-bride and mother-of-the-groom. She'd made special efforts to attend her grandchildren's birthday celebrations regardless of how far she had to travel. She delighted in giving her grandkids special treats when they visited. But babysitting and long visits with the little ones were not for her. Her son-in-law, Andy, thought this was strange: How could she not want hours with his pride and joy! Her daughter-in-law, Bonnie, just wanted a night out with her sweetie, away from the kids and extended family. Jennifer was neither interested in babysitting nor in finding a sitter. The result was that her times with her grandchildren were tense. Both the parents and the grandchildren wanted more from her than she could give.

All of life's joys are mixed. Those who rave about grandparenting are not lying. They are just telling part of the story and some of their feelings. If we believe only the idealized visions of grandparenting, we wonder what is wrong with us when we feel more mixed emotions. As is true throughout life, if we believe only the positives, we are sure to be disillusioned by life's complexities. Some grandparents are so happy that they finally are free from the annoyances of young children that they do not want to bother with the newest offspring. Some are overjoyed and want to be involved. In fact, they would be happy to take over.

Some grandparents love babysitting; others don't. Some do not want to be with the grandchildren at all. Some like the little ones, and others prefer the big ones. Some grandparents assume that they have license to spoil the grandchildren, while others walk on eggshells trying to please the parents. Most grandparents do both. Some see their grandparenting as a chance to redress the wrongs of their own parenting. Perhaps they were not attentive enough or were too strict or too lenient or too critical or not critical enough. Others view their grandchildren as a chance to influence the future or to obtain a kind of immortality by living on in the grandchild's memory. Still others are entering their later years, when their friends and outside activities are diminishing. To them, family becomes more important. They need the grandchildren.

*   *   *

Some grandparents say grandparenting is great because they can have a good time with the grandkids and then are able to send them back to their parents. For others, the joy is more profound than just being able to take the good parts and leave the hard parts for the parents. Their delight is in finally being mature enough to have perspective, to have priorities straight, to finally have the acceptance of both the good and the bad in children and to cherish all of it because it really is fleeting. Often parents complain about or ignore grandparental advice. In the grandparents' mind, their years of parenting give them some knowledge and therefore should also give them credibility. Instead, they find their opinions disregarded. Perhaps the suggestions of the older generation fall on deaf ears because the individual perspectives are so different, not merely because of rudeness or dislike. Or maybe the parents are just too anxious to accept any advice.

José and Gertrude visited their three-month-old grandson and agreed to babysit while the new parents went out to do errands and grab a cup of coffee. It was a gorgeous day, so the grandparents put the baby in the stroller and went for a walk. When the parents arrived home, the grandparents waxed eloquent about how the baby enjoyed the fresh air and the leaves. Their daughter-in-law, Meredith, screamed, "How dare you take out my baby for a walk without asking my permission!" The in-laws recoiled. They meant well and used their judgment, but Meredith expected them to not only follow her instructions, but also essentially to read her mind. Fortunately José and Gertrude, though completely deflated, merely apologized. They understood that their daughter-in-law only wanted to protect the child and that as a new mother, she was just learning what that meant.

From that time on, they asked detailed questions before they did anything with the child. They adhered strictly to the instructions. They could have been insulted that their daughter-in-law thought they were not capable, but they instead chose to follow her wishes. Perhaps when she is more secure as a mother they will raise the issues of independent thinking again. These grandparents understood that their daughter-in-law was not distraught about their actions, but that she was anxious about something happening to her child. They wisely reacted out of that understanding rather than arguing that a little fresh air would not hurt the baby.

* * *

Some grandparents are young and spry. Others are not quite as agile as they once were. They may not be able to lift a 30-pound toddler or go from sitting on the floor to sprinting across it in a nanosecond, which is a necessary skill in chasing toddlers. The parents may be reluctant to allow the grandparents to babysit, fearing that the grandparents may not be able to handle an emergency, knowing that dangers abound in a toddler's world and that accidents do happen. When grandparents babysit, they are taking care of two generations and must address the needs of both. Parents' worries are real and a sign of love.

Grandparents may be physically capable but unable to speak English well enough to call for help, or they may require so many instructions that it feels burdensome to the parents. Some parents may be wary of insulting the grandparents and thus do not mention the real reasons behind their reluctance to hand over their children. In-law children particularly are uncertain of how such a message will be received. They do not want to insult their in-laws or they just want things done their way. Some grandparents are hurt by their children's refusal to let them take care of the grandchildren.

> *Larry is babysitting his grandson Jonah, who is nine months old, while Jonah's parents and grandmother are out. Larry is outside on the hammock, equipped with the requisite baby monitor so that he can be fully aware of the baby inside and two flights up. His daughter-in-law has told him to be sure to put the cell phone beside him, but he insists he will hear the house phone since it is just inside. Armed with a list of instructions about how to feed, diaper, and hold the baby, he feels quite in control of the situation. Although Larry insists that his hearing is fine, he does not hear the house phone and has forgotten where he put his cell phone. After an hour, his daughter-in-law, Jonah's mother, calls on both lines, but he does not hear them ring. The mother is beside herself with worry. She returns immediately.*

Larry forgot that he was not only taking care of the baby, but also tending to his daughter-in-law's concerns. He was unprepared to do the latter. Larry's rejection of any hint that his hearing was diminishing made it awkward for his wife and the child's mother to insist that he keep the phone nearby. Sometimes when the parents leave a long list of instructions on how to care for their children and in what environment, they are not necessarily being overly concerned but merely dealing with reality. The older generation must deal with it as well.

How grandparents adjust when grandchildren arrive in nontraditional ways—out of wedlock, by a sperm or egg donor, by adoption, or by remarriage—can color relationships for a long time. Parents may expect their kids to have kids in their 20s, but the adult kids may be planning to wait until their 30s or even their 40s. If grandparents want a relationship with the grandchildren, good relationships with the parents of their grandchildren are key, including the daughter- or son-in-law. They must also follow the parental rules unless they discuss why they are deviating.

FORGET PERFECT; SETTLE FOR OK

Both parents and grandparents have dreams and idealized visions of the future. The dreams of in-laws do not stem from the same source as those of the related parents and grandparents, so any difficulty in the intergenerational relationship is magnified when the relationship is by marriage. One mother wants her parents fully involved in all phases of her child's life. The father wants to build his own unit. The grandparents may want to be included but are not sure how. Or they may want to be off fulfilling their own dreams. Another mother sees her parents as role models. The father sees them as neglectful. The grandparents want to travel. One father doesn't trust his mom to babysit. His wife thinks he is overprotective. The grandmother is just hurt.

Most likely, the future will not fulfill perfect grandparenting fantasies; instead, it will create a tapestry of highs and lows. Whatever it includes, children in families that support each other fare better. Parents who are part of a family do better, and grandparents who are included positively in their grandchildren's lives have a greater sense of well-being.[6] Good relationships are a win-win-win, but they are hard to develop and maintain. It is in the interest of all three generations to maintain close relationships. Yet often grandparents subvert their own interests.

> *It's easy for me now. My in-laws decided not to speak to me and to pretend I do not exist. I would go to family funerals to support my husband, and they would not even say hello. I was hurt and devastated. Even if I am from a different religion, I am a nice person. Now I have two children, and I realize how his parents have cheated themselves. I am not the problem. I feel sad that my children see their grandparents only once a year when my husband visits without me. I do not want to feel the disappointment and anger of his parents, so I stay home or use the time to visit with friends. I have a great life, and they are not part of it. I have given up trying with them.*

Sometimes parents think their disapproval will change their children's behavior, and it does—but not always in the way they had hoped.

Shunning may work well to keep communities together, but it usually is at the expense of the individuals. Parents who are rude or insensitive to their in-law children gain little. They punish themselves. At some point, one side or the other will give up and move on, and the discourteous family members will be left with only the corrosive justification that they were right and their in-law child was wrong. Both in-law parents and in-law children should be at least as nice and inclusive to in-law family members as they would be to strangers or coworkers. There is rarely a downside to being courteous.

CULTURAL EXPECTATIONS

Differences in cultural expectations, especially between the grandparents and the in-law child, can be a source of problems. In many Asian cultures, for example, grandparents are honored as sources of wisdom. The elders are respected for their knowledge and experience in raising children. They pass on the traditions. In American culture, grandmothers—particularly women who "only raised children"—often command little respect in the family. Although they were once looked at as a useful resource, it is now common for them to feel as though their opinions are discarded. Grandparents who have expectations of being revered are hurt when their American in-law children or grandchildren do not honor them properly.

In-law grandparents and in-law parents are particularly prone to misinterpret behaviors due to cultural expectations. Some believe that encouraging children to pursue their passions and providing positive reinforcement and a nurturing environment are the foundation of upbringing. Others believe that the best way to protect their children is by preparing them for the future with skills, work habits, and inner confidence that no one can ever take away. In her bestselling book, *Battle Hymn of the Tiger Mother*, Amy Chua captures the way Western parents try to "respect their children's individuality." In her view, this runs counter to the more important task of preparing the child for the future.[7] Much of parenting is a matter of perspective and attitudes toward the future and the past. Some of these attitudes are so subtle that few of us can articulate them, though they often serve to make us closed to opposing views. We assume our way is the best or only way. Some families believe in seizing the moment, and others believe in deferring pleasure. Some families believe thrift and hard work are essential, and others think they should help their children in any way they can.[8] There is value in many child-rearing philosophies. If there were an agreed-upon best way to raise children, most of us would do it. One doesn't need to be from an overtly different culture to have disagreements with in-laws.

> *Tad is a well-educated businessman from rural Montana. He hunts and fishes regularly. His in-laws are both professors at an elite East Coast college. They spend several weekends camping with him and his wife. However, once the children are born, his mother-in-law, Prudence, true to her name, asks if he has locked up his guns every time she enters the house.*

Tad considers himself a responsible sportsman. He also loves his children. When his mother-in-law inquires about the guns, he is insulted. He feels Prudence gives him no credit for good judgment. Prudence is scared of keeping guns at home and reads every article about firearms going off accidentally and killing a child. Both are focusing on the facts instead of on the feelings of the other. Tad could show his mother-in-law the gun lockbox and gently tease her that he loves his children as much as she does. And Prudence could ask Tad to assure her that he really has heard her and that he has bought a double-combination lock to ensure the safety of his children. There is a clash of cultures here related to different geographic heritages, though both are from the same socioeconomic class, race, and religion.

Disagreeing with in-laws happens regularly. Grandparents worry that their child or child-in-law may not be raising their grandchild "properly." The parents have too many or too few rules. The grandchildren eat too many sweets or not enough of them. All of these are valid concerns of well-meaning grandparents, but they are a headache to in-law children. For many grandparents, their biggest fear is not being able to see their grandchildren: "*I live in fear that my in-law child will not want to make the effort to come see me, or even worse—that I will be unable to see my grandchildren"* or *"Frankly, I feel cheated. I devoted years to those kids. I gave up opportunities and now I have nothing. Don't I deserve something?"*

Sometimes this fear is exploited by the daughter-in-law in order to control her mother-in-law. The children become bargaining chips. One doctor who read my first book, *Don't Bite Your Tongue*, wrote me asking for advice: *"I am a physician in private practice in northern Virginia, and I have sent several of my elderly patients for counseling after being bullied by their daughters-in-law!! They seem to use the grandchildren as ammunition, and my patients live in mortal fear of being cut off from them."*

For many in the parent generation, experts have supplanted the role of the wise elder. Parents read every book they can find, leaving little room for grandmothers who still wish to play the traditional role.

For grandmothers who followed the traditional gender roles and made the children the primary focus of their lives, this change in status can be devastating. They feel vulnerable and undervalued. Their knowledge and skills are discounted because they have no credentials and no paid work experience. However, fathers, too, can chafe at their new auxiliary role. They may blame their sons-in-law for replacing them. Even those who have their own interests and are happy in their own lives may still feel the loss of intergenerational respect.

* * *

Vanessa is a "macrobiotic nut" according to her mother-in-law, Shirley. She feeds the kids only seafood flakes and seeds—no animal protein. Shirley has come to terms with the fact that there are many ways to feed children. All over the world, children grow without animal protein. While she sees that her grandchildren are above average in both height and weight, she still worries about the long-term consequences of no animal protein. She has tried hard to educate herself about macrobiotic eating. She is concerned, however, about their mental health. She fears that her daughter-in-law's rigidity will restrict the children's ability to develop wholesome eating habits. Will they become obese

the first time they attend a birthday party and taste sugar and subse-
quently gorge on it time and time again? Will they not differentiate
between cocaine and white bread and grape jelly? She knows that
parents have total control over their children for a very short time.
She worries about the battles that will ensue. Because she knows how
passionately her daughter-in-law feels about this diet, she fears that if
she says anything, her daughter-in-law will not only blow up at her,
but also not trust her to take care of the children. Her son does not
share her concerns.

There are many contentious issues. Some matter in the big picture and
some don't. Shirley worries about her grandchildren's health and believes
that if the children are too tightly controlled, they will rebel. She does
not feel comfortable talking about her concerns with her daughter-in-
law because she fears Vanessa will lecture her—or worse. To date, they
have never had an argument, but she is not sure her relationship is
strong enough to withstand a disagreement. She knows she may be raising her worries to the catastrophic level as many of us do, but she also
knows her concerns have some merit. She is not certain if, as long as the
children are healthy and the pediatrician is in agreement with the diet,
there is any real health danger. She cannot sort out whether this issue is
important enough to risk losing her daughter-in-law's affection, so she
remains uncomfortable. Her relationship with Vanessa will probably
remain at this unsatisfying level unless she risks raising her concerns.
From experience with her own children, she knows her grandchildren
will let their mother know when they will no longer acquiesce to her
rigid diet. She knows that her worries about their mental health may
be overblown.

Many grandparents think that their kids are neurotic about food,
and there is some basis for this notion. Some of our most commonly
held notions of food dangers are not supported by science.[9] Since food
serves for more than just nourishing the body, it is often a battleground
on which issues of control, power, and belonging are fought. One of the
underlying issues is who has the right to make these choices for the children. Grandmother Shirley feels completely disregarded. Her concerns
for her grandchildren and their future social life and eating habits have

some validity. On the other hand, Vanessa's concerns about eating also have some validity.

Shirley can learn even more about macrobiotic eating, and in that way, if she chooses to talk with her daughter-in-law, she will have the correct facts. Her worries about the future decision-making ability of her grandchildren also have some validity. Children who are too tightly controlled often do rebel. Here again, instead of predicting calamity, she could discuss with Vanessa the pros and cons of strict controls on children—but to do that successfully, she will need to seek examples of the benefits of controlling one's appetites of any kind.

Another underlying matter is the comfort that can be found in adhering to strict ideologies. Vanessa wants to protect her children from the vagaries of nature. She may think that if she trains her children in her eating style, they will forever remain true to her teachings. Many grandparents and parents cling to child-rearing rules in an attempt to ward off the evils of life. Shirley and Vanessa have a mutual concern—the health of these children—but they differ on the method of achieving it. Their mutual interest could be the beginning of rapprochement. Both Shirley and Vanessa will need to acknowledge each other's deep fears. Shirley's version of rolling her eyes—that is, calling her daughter-in-law a "macrobiotic nut"—prevents her from understanding Vanessa's anxieties and fears.

Gifts, food, discipline—all of these can cause serious problems. Rules around gift giving often feel like rude directives. If an in-law parent is specific about what or how many gifts the children are allowed, it's worthwhile following his or her instructions. Gifts are merely a vehicle for showing affection. If grandparents really object to the suggested gifts, they can give an activity such as going to a museum or a park. As far as discipline goes, there are many ways to bring up good citizens. Unless the issues are life threatening or emotionally damaging, the grandparents can either overlook the parents' methods or discuss what modes of discipline they feel comfortable following. Many people feel more comfortable having these discussions with their own children rather than their in-law children. Discipline, gifts, and food are symptoms that mask more fundamental issues, such as the right to educate the child, how to protect the child, and how to prepare him or her for the future. Focusing on the symptoms will not lead to resolution.

In the United States, the parents, in most cases, are the legal guardians and thus have the right to make decisions for the children. Many grandparents are aggravated by some of the decisions the parents make. However, grandparents had their chance to be the decision makers. It is now time to trust their children and in-law children and let them gain wisdom on their own.

Sometimes parents are disappointed with the grandparents because they are otherwise occupied.

* * *

Gail is proudly pregnant with her first child. When she announces this to her father-in-law, he is pleased and counters with, "My new wife, too, is pregnant." Gail is crestfallen. She thought this was her time for the limelight, but her father-in-law is focused on his new wife and will not be available to grandparent her child.

Our life courses are not always in sync. Parents' expectations may be dashed when grandparents do not make their children the primary focus of their lives. They also may be disappointed when grandparents from either side of the family are not readily available to serve their needs, although they have no right to expect these babysitting services in the first place.

IN THE CASE OF DIVORCE

Divorce's forgotten victims are the grandparents. Some parents-in-law feel that they are on the outside looking in as their children's families unravel. Will they be allowed to see their grandchildren? Are they still factored in when the divorced children get remarry? And what happens if they aren't? Grandparents' positions are constantly changing both in and out of marriage, with no given definition of how things should be. In-law grandparents are particularly vulnerable to losing the right to visit with their grandchildren when the in-law is the custodial parent.

Andrea and Mario divorced after seven years of marriage. Their children were four and seven at the time of the divorce. Andrea's parents were relieved that they never again would have to be involved with her husband, Mario, whom they had never liked. They were pleased that Andrea was granted custody of the children, as this enabled them to see their grandchildren regularly. However, when their grandson, Blake, turned 14, he begged to live with his father. Andrea was having trouble reining him in. Blake had begun drinking and staying out very late at night. So she consented to this new custody arrangement. The grandparents who had been a regular fixture in Blake's life were unable to come to an agreement with their ex-son-in-law about visitation. As far as Mario was concerned, his ex-in-laws were no longer part of his life. They might have preserved their relationship by being more neutral or supportive toward Mario after the divorce.

Once children are born, grandparents have no choice but to interact positively with both parents of the grandchild if they want to be a part of the grandchildren's lives. Grandparental rights to visit with their grandchildren are not guaranteed. They are a product of emotional connection and are not necessarily protected by the law. The American Bar Association has a grandparent visitation report in the hopes that a federal law will support grandparenting rights. However, to date, in the United States, parents' rights come from the due process clause of the Constitution: "No state shall...deprive a person of life, liberty, or property without due process of law." Liberty includes the right to marry, establish a home, and bring up children. Grandparents are granted no such rights. Laws regarding grandparents' rights derive from the state legislatures as interpreted by local courts.[10]

Some states require grandparents to prove that the grandchildren will be harmed if they do not see their grandparents. Others only require proof that it is in the best interest of the child to have contact with his or her grandparents.[11] In some states, that means showing that grandparents already have a meaningful relationship with the children. This can be problematic if they do not have good relationships with the custodial parent.[12] In some states, grandparental visitation rights may be limited or nonexistent. Some states make no provision at all, leaving it up to the discretion of the parents. Regardless of the local law, it is almost always in the interest of everyone involved to have good relationships with their children and in-law children.

After the younger generation divorces, parents often find that if they want to see their grandchildren, they must continue their relationship with their former in-law child and his or her new spouse. For the older generation, anything they can do to mitigate the difficulties is worthwhile in terms of enriching their own lives. However, keeping a relationship with the ex-child-in-law is complicated. Your child may call you disloyal for cavorting with the enemy. The ex-in-law may marry or couple with someone who does not like you or vice versa. Regardless of our likes or dislikes of our in-laws, I repeat: if you want to have good relationships with your grandchildren, it is easiest if you maintain good relationships with your ex-in-laws. You don't necessarily have to like them, but you may need to be polite in order to maintain any sort of relationships with them.

* * *

If your child's divorce was an acrimonious one, you as a parent may be painted with the brush of animosity that goes with the divorce. Grandparents often find it difficult to maintain contact with their grandchildren when the custodial parent is not their own child. If your in-law child has custody of your grandchildren and you say or do the wrong thing, you could lose your privileges of seeing your grandchildren. Anything grandparents can do to mitigate the difficulties is worthwhile, but what should be done is not always clear.

> Carl and Irma married, bought a house, and had two children. But then troubles began. The accusations flew—infidelity, money grabbing, unequal distribution of family labor. The bitterness escalated until finally they divorced. Irma's mother retained her closeness with the grandchildren. For Carl's mother, it was harder. Irma blamed her for his lazy ways and for not bringing him up with ambition. Carl's mother, however, never took sides. She would call

her ex-daughter-in-law and offer help, she sent gifts to the children and to Irma, and she invited her and the children for the holidays. Irma eventually had the good sense to see that her ex-mother-in-law was a nice person and that Carl, as an independent adult, could have acted differently. She saw that her children thrived when they saw their grandmother, so she finally allowed her ex-mother-in-law back into the family.

Carl's mother had the wisdom to keep trying until the raw wounds of divorce lessened over time.[13]

Fighting with in-laws, though it may seem unavoidable at the time, is often pointless when everyone is honestly looking out for the children's best interest. Any personal problems that may occur between you and your in-laws have the consequence of depriving the parents of help and the children of a more extensive support system. Divorce is between two people, but it involves the whole family.

TALK, WALK, ROCK

One approach is to have a direct conversation with the in-law child. It could be something along the lines of, "Everything that I read tells me that having grandparents in a child's life is beneficial, and I would like to be helpful to both you and my grandchildren. I don't feel it's working now. What might I do to make it better?" By using *I* instead of *you*, there is no blame. You are being honestly concerned about your relationship with your in-law child and your grandchildren. You could also suggest things that you would like to do. For example, maybe there are certain days when you would be available to babysit, or maybe you would like to take your grandchildren to the park one weekend. By running these plans by your in-law children first, it lets them know that you are not a threat. You are just trying to be a part of their lives.

The first step in grandparenting is supporting the parents. Talking about what parents want can help, but because feelings are so complex, we need to attend to other clues—body language, timing, and attitude. Obviously this is harder for in-laws since they do not have years of living together to learn each other's silent communication modes. However grandparents and parents "hear" each other, they must then demonstrate their willingness to modify their own behaviors by accommodating. Only after the talk, whether in words or observations, and the demonstration that they have listened so they can "walk the talk" do grandparents get to rock the babies.

Some grandparents need to fill their own lives with activities that make them feel good about themselves. Then the grandparents are not burdening children and in-law children with the responsibility for grandparental happiness.

WHAT TO DO

Giving advice at any time can cause huge conflicts. Grandparents may think that they are being helpful, but the parents may take their comments as harsh criticism. Unfortunately, there is a fine line between giving helpful hints and criticism. Parents may think that they should learn things on their own or that they already know enough to raise their children properly. Sometimes sharing what you did and why it worked helps. At other times, that feels too intrusive. Where safety is concerned, honest feedback or even criticism may be warranted.

Timing matters. Don't give advice in the heat of the crisis or in front of others or when someone is upset. It might be that grandparental criticisms are out of date. It is easy to say that the grandchildren have no manners, no values, and no consideration for others, but the manners and values taught to them by their parents may simply be different. For example, acknowledging a gift by texting rather than writing a note on paper is not only faster, but it might be better for the planet. In this electronic age, even the most basic of social niceties are changing. The core value of acknowledging a kindness remains; the form it takes, however, morphs with time and technology.

It is important to be positive. Rather than dreading the next time you will see each other, smile and say hello. Ask about your in-law's life. Hanging on to resentment is, as they say, like taking poison and expecting the other person to die. Being angry will get you nowhere other than being miserable. Instead of focusing on the things that your in-law does that annoy you, focus on the big issues. Do your grandchildren feel loved? By looking for a shared understanding and admitting our fears to our children and in-law children, our relationships with them will become stronger and less complicated. Happiness is a choice and, with work, can become a habit. By being open and honest with each other and looking on the brighter side of things, we allow ourselves happiness.

Both parents and grandparents need forbearance. As long as the rules are reasonable and nonviolent, rules at one house do not have to reflect rules at the other generation's home and vice versa. This, of course, does not mean that you should avoid discussing them. By making sure that all adults agree with the most important rules, relationships can remain uncompromised. Both grandparents and parents must weigh the cost of severing supportive and important relationships over a couple of days of nonorganic milk or dessert before dinner. Kids are smart enough to figure out the difference between what they should and should not be doing, and by allowing them to figure out this difference early on, you enable them to make better choices when they are adults.[14]

Both in-laws and grandparents can benefit from learning how others handle situations. Talking with people in both the same generation and different generations gives us all new ideas on how to interact in ways that bring more harmony and less tension. Intergenerational conversations not only give us a different perspective but also help us see how much has changed since "we were young."[15]

ADDITIONAL HINTS

Remember that there are at least two sides to every story. What you may think you see may not be the entire truth. Ask questions. Find out the rest of the story before throwing out advice.

Go the extra mile. Ultimately, different views on bringing up children don't matter. Find a way to see the other point of view instead of judging. What matters most is that children feel loved and cared for in both environments.

Respect isn't given; it is earned. Both generations are learning new roles together. Hopefully, they can teach each other how to be helpful, loving, and useful.

QUESTIONS

- How has your image of yourself as a parent or grandparent been tempered by reality?
- Have you ever been reluctant to discuss an issue that was troubling you with an in-law? If so, what was the issue?
- In retrospect, how might you have raised the topic to lead to a productive conversation?
- What annoys you most about your in-laws' parenting styles?
- What do your in-laws do well as parents or grandparents?
- When did your in-laws help you out with the children? Did you need to make any compromises to gain their help? Was it worth the changes?
- How could you help each other with the children?
- What physical limits do you have that prevent you from taking care of your grandchildren? How could you work with these to make yourself a good sitter?
- How do you and your in-laws differ in terms of expectations for parents and grandparents?
- If there is divorce in your family, how can you gain assistance from your ex-in-laws, or how can you be helpful to them?

CHAPTER 9

More Money, More Problems, Less Money, Still Problems

Money may buy temporary happiness, but its presence can create jealousy and animosity. Its absence can put one at a disadvantage—perhaps leaving a parent at the whim of family members or leaving an adult child feeling like a failure. For many, money is a proxy for status, a measure of success or failure. It is often surrounded by secrecy. For some, hard work and thrift lead to financial success. For others, showing status can create the illusion of success and with that, they hope, respect. Talking about money (earning it, saving it, spending it) is difficult enough within a nuclear family; adding in-laws complicates the picture even further. Economic disparity, competition, and different values among adult children are the bugaboos in the discussion. Conversations about money can come up frequently and unexpectedly. Perhaps an adult child wants to buy a house or a new TV and needs a loan. Maybe at the same time, a dependent child needs tutoring or special therapy. Perhaps an adult of either generation returns to school or loses a job, or sickness afflicts one of the wage earners. All of these situations change the financial status of the family. Because the way each of us spends money is often conflated with what kind of a person we are, each one of these situations not only gives rise to monetary concerns, but also invites judgment. One person or generation may think an expense is necessary while another is convinced that it is frivolous.

In-laws of all types—parents, adult children, siblings—may have very different views of how money should be spent. Adults differ on the continuum between immediate gratification and long-term satisfaction. Most of us are quick to judge others who spend money differently than we would. Because families are called upon to help each other in times of need, the question of how a parent-in-law or child-in-law spends money becomes a subject of genuine concern. If, for example, the older generation spends all of its funds on trips and saves nothing for a rainy day, an adult child may be asked to help out in an emergency. Or, an in-law child may squander money on material goods and save nothing for a health emergency, or either generation may lose a job, causing the other to feel called upon to pitch in. All persons involved may find themselves with divided loyalties. When definitions of family obligation differ, the resultant rifts can cause resentment. A daughter-in-law may feel no obligation to support parents who, in her mind, squander their resources, whereas her husband may believe he owes his parents financial support because they raised him. The son-in-law believes they have worked hard for their earnings and deserve a condo in Florida, while his wife believes they should help the grandchildren.

Money can ease short-term issues like job loss, a return to school, or a sudden accident. In these cases, some parents may be willing and able to give money and shelter or provide services such as child care. But whatever parents give to one child can cause problems with another. If the other sibling's spouse has a contrasting view of the appropriate way for families to support each other, the support of one can cause or exacerbate rivalry.

How can parents mitigate tensions around varying incomes, inheritance, and end-of-life plans when their own children and their in-law children may have different expectations? How does one develop a special bond with a stranger who may have legal rights to his or her money and grandchildren? Should the older generation husband its resources to ensure a secure retirement instead of helping out the younger generation? How can people balance their own future needs and the current needs of their children and grandchildren?

CONTENTIOUS FINANCIAL
RELATIONSHIPS WITH IN-LAWS

Sometimes money is part and parcel of other long-standing issues. A parent may be compensating a child who has always felt unloved. Money may be a source of control and disagreement within either generation. Or, where divorce or death has occurred, an adult child or a parent feels obligations to numerous parental and grand-parental groups. Further complicating matters in many families, financial situations remain clothed in mystery. Even talking about money is taboo.

An in-law is not privy to the whole history of hurts and past events that may be played out in a specific financial request. Nor is an in-law necessarily knowledgeable about what other obligations family members have to the extended clan. Different financial backgrounds make negotiations difficult. An in-law from a dirt-poor family may presume that a family who owns their small home is not only wealthy, but also has disposable income. People who have always had disposable income may have never needed to make financial trade-offs. They may not understand the reluctance of their less affluent in-laws to be what they call generous. Or the less affluent who are used to sharing cannot understand why the wealthy in-laws withhold funds.

Felix benefited greatly from generations of family wealth. He lacked for nothing. He went to the best private schools, had tutors when necessary, and attended fabulous summer programs. His wife, Marinda, is from a solidly middle-class family. Her parents have a satisfying lifestyle, but it is not stress-free financially, and there is little cushion. She and her two siblings all earned money to pay for their educations. Several years into Marinda and Felix's marriage, Marinda's sister is in a horrible accident. She is expected to be bedridden for a year, needing almost constant support. Her mother has to leave work to care for her injured daughter. Since Marinda knows one can live a perfectly happy life with fewer material possessions than she now has, she wants to cut back on expenses to contribute to her natal family's coffers. However, Felix feels that as a financial advisor, he must display an affluent lifestyle; otherwise, clients will be reluctant to come to him. Being a

*member of the country club is essential, and sending their children to
private schools is important not only for their education, but so he can
meet the other parents who are people of means and potential clients.
Felix has been generous but is unwilling to give as much money to
her family as she believes is necessary. Marinda's parents see her and
her family living the high life and wonder why they cannot help out
more in this catastrophe. What her parents do not know is that Felix
has a brother who is severely mentally challenged and living in an
institution. The family rarely mentions this son. Felix feels responsible
to help his parents support his brother's care. He is willing to help out
Marinda's family, but only a little bit. He fears that the assets intended
for their own children could be absorbed by their two siblings' needs.*

The two families have very different assumptions about what is necessary for a good life. Because Marinda's parents make all financial decisions together, they incorrectly assume that their daughter's marriage
operates similarly, but in Marinda's marriage, Felix's financial views carry
greater weight. Marinda's family has no inkling that Felix feels obligated
to provide for his disabled brother. However, his wife's obligations are
relatively short-term and likely to diminish. If Felix can discuss with
his parents a temporary reduction in his sharing in his brother's support, perhaps he could contribute more to his in-law family in this crisis
period. Felix could give a general outline of his finances and obligations
to his in-laws and explain why he feels constrained in what he can do
for them.

Complicating the whole discussion is the underlying theme between
the couple. Like so many couples, Marinda and Felix have different
ideas on what they are morally required to do for their children. Felix
feels they must provide financial support for the very best education,
and Marinda feels they must enable their children to provide for their
own learning. Both want to do what was done for them. Any discussion
of money with either set of parents is colored by this past history. Both
of them may feel disloyal to their family values if they suggest an alternative. The couple would benefit from a frank discussion about what
financial help they received growing up and how it shaped their assumptions about what parents "should" give their children. Money is often

part and parcel of other values. Perhaps Marinda and Felix can come up with ways in which they could cut the family budget that would not adversely affect Felix's status or jeopardize his professional prospects. This might even be an opportunity for them to reevaluate their priorities, including the importance of private school. Their conversation with both sets of in-laws will go more smoothly if they are clear about their own values and how they might modify their own finances.

It is no more likely that the two sets of in-laws will share their Dun and Bradstreet ratings, or lack thereof, than would be the case among other acquaintances. But if they accept whatever gifts of time or money the other family offers rather than wanting and expecting more, they are likely to have kinder feelings for each other. No family understands the internal politics of another. When one child is more successful than another or marries into a more financially secure situation or is more able than another, parents allocate whatever resources they have according to what they feel is right. Some give to each child equal amounts, and others give according to the children's needs. How one allocates funds within a family can cause real tension, especially with in-laws, who rarely know all of the facts. Because in some families money equals love—that is, it is a proxy for the parents' caring—an in-law child can be hurt because the in-law parents give more money to a sibling-in-law. Or in-law children may take on the mantle of hurt they see in their spouse who feels unloved because he or she perceives that a sibling gets more money.

* * *

Though many Americans profess to expect nothing from their children, many parents hope that family members will help them out during financially tough times. Often the anxieties about their own futures play out in criticisms of their in-law children.

> *My children and their spouses have made choices that I would never make. They spend money on takeout food, send their kids to private schools, and go on expensive vacations. I did not bring up my children this way, but their spouses like the finer things. I constantly suggest less*

*expensive alternatives. They think I am criticizing them, but I am only
trying to help them prepare for the future. Frankly, I do worry about
money. I know I don't have enough for my retirement. I spent it all on
my kids and could not save. I worry that I will not be able to count
on my children for any help, as they just spend too much. I worry that
if hard times came to them, they would turn to me for help. I need to
count on our relationship in the future. I don't want to be alone and
uncared for. To tell you the truth, they may not know it, but they will
need me, too, if things don't continue to go well for them.*

Margaret's concerns about her children's spending habits are actually
concerns about her own future. She knows she does not have enough
money for her old age. Instead of discussing this fact, of which she is
ashamed, she berates her children's spending, all the while justifying
her comments as helpful hints. She blames her in-law children for their
financial habits when it might be her own children who want to give their
families more than they themselves ever had. To blame her own children
would make her feel like a failure, a mother who raised ungrateful and
thoughtless children, and thus she blames her in-law children. Before
Margaret can even consider talking to the younger generation about her
financial situation, she must acknowledge to herself her own insecurities
about both her parenting and her wallet. Being honest with herself will
not be an easy task, but she may find that when she stops blaming and
criticizing others, it becomes easier to talk about her own situation.

Many of us are not talkers, but maybe we can share our financial
concerns by discussing our monthly income and needs. Or we can hire
an intermediary to share our concerns. Or we can write them down.
Neither our children nor anyone else can help us plan for our futures if
we do not speak honestly to them about our situation and our worries.
But reticence may dominate. Thoughts like, "How can I ask for help
when my in-law kids think that having me over for dinner is 'above and
beyond'?" only reinforce that reticence.

Margaret's children may not be obligated to support her, but if they
understood her concerns, they might change either their spending habits or their attitudes. Too often neither adult children nor their parents have accurate ideas about the amount of money each has and how

much is needed. And often, the adult children do not know how the older generation will distribute what remains. Many of us believe it is not appropriate to share this information. The older generation may be embarrassed by their lack of resources or not want to inhibit the ambition of the younger generation. The younger generation may not want anyone meddling in their business.

* * *

In some families, the younger generation must sort out what resources they will contribute to the older generation. One person may be dealing with very different expectations from two different sets of in-law children or in-law parents. It would help if both generations had a broad outline of the other's financial assets and commitments. Financial problems are often conflated with social expectations. The third season of the HBO TV show *In Treatment* poignantly shows how culture and financial differences are intertwined.

> *A young, two-career professional family with two children has an upper middle-class lifestyle. The wife's choices dominate, except in one area. Sunil, the newly widowed, still-grieving father-in-law, is brought into the home from India. His money supported his son through college and medical school and paid his wife's huge medical bills, leaving him with no financial resources. Sunil feels totally lost as a human being. His son, as any good Indian son would, feels obligated by his promise to his dying mother to care for his father both financially and emotionally. His daughter-in-law shows no respect and little sympathy for Sunil. As the financial planner in the home, she puts her father-in-law on a limited allowance and resents anything her husband does for his father.*

Although finances are not a problem, the wife focuses her resentment on every penny the family spends on her father-in-law when what she really resents is his intrusion on her life. When money rules, discussions suffer, as do those who are dependent. Her husband's filial obligations are clear to him, but he does not make them clear to his wife, nor does she intuit them. Instead, they send the father for psychological treatment. While the father may indeed benefit from some therapy, it is the couple themselves who must negotiate their differences.

Again, in-laws become the convenient dumping ground for marital difficulties, and it goes both ways: Sunil neither respects nor understands his daughter-in-law, and vice versa. The couple here has very different cultural expectations. The wife does not understand that, in marrying her husband, she married into a very different culture—one that requires men to take care of their parents. She resents having her father-in-law in her home. For her, he is an intruder. The son can try to mitigate the inconvenience by helping his father find activities that take him out of the house so he is not in his wife's way, but that cannot be a 24/7 solution. Ultimately, the wife must decide whether she wants to remain in the marriage and accept obligations she had not fully understood or expected when they married. She can, however, reflect on how to make the situation more livable for herself and her father-in-law. Merely tossing her father-in-law out is clearly not an option that would work for Sunil or that would allow her husband to retain his self-respect. She needs to give serious consideration to what options would be most effective and acceptable. Life brings with it unexpected challenges. All parties in this scenario will need to reevaluate their own priorities and modify their expectations. Perhaps then, and maybe with some neutral-party participation, effective communication can occur.

* * *

The current economic downturn has forced many families to share resources. In some cases, one generation has to help out the other with money. In others, they come into unexpected proximity with their in-laws as adult kids and parents move in together.[1] Not only must the in-laws negotiate an unexpected intimacy, but siblings-in-law of those who have returned to the nest may wonder if they, too, will get the resources the family is spending on the ones who are down on their luck. Maybe they want to move back to the family home to ease their own financial burdens. The other in-laws who are not on site may be jealous of the new intimacy their shared children have with the other family. Those who take in parents may expect compensation from their siblings or siblings-in-law. Alternatively, the siblings and siblings-in-law may be upset or relieved that they cannot provide the same services.

> *Louise's parents want to do all they can to support her and her family during this period when both she and her husband, Gilbert, have fewer hours at work. Gilbert resents his in-laws' active participation in their lives. It makes him uncomfortable, in part, because he sees the absence of his own parents' role, financially and otherwise. Louise perceives her in-laws' lack of interest as a personal affront. After all, they have financial means. Besides, in her view, they could contribute in many other ways—not just by giving money. They could provide child care and even pass on pictures or furniture that they store rather than use, but they do none of these things.*

Neither Gilbert nor Louise has asked for assistance. His parents may not want to intervene without permission. Her parents dote on her, in part, because she's their only child. Gilbert has two siblings. His parents may fear that helping one of their children will require that they do the same for another.

Unless the children talk together and then with their families about what they need, each will continue to feel that the other is not living up to expectations. Sometimes in-law children need to ask their spouses to talk with their own parents, since they do not have the full understanding of the family paradigm. However, it may not be easy to talk about financial matters even with those to whom we feel closest. The internal politics of families are always delicate.

Financial decisions can be overwhelming when you are looking at how to best invest your income, how to pay the mortgage, or when and if you can retire. Expenses and attitudes toward these issues differ in every household and for each person. What one might think absolutely necessary, the other may consider useless. What one person sees as a fixed expense, another may reduce or eliminate. Some call gifts discretionary, while others feel they are essential in fostering relation-ships.[2] Some people are bred on fear and anxiety about money; others rarely worry. Some are risk takers; others are not. Money concerns are based on personality differences as well as objective realities. Money can cause some of the most problematic issues within families, in part, because many of us do not understand the anxiety that underlies our financial viewpoint.

LOANS AND/OR GIFTS

Parents can spend whatever they want on dependent children, but the law limits tax-free gifts to adult children, in-law children, and parents. On the one hand, families' generations are tied by obli-gation and affection and sometimes with a desire to offer mon-etary support. On the other hand, the government considers the generations as independent entities with tax obligations related to the transfer of money—thus, the murkiness of familial reciproc-ity. Some families feel that they should do what banks do and put everything in writing and charge interest before they give a penny to a relative. Others feel that, even if there are very few resources, they are obligated to give what they have if a child or a parent asks. Needless to say, adult children and in-laws are often critical of the choices made by their spouses' families.

Financial transactions within families can go in both generational directions. Gifts or loans to family members have many repercussions. Sometimes, a gift is given as an advance against inheritance. Too often, the best of intentions are not fulfilled. The parents might use all of their remaining resources for their own end-of-life care and have no resources for the other child who expected to be compensated in the will for what other siblings have already received. Sometimes, a loan or gift to one child signals to the other children that they might be entitled to similar support. However, the parents may not be able to do so for all at the same time. If the child who received the loan fails to repay it, this angers not only the lender parents but also other fam-ily members who might have made better use of the money and been able to repay the loan. Grandparents who promised to help with the college expenses of their grandchildren and who did put money aside may have found that the downturn in the stock market wiped out their savings. They can no longer keep their promise. Their children and grandchildren now face a huge unexpected expense and are not happy. Because financial gifts to family members can lead to animosity and loss of contact, many families choose to make loans if they give money at all.

In most families, both generations are juggling current expenses and expected future costs for themselves and their progeny. Both individuals in either generation must agree on the terms and affordability of any loans. Because foreclosing loans to relatives results in the loss of more than just money, making sure that both lenders and borrowers can afford the loan is most important. To save the frustration and anger of personal devastation if a family loan is not paid, many families keep a cushion of cash should their fortunes change or unexpected expenses arise. While this is standard behavior with most loans, when family is involved, each person in the family will have a different view on what is the right amount to set aside. Some will be willing to lose the money they lend; others will not. Most financial advisors recommend that the loan terms—including interest rate, repayment schedule, and the consequences of a failure to meet the payments—be put in writing. They would urge you to check the tax consequences with an accountant or attorney. This is good advice, but in some families, anyone who suggests such steps is suspect. Your in-laws might find such documents unloving. But the loan agreement can act as a family mediator as well as a financial tool. Having a written document prevents future squabbles should the lender forget the terms of the agreement due to Alzheimer's or should various family members have differing recollections of the terms.

In addition, family members can be confused between helping and controlling when they lend money. Helping is lending money; controlling is dictating how it is spent. Trying to control the behavior and choices of the recipients is usually not considered supportive—nor is it welcome.

Uncle Alvin is wealthy. He offers, and then insists, that Jonathan, his nephew, borrow from him rather than from the bank for the down payment on a house. Uncle Alvin graciously charges a below-market rate. Jonathan and his wife, Nancy, appreciate Alvin's generosity and want to honor and thank him. Knowing that he is a frugal man, they send a lovely, modest box of candy and fruit for Christmas. Uncle Alvin is furious. He says, "You borrowed money from me, and you're wasting money on unnecessary gifts." Nancy is very upset. She feels that by taking the loan, their relationship with her husband's uncle changed forever. Uncle Alvin thinks that because he lent them money he now owns other decisions in their life. He had attached the classic "strings" to the transaction. To help mend the relationship, Nancy sends a lovely letter saying, "I'm sorry we offended you," and she explains that they did not use the money he lent them. The uncle writes back and suggests that Nancy should get a job. In his view, his support bought the right to interfere in, or "advise" on, all aspects of their lives.

The uncle's initial generosity becomes an ongoing problem for the young couple. Uncle Alvin assumes that his generosity gives him the right to intervene in the couple's every financial decision. He interprets the gift they sent out of gratitude as profligate spending. They now wish that they had borrowed money from a bank because Alvin's behavior toward them has become eccentric, rude, and invasive. The loan has led to tension.

*   *   *

As crazy as it sounds, if the loan goes bad, the debtors may be angry at the lender for "allowing" them to get into this mess.

Claire lends her son-in-law, Miguel, money to buy a second home in a ski area. He plans to rent it out. It looks like a good invest-ment. Miguel, wanting to make it a good deal for his mother-in-law, agrees to pay 8 percent interest, which is much higher than the mar-ket. However, when the economy tanks, Miguel can neither rent out the home nor repay the loan. Suddenly the good relationship Claire had with her son-in-law goes sour, right along with the investment. Miguel berates his mother-in-law for allowing him to agree to pay such a high interest rate.

Miguel was trying to be generous, but like so many others with "get-rich-quick schemes," he floundered. Claire could have refused to lend him the money. However, she felt awkward questioning his business acumen. Miguel blames his mother-in-law because it is easier to blame others than to accept responsibility. Mixing business with family can be very satisfying and successful, but like mixing business and friendship, it can be fraught with complications of all sorts. Rather than minimize or ignore them, prepare for them.

Fairness depends on how you look at a situation. An in-law who comes with a different definition of fairness can rile his or her spouse. Although it is difficult, sometimes not viewing a transaction as a business deal can lead to unintended consequences.

* * *

Francine and Mitchell want to move from their starter house into a larger one, as they are anticipating the arrival of their second child. Financial support from both sets of parents will make this possible. Mitchell's parents make their assistance a gift, while Francine's agree to arrange a formal loan with a bank. Both are doing what works for them in their own financial situations. The younger generation has their down payment on their new home. All is well except that Mitchell feels it is unfair that his parents gave the money while his in-laws only facilitated a loan. Mitchell's resentment turns into anger when the combined loan and mortgage payments prove to be too much for the young couple.

Mitchell and Francine were unrealistic in their initial expectations. They failed to plan realistically, and no one advised them how to do so. Both sets of parents, in trying to be cooperative, actually facilitated the couple's extravagance. In the end, Francine's parents have to meet some of the loan payments so that the couple can keep their home. This embarrasses the young couple, especially the son-in-law, who is the primary bread-winner. Mitchell asks Francine's parents to consider these payments a gift, rather than an expansion of the loan. This is much more than his in-laws had intended. Francine's siblings are irate and feel that Mitchell has been financially reckless. They are annoyed that he would request a gift rather than a loan since the parents need to secure their retirement.

Mitchell never considered his in-laws' need to secure their retire-ment. Francine's parents had discussed the loan-versus-gift question with their other children. They wanted to be open and honest about their participation. On the one hand, this openness allowed the other siblings to understand their parents' intent. On the other, it did cre-ate some resentment. Financial discussions bring up many complicated emotions. In general, parents need to be sure that they have money for their own short- and long-term requirements before lending money. And children need to do the same. This is especially true when the loan may never be repaid, thus requring the lenders to make the loan pay-ments themselves.

As time goes on, circumstances inevitably change and com-plicate both finances and family relations. Children are born. Divorces, remarriages, and deaths happen. A successful child or parent becomes ill. Parents who have gone into debt to finance one child's education may yet call on another child to take care of them in their old age.

* * *

Judy and Craig have a child with disabilities. He can neither walk nor talk. He is, however, quite expressive. Judy's parents have been very generous in paying for the numerous supplements to his education and for some assistive technology, and they also left most of their assets for his care in their wills. Disability is expensive, and insurance does not cover every item. Soon after Judy's father dies, her mother is diagnosed with leukemia. Craig and Judy are still taking care of their son at home. Judy's mother, Eve, knows that she will need family support.

She brings her children and their spouses all together to explain her financial situation and her likely physical needs. She tells them that if she dies, Craig and Judy will inherit every asset she has because of their son. Eve also tells them that she has enough resources to support herself during this period when she will make no income. She stresses that the resources she and her husband had given to Judy and Craig were given to help their child. Sadly, Eve admits that she is not in a position to give that amount to her other daughter, Heidi. However, she really hopes that Heidi and her husband, Ethan, will understand the uniqueness of her grandson's (their nephew's) situation. What Eve and her husband have done was out of necessity, not out of preference for one sister over the other. Then Eve tells her family about her upcoming needs as she undergoes a bone-marrow transplant. She then asks the children to figure out how they might be willing to take care of her and who might take charge of that task.

Judy's mother honored her children by taking them into her confidence. She minimized potential problems by including her in-law children in the discussion. In this way, she assured that her motives were clear to everyone involved. She openly expressed her regret that she could not equalize the financial contributions to both of her daughters' families. She honored them, too, by not minimizing her own needs and allowing them to decide who would care for her. Not surprisingly, all agree that Heidi, as the less busy of the two sisters, will take charge of their mother's care. Had Eve not shared her reasoning with her children, Heidi may have felt it unfair that she would be their mother's caretaker while her sister had received much more money than she had over the years.

In this case, being open about money helped both sides see that the relationship wasn't based on it; in the following case, you will see how money can also aid in situations where the obligations are ambiguous.

Tiffany and Anish married after graduate school. Neither set of parents-in-law was thrilled with the match initially; however, the couple showed great maturity in understanding why Tiffany's Midwestern family would be shocked by her bringing home an Indian village boy and why his family would be shocked by a blond-haired, blue-eyed American. They each slowly introduced the other to their families—a walk, then dinner, then a weekend for the Midwesterners and a meeting outside the village to avoid gossip for the Indians. Eventually they all became comfortable with each other. Both sets of parents grew fond of their in-law child. After 20 years of a happy marriage, two children, and many trips to India and to the Midwest, Anish was killed in a traffic accident. Both families were bereft. Fortunately Anish had a good life insurance policy and had done quite well financially, and Tiffany had a superb job. While Tiffany had no obligation to support her in-laws, she knew that her husband had felt that responsibility and had sent them monthly checks. After his death, she continued to give his parents a stipend. She also continued to visit India.

Because the Indian family had become so fond of Tiffany and their grandchildren, they probably would have continued their relationship with her without the money, but Tiffany honored both her husband's memory and her in-laws by fulfilling his filial duty. She was not required by law to do this.

Money can complicate or facilitate family interactions. In either case, breaking taboos against discussing money can be helpful.

QUESTIONS

- Have you ever asked for a family loan? If you received it, what has your attitude been toward the person(s) who gave it to you? Conversely, if you were denied it, what has your attitude been?
- Have you ever loaned money to a family member? When do you think doing so is appropriate?
- Have you ever regretted *not* giving money to an in-law?

- Do you think that loans to family members are an obligation or a business transaction?
- Have you and your in-laws ever viewed a financial transaction differently? When?
- Do you approve of the way your in-law parents or your in-law children spend money?

CHAPTER 10

Until Death Do Us Part: Prepare for Illness and Death

None of us wants to get sick or die, but we do. Some will face bouts of illness; others will suffer chronic health problems. Accidents may randomly hurt one or more individuals in a family. In-laws are as much affected by these circumstances as those born into or adopted by the family. Like others in the clan, they may be called upon for everything from driving to doctors' appointments to providing housing. An unanticipated accident, illness, or death can disrupt a family or can be an opportunity to think through what we mean to each other. Ill fortune gives us a chance to turn good intentions into good behavior. It focuses us on our shared responsibility and underscores the importance of our relationships.

Accepting such possibilities encourages families to plan ahead. Because families take care of their own,[1] and because illness requires much work and time, health misfortunes are better weathered with a strong, healthy family support system. The family may need to rearrange its own plans or hire help. It may need to work out new living arrangements for the person who is sick. All of this requires family coordination. Both the conversations and the execution of the plans will fare better when families have cordial or, even better, warm relationships.

Inevitably, many of us will need help with bill paying, financial management, relocation, medicine management, and the chores of daily life. We will also need emotional support, even if we are in long-term, stable relationships. The younger generation may need help carpooling or babysitting or with visiting the hospital or nursing home. Discussing with family members the help we will need at some point in our lives can create incentives for getting along. We fear these conversations in part because it is not fun to contemplate our own demise, but also because we fear our families will not be willing to care for us as we had hoped. It also may give clear signals about when we cannot count on our families and suggests the necessity of planning for alternatives.[2] These deliberations help us think about the advisability of moving closer to each other or moving in with our children.[3]

If this is not possible or advisable, the older generation may want to look at continuing care retirement communities (CCRCs), which are usually pricy, or joining or helping to establish an "aging in place" community near their home. These are retirement communities without walls, sometimes known as naturally occurring retirement communities (NORCs). Another possibility that is more in the average person's budget is the "Golden Girls" model, in which older people live together, pool their resources, and help take care of each other as they age.[4] This provides a better standard of living for all of them, plus access to help of various kinds from one another. Some couples may want to consider purchasing long-term-care insurance, which can cover nursing-home stays, home care, and even care provided at home by a family member or friend. (Many families do not realize that Medicare covers only short-term nursing-home stays following a hospital stay.) This can mitigate or eliminate the need to discuss spending down assets to qualify for Medicaid. Options should, of course, be carefully evaluated, as with the purchase of any insurance, and it might be wise to seek professional advice before making a commitment.

The younger generation will want to build support networks—people they can call on in case of an emergency. No matter how awkward these conversations may be, they give us each a chance to make clear our preferences. Because these intimate conversations involve sharing our most profound thoughts, they can help make in-laws into family. Together, you can build a mutual aid society for yourselves based on reciprocity. Generally, the reciprocity is implied rather than discussed explicitly in terms of trading services.

Your own child may be unwilling or unable to drive you around to various appointments, but your in-law child may be willing. Your own sister or brother might be unavailable to assist, but a sibling-in-law might take over. Sometimes in-law children are the ones who support their parents-in-law. My cousin's husband supported her mother for years. My neighbor has seen to the daily care of her stroke-stricken mother-in-law. These reciprocal relationships begin with small exchanges. Building a good foundation benefits us all.

> *Marcie and her ex-brother-in-law, Jack, had many conference calls about what to do with Marcie's mother, Genevieve, now that a stroke had left her with no speech and little mobility. Marcie's sister—Jack's ex-wife—had left the family years ago, but everyone loved Jack, so he remained in the family circle. Marcie did not feel she could take her mother in, nor did she know the community where her mother lived. Jack lived near Genevieve, so he picked the nursing home. Marcie supported Jack's decision until she visited her mother and found that the other residents were more disabled than her mother. Marcie felt her mother wasn't getting the stimulation she needed. Jack's decision was based on affordability, proximity, and cleanliness. Marcie angrily reproached her ex-brother-in-law for shoddy research. Marcie and Jack became estranged.*

Had Genevieve selected a nursing home before her stoke, Marcie and Jack might have avoided this argument. It is not uncommon for ex-in-laws to remain in the family. Nor is it uncommon for in-laws to choose the eldercare. Jack had no obligation to help, but he liked his former mother-in-law. His ex-sister-in-law attacked him in part because she was distressed about her mother's situation and frustrated that living far away meant that she could not provide assistance herself. She also blamed Jack because she felt that she herself had been remiss in not checking on the arrangements.

In the trenches of care giving, many of us say words we wish we could retract. Accusations and blame can cause family arguments. Those who acknowledge each other's efforts tend to do better. Those who plan ahead minimize the risk. The older generation might hope their children will care for them in old age, but they may not want to either move in with their kids or burden them with paying for a nursing home. Their in-law children may or may not want to take on any part of these filial obligations. The expectation of how and what money and services are exchanged between the generations varies by family and certainly by culture, personality, and family history. In some cultures, the obligations are clear; children in India, for example, are obligated to support the husband's parents. In the United States, the obligations are unclear.

FILIAL OBLIGATIONS

Parents are responsible for caring for their children. If they do not provide for them, the state can take them away. The same is not entirely true when it is the parents who need the care. There used to be laws requiring children to take care of their parents. The rationale behind these laws goes back to ancient Roman law in which children had a duty to care for their parents. Taking care of parents now is mostly a matter of ethics, a sense of responsibility, and reciprocity. However, it's no urban legend that the state could come after grown children who fail to support their parents. In Massachusetts, for instance, an adult child who "unreasonably neglects" to support a parent who is destitute or too infirm to maintain himself or herself could face up to a year in prison plus a $200 fine.[5] The small monetary penalty makes it clear that this is an old provision. However, the provision that one could be jailed for a year does sound menacing. Many states have taken these laws off the books, signifying the change in American attitudes.[6] In most states, even Massachusetts, these laws are seldom enforced. Now, the only real clout remaining in the ancient law is the moral obligation to support one's parents. Sadly, not all adult children feel its force to the same degree, leaving children and in-law children squabbling over what is the appropriate financial and time commitment due to parents.

Illness provides an opportunity for family closeness as well as for the challenges of unmet expectations.

Carl has a stroke and spends two weeks in the hospital. Before he is released, his doctor says that he can no longer live alone. None of his children wants to take him in because they say he talks a lot and is self-absorbed. His daughter-in-law, whose grandparents lived with her when she was young, insists that she and her husband take him in for at least a six-month trial. She had nursed her own father in his final days and believes that children should care for their elders. When the other siblings see what this in-law is willing to do, they chip in. The brother who lives close by provides weekly respite care and takes his dad to the doctor. The one child who lives far away provides vacation care. Both brothers agree to pay the added expense that comes with illness since Carl has only his Social Security check on which to live. The family grows closer from their shared responsibility.

In this case, the daughter-in-law's family upbringing prevails. Her past experience helped her craft a way for her brothers-in-law to help so that she would not be overburdened. Had she not done that, she or her husband might have become resentful. If this arrangement becomes permanent, the family might want to discuss whether the daughter-in-law should be compensated for her work. Sometimes when a family member forgoes income to care for another, the other family members provide some income. Many older people like Carl have little or no disposable income. Often, different family members may have different means, which may either simplify or complicate conversations about who should cover costs for an aging parent. This family worked together to decide who could furnish monetary support and who could provide needed services.

The ideal time to take care of our health and financial matters is before anyone gets sick. The sick are vulnerable. If you are ill, you may or may not have the emotional energy or the capacity to make decisions. Others will make them with or without knowing your intentions. This applies to both generations. Both need guidance about health costs and retirement costs because none of us knows whether or when an accident will happen or ill health will befall us.

The older generation might want to avoid taxes and help their children provide for their care. They can do so, but *not* by giving away all of their assets to become eligible for Medicaid-funded nursing-home care. Medicaid look-back rules are enforced and do not allow transfers of assets within (currently) five years of applying for Medicaid benefits. That is, parents cannot give away their assets and then ask for Medicaid benefits for long-term care unless they transfer their assets well in advance of any need for long-term care. They can, however, arrange for other kinds of long-term care from assisted living to retirement living. As discussed earlier, having long-term-care insurance may significantly ease the financial burdens on a family if such care is needed. However, not everyone is eligible, and it is expensive. These are major decisions for most families because there is no way to know whether long-term care will be needed tomorrow, far in the future, or not at all.

MEDICAL DOCUMENTS

Without proper health-care proxies, powers of attorney, and living wills, medical-care choices are hampered at the time they are most needed. Drafting and signing all of the documents required for medical care makes our intentions clear and can mitigate future family squabbles and hurts. However, each one is rife with potential family problems. Many of us shy away from facing unpleasant topics, particularly ones that are frightening. Each one of the legal documents helps focus the family, but they can also bring up long-standing family rivalries.

Families should take steps to ensure that their family members or people they trust to assist in making health-care decisions are legally empowered to do so should circumstances require. Because the Health Insurance Portability and Accountability Act of 1996 (HIPAA) requires that health information be given only to you and the person(s) you designate, we all need to have a note on file with our doctor about who can get information about our medical condition. Families should discuss with their physicians or estate-planning advisors how best to arrange for *health-care proxies* and/or *health-care powers of attorney*.[7] Many people designate their own adult children for all of these roles. However, in some families, other people are chosen, often for good reasons. Choosing someone other than your adult children may be controversial or considered hurtful. The in-law child, who is a doctor or a social worker, may have the expertise, but the biological or adoptive children may feel they deserve the honor and should have the authority (and the work). You might also want to craft a living *will* that advises physicians and family members of your wishes should you be on life support. Although this document is not recognized in every state, it makes your wishes clear.

Family members can end up in battles, each believing that he or she knows what you want. *Health-care proxies* and *health-care powers of attorney* ensure that the person you have chosen represents your interests with your doctors. When you discuss these documents with your family, you have an opportunity to share your philosophy and your decision-making process. Letting all family members know how you would like to be treated at the end of your life relieves families of arguing over their own beliefs and guessing what you would want.[8]

> *Stuart's mother lay in the hospital after a severe heart attack. Her brain waves were flat. Stuart wanted all of the machines turned off. He felt that his mother would not want to live in a vegetative state, but she had not expressed her actual wishes. He also believed that the machines represented humans intervening in God's plan. His wife, Faith, felt that stopping the medical machinery was tantamount to killing her mother-in-law. Faith told Stuart that she would forever see him as a murderer if he suggested such a move.*

In-laws from different religious backgrounds can have strong feelings about God's intent. Had Stuart's mother made her feelings clear, a difficult situation for her son and daughter-in-law could have been moderated.

GUARDIANSHIP

Because death does not discriminate on the basis of age, young parents can and should plan for the guardianship of their children. This is a delicate matter when several siblings on both sides of the family and one or more sets of grandparents will feel hurt if they are not chosen to fulfill this role. When you choose a guardian, you are also confirming that you trust that person and his or her values enough to allow him or her to rear your children. Explain why you have chosen one family over the other. If you choose a friend rather than an in-law, that decision, too, must be explained, since many believe that family should be chosen first. Geographical location might be one reason, age of cousins might be another, and lifestyle is clearly a third. There are others. Perhaps you can suggest that the person you choose may want to give visiting rights to the other family members and put that in writing. While it may not be legally binding, it does declare your intent and can reduce the competition between in-laws. Reevaluate your decision as your children and family circumstances change, and share these deliberations with the potential guardians. Conversations surrounding these documents give in-laws a chance to talk about their intentions, hopes, and desires and a chance to work out some of the existing problems. Of course, there are other families in which no family member is willing to take on the task of rearing children. Knowing this propels individuals to look elsewhere in their networks for guardians.

If either generation has a child whose disabilities are so great that he or she needs lifetime supervision, whoever is expected to take over the guardianship should know and participate in making provisions for that child's care. Make sure that all of the family members including any in-law children understand your intent in all of the monetary, social, and housing provisions you have made.

RETIREMENT PLANNING

Another way we prepare for the unexpected is by preparing for retirement. We all hope that it will come when we want, but life events may bring retirement earlier than we expected. Financial planning is complex, and it cannot be divorced from life planning. Both before and after retirement, it is wise to talk with your children and in-law children about your aspirations. It is easier to forgive grandparents who do not babysit when they have made known that they are following a lifelong dream, rather than just being selfish. Letting your children and in-law children know that you are working with more variables than just their needs can lessen their disappointment when you are not available to them. Of course, the older couple may not agree with each other on their own goals for their later years. One partner might want to travel and the other might want to stick around and help take care of the grandkids. Discussions among both generations help sort out priorities.[9]

The older generation must think about what they want and need in retirement as well as what they may want to leave to their children and grandchildren. The younger generation, too, needs to consider their goals over a lifetime. Planning cannot deal with every possibility, but it can help us think about our goals. Here are a few questions that you should be answering: Do you have an IRA or a 401(k)?[10] Do you need life insurance or long-term-care insurance? Do you need a supplemental health-care policy to add to Medicare benefits? AARP.org[11] has a complete list for you to consider. For many of us, it is overwhelming to think of all that we must do to secure our futures, but the generations can share their knowledge, and in-laws may have new perspectives to share.

INHERITANCE AND WILLS

Regardless of whether you have any material assets to leave, you can provide an *ethical will* in which you share your values, hopes, and dreams for the future, and your love. It is not a legal document, but it is perhaps the most important "thing" to leave. Of course, beautiful words do not replace a lifetime of bad behavior. Our families learn by what we do, not what we write. Many use the writing of an ethical will to take stock, to see whether their actions are leading to the kind of ethical legacy they hope to leave. If not, they still have time to change their actions.

How the older generation writes its wills sets a tone in intergenerational and in-law relationships. Once grandchildren arrive, both generations need wills. They will need to ask similar questions. Is the in-law child included? If so, how? If not, are the reasons evident and fair, or at least understandable? This is an area ripe for invidious comparison: "My parents can do so little compared to yours" or "Your parents obviously don't appreciate me." These issues and choices all have implications well beyond the writers of the wills. Their impact may depend, in part, on the openness of the intergenerational relationship. However difficult, when intentions are explained, they are more likely to be accepted.

One of the more potentially contentious documents we leave is a *last will and testament,* or *will.* It directs the disposal of our material goods. In more complex estates, a *trust* is often created to minimize estate and income tax liability for heirs. It also facilitates processing the estate since it bypasses probate court. Unless your assets are truly minimal and uncomplicated, consulting an estate lawyer both in planning and periodically to keep wills up to date is good practice. Congress changes the rules from time to time, and our life circumstances, too, can change. It is important to appoint an executor of your will who will distribute your assets as directed in the will. If you have your assets in trusts, you need to appoint a trustee to administer assets that are not immediately available to the beneficiary but are instead tied up in a trust—which may stretch over time for a particular purpose. Again, your in-law child who may be a lawyer or who may be experienced in these matters may be hurt if he or she is not chosen for these positions. Or your own child may resent that you chose an in-law rather than him or her.

The danger of using any family member as your legal counsel is that it may be difficult to ensure the appearance of impartiality. Other family members may be angered if they do not get what they expect. You may want to take other family members with you for these discussions, or you may not; in either case, you should let the family know your intentions. Family members may expect that you will leave your fortune to them but you instead decide to leave it to charity. It is important to update these documents periodically and while you are in relatively good health; it is also important to share your intentions with your family, making it possible to clear up potential future misunderstandings.

For the older generation, many issues can prove to be touchy. We may think our children are in strong, healthy marriages only to find out that they are about to divorce. We want to protect our progeny and not hurt the in-laws who have become part of the fabric of our lives. Some opt for equality among siblings, regardless of the adult children's marital or financial status. Others focus on need, and they expect or hope that the less needy will understand. Some choose to include in-law children in ways that acknowledge their importance; others do not. Some give in-law children monetary gifts, and others give token mementos to help the in-laws know that they are appreciated. Some take into consideration the resources the other family may leave the adult children and grandchildren; others feel that marriage is so fragile that counting on the other in-laws to protect their children is folly. They do not take the potential in-law inheritance into consideration when writing their own wills. Others do not feel obliged to leave anything of monetary value to their children as a matter of principle.

A parent's remarriage or a new coupling can cause both social and monetary concerns for the younger generation. The new partner not only takes the time and attention of the parent, but the parent's money. What the younger generation may find to be still worse is if a new family is created or inherited by the new unit. Regardless of whether money was ever discussed, children often have fantasies about what is coming to them. They may not like it when the new in-law's family dips into what they assume will be their inheritance, even if the reasons are very good.

Morton was 60 when he married Sheila, age 50. Her son, Lee, is a college graduate with a good job. Suddenly, however, Lee loses his job and confesses his addiction to drugs. His mother has no funds to send him to a rehabilitation program. Morton had been successful in business, likes the boy, and feels that he can and, therefore, should help. He agrees to pay for rehabilitation. When Morton's biological children find out, they are incensed. In their minds, Lee is not their father's responsibility. He is an adult stepchild. From their point of view, Morton is rewarding bad behavior and spending their expected inheritance.

Sheila is shamed and embarrassed. She does not want to discuss her son's addiction with anyone. Addiction is corrosive to families as well as individuals. While some treatment programs work, others do not. None works without the cooperation of the addict. It is hard for family members to know when helping is beneficial and when it is reinforcing irresponsible behavior. Accusations fly. Morton, of course, has the right to spend his money however he wants. For him, his stepchild is part of the package that comes with his wife. The children see Lee and, by association, his mother as competitors within the family. Though Morton's children have no right to expect his money, their expectations and Lee's problems create unrest within his family.

* * *

Frequently, children from the first marriage worry that they will be disinherited once a parent remarries. Money that they thought might be coming to them is going to a second wife or the children of the second marriage. Sometimes a conversation can avert problems before they start.

> *Flossy, in her 70s, married Jeffrey, in his 80s. They found tremendous joy in sharing their love of gardening and music. Flossy sensed a palpable resistance to their union by Jeffrey's children. Although she did not need to do this, she gathered all of her spouse's children together and outlined her own financial situation so that the stepchildren could see that she could manage quite well without their father's assets. She assured them that she would forgo any inheritance from their father, so theirs would remain intact.*

Flossy sensed that she was being demonized as a gold digger. She understood that she had no obligation to explain her finances to her future stepchildren, but by doing so, she would head off problems. She did not try to justify or erase their concerns, nor was she angry with them for worrying. Instead, she used maturity, compassion, perspective, and empathy to head off problems.

Of course, not all of us can afford to be as generous as Flossy.

* * *

> *Meredith was a single mom from age 25 until she turned 44. When she married Fernando, she was not only happy to have found a soul mate but also relieved to have another income. Fernando was by no means wealthy. He had a steady job with a modest pension. He managed to*

get his own four children through high school and help them here and there while they worked themselves through community college. After 15 years of marriage to Meredith, he wrote a will. Meredith did not want to return to her former hand-to-mouth existence. She encouraged Fernando to make her—not his children—the beneficiary of his pension. She also asked him to tell his children. Of course, they had no right to expect the little money he might leave, but she worried that after all of her hard work of incorporating them into her life, they would be left with anger toward her. He could not talk with them; it felt too macabre to him. However, he did leave a note with his will explaining that he felt that Meredith had brought him happiness and that his obligations as a parent were over. He wanted to ensure her financial future.

Meredith and Fernando's feelings were different from Flossy's. They felt that they had worked hard to give their children a good start in life and that now they should focus on their own futures. They tried to avert ill feelings by at least letting the younger generation know their reasoning and that there was no malicious intent.

* * *

It is hard for the younger generation to plan without knowledge of future obligations and future resources.

Lois died of breast cancer at age 36, leaving two toddlers. Her husband, Gregory, took over as mother and father and worked full time as a teacher. He has recently remarried, but he continues to facilitate his children's close contact with Lois's parents. His former father-in-law, Zeke, is a nice man, with considerable economic means. When Greg was married to Lois, Zeke gave annual monetary gifts to the couple. Greg is doing some estate planning and wants to know whether his former father-in-law is planning to leave money to his grandchildren. Greg will find a way to educate his children, but it will help his planning if he knows what to expect. He would hate to deprive his kids of piano lessons now if his former father-in-law is planning to pay for their college educations.

Although it is unclear whether Zeke and Greg are still related, Greg's children are, and will always be, Zeke's grandchildren. Greg anticipates that Zeke will leave or give money to his grandchildren. Greg needs to know this information in order to properly care for his children. Unless Zeke shares his plans with his former son-in-law, Greg will have to make financial decisions without the facts.

Children often provide care for elderly parents, and parents often provide primary or secondary income for grandchildren and their education. Either in-law generation or either individual within the generations may be making very different assumptions about what financial contribution is necessary or forthcoming. It is incumbent on each of us to explain our desires and intentions to both our children and our in-law children.

Unlike spouses, long-term partners do not automatically inherit unless something else is stated in wills. Adult children may not consider these quasi in-laws worthy of inheritance. If it is your desire that your partner receive any of your assets, share that with your children. Conversely, if your child has been coupled, but not married, your quasi in-law child may be deeply hurt if you give him or her no mention in your will.

One way to reduce problems is to discuss your intent with both your children and your in-law children. If you feel that each child should receive according to his or her need and your resources, disclose that. Those who assume parents have an obligation to leave whatever money they have to their neediest child will be miffed if, instead, the money is divided equally. Alternatively, those who believe that, in the absence of a disabled heir, parents should divide their money equally among their children regardless of their relative means will be annoyed if the neediest gets a bigger share. And of course, those who assume parents should leave money to their children will be sorely disappointed if the parents do otherwise, as many do. If you have paid for one child's housing, do you plan to equalize this big expense in your will? Whatever your thoughts are about whatever you have to give your children, share those thoughts with them. Conversely, if your intent is to even off the contribution by giving time, services, or money to the other child, let them know that. Both even exchanges and providing for needs are valid ways of helping family members, but other family members may use different measures from yours. Similarly, if children are giving money or services to one set of in-laws, they may want to let the other set know why they are doing so and whether the other set can expect the same in the future. What appears unfair may actually be appropriate. Conflict and competition may sell newspapers and be great for TV, but cooperation works best in families. Knowledge fosters cooperation.

QUESTIONS

- What obligation do you feel to take care of your own parents?
- What obligation do you feel to take care of your in-law parents?
- What obligation does your spouse or para-spouse feel to take care of his or her own parents?
- What obligation does your spouse or para-spouse feel to take care of your parents?
- Have you talked with your family about your end-of-life wishes? If not, why?
- Have you arranged for guardianship of those dependent on you?
- Is there a person with long-term disabilities in your family? If yes, have you and your spouse talked about your roles in his or her care?
- What are your plans if you become disabled?
- Have you prepared any of the legal documents in preparation for death or infirmity? If yes, which ones? If no, why not?
- Do you have a will?

Chapter 11

Do Unto Your In-Laws

I wish I could end this book with simple, easy-to-follow lessons to instantly improve your connections with your in-laws. That would be unrealistic. If there were simple answers, I suspect you would not need this book. I can, however, give you a handful of approaches that, over time, might improve your lot. All of these will require change. You finally find a way to communicate with your father-in-law, but then he develops Alzheimer's disease. Or you eventually realize that your daughter-in-law will never be close to you. You create an amicable distance, but then she is diagnosed with breast cancer, which you had, and this utterly transforms your relationship. Or your ne'er-do-well son becomes the next entrepreneurial sensation. Or your sister marries or divorces someone you detest.

Rolling our eyes is a gut-level, instinctive way in which we show disapproval. However, if your aim is to relate well to others, you must not roll your eyes. Families that get along do so in part because they decide to get along. They decide that they are on the same team. They decide that anyone who loves their children at least has good taste and judgment. The in-law children conclude that the people who brought up the person they love is worthy of some respect. With small and continually growing acts of kindness, we can begin to build our relationships. We may not love or even respect our in-laws, but we can work with them. After all, in the office or at the factory, we work with all sorts of people, some of whom we detest.

We can change if we imagine ourselves differently.[1] The first step in that imagining is to see ourselves truthfully. We do this by observing our actions, examining their results, and then changing our behaviors and attitudes to achieve better results. We all can benefit from self-awareness so that we do not accuse others of causing our displeasure, when the dissatisfaction really lies within ourselves.

You and I can take comfort in knowing that humans have been trying to figure out how to get along better since at least the second century, as is evident in this quote by Rabbi Nathan:

> *If you have done your fellow a slight wrong,*
> *let it be a serious matter in your eyes;*
> *but if you have done your fellow much good,*
> *let it be a small thing in your eyes.*
> *And if your fellow has done you a small favor,*
> *let it be a great thing in your eyes;*
> *but if your fellow has done you a great evil,*
> *let it be a little thing in your eyes.*[2]

If we substitute *in-law* for *fellow* in this quotation, we have the recipe for improving relationships. However, the recipe alone does not make all troubles disappear; as cooks do with so many recipes, we must add our own special personal/secret ingredients to make it work. It takes time, energy, compassion, understanding, and personal discipline. Relationships do not have to be perfect in order to be rewarding. In the two millennia since Rabbi Nathan made the aforementioned statement, no one has invented shortcuts to creating relationships that give more pleasure than pain. Then as now, pride, stubbornness, and a fear of letting the other person win prevent us from following Rabbi Nathan's advice. Instead of simple answers, I list some pointers you can try that you might find helpful over time. They take practice, practice, practice.

1. REFRAME WITH A POSITIVE VIEW

If your daughter-in-law clears the table too soon, rather than assume that she was trying to rush you out of the house, assume instead that she misunderstood and thought you were finished. When your father-in-law picks up the baby, consider that he is trying to be helpful, not criticizing your parenting or trying to take over. When your mother-in-law checks her e-mail while talking with you, assume that she is busy at work, rather than avoiding you. And when your mother-in-law comments on a situation, assume that she is trying to help, not trying to control the outcome.

Once you fall into the trap of negativity, you interpret every action as hurtful. You create self-fulfilling prophecies that ultimately damage relationships. You expect your in-laws to refuse your invitations, so you stop inviting them. You expect your in-law child to fumble, and you make him so tense that he does. A critical attitude might serve a book or theater reviewer, but it does not help human friendships. My dog-lover friends tell me that there's a school of dog training that ignores the bad and praises the good. By envisioning and emphasizing the positive, we train ourselves and others to accept the best we have to offer.

2. DEAL WITH WHAT YOU HAVE, NOT WHAT YOU WANT

Forget the stereotypes. Forget the hopes and fantasies. Preexisting expectations are disappointments waiting to happen. Both generations must cope with them, examine them, and modify them. Whether you hoped you would never see your in-laws or hoped you would be close, either way, forget what you wanted. Make what you actually have more satisfying. If you see your in-laws only once a year and want more closeness, be inventive with technology. If either generation of in-laws comes for long periods that you find stressful, think of interesting things for them to do. Ask if they would like to help with home projects or cooking, or ask them to help with your errands. If your sibling attends to his spouse before you, focus on their happiness and your freedom to make new friends.

3. PUT A STATUTE OF LIMITATIONS ON SLIGHTS

Each relationship takes work. Misunderstandings and miscommunications happen often and regularly in established relationships. They occur even more frequently in developing ones. Because in-laws are still relative strangers, jumping to conclusions and letting anger and resentment get the best of you lead nowhere. Holding on to real and perceived misunderstandings suffocates relationships. It freezes them in misery. It impedes the way to improvement. As for grudges from former marriages or childhood days, don't pass them to the next generation. Don't hold onto old hurts. Talk things out when you can. When stymied, talk to friends, peers, spiritual advisors, or counselors. Holding onto resentments does not help anyone, especially you. Forget a past slight; that was then, this is now! We can't change the past, but we can create a new present.

4. LISTEN INSTEAD OF JUDGING

Instead of accusing and calling names, try to listen to what is subtle, implicit, and even silent in each other's views. You can then begin to understand, if not agree with, one another. My three terms in the New Hampshire legislature taught me that people are not stupid. They have reasons for what they think, although their conclusions may differ from yours or mine. Understanding why others believe what they do is usually fascinating. It gives insight into them as people. Besides, you may just find that there is a grain of truth in their thoughts and actions. Your sense of reality and possibility can be extended. Forget the name-calling. Use differences of opinion as an opportunity to learn. If the gap is too wide, agree to disagree and find other "safer" topics of communication and areas of activity. You may be a Republican; they may be Democrats. You may not be a sports fan; they may avoid museums. You could all probably enjoy going to a child's school play together. Gender roles, manners, and ways of communicating are changing at lightning speed, and this makes it hard for us to understand and accept one another.

5. TAKE THE LONG VIEW—THINGS CHANGE OVER TIME AND OVER LIFE STAGES

As we know, change is the miserable, intractable, and sometimes joyous constant in our lives. The coupling of your parent or of your child will bring new alliances. Embrace them. Focus on your reduced responsibilities rather than your loss. A new relationship is like a new baby—it takes time and patience, but it can give pleasure. We are all on different learning curves. Some of us learn to juggle many tasks at a young age, while others of us need to focus and only later learn to multitask. Some of us have social graces from birth, and others of us learn over time and after many mistakes. None of us grows without a combination of support and challenge. Sometimes we rise to the challenge on day one; other times we need support. It takes a while to grow up at any age, but we all can keep growing. Make allowances for mistakes along the way. When we look at our children's or parents' marriages, it is a good time to take an honest look at our own marriage. We can criticize someone else's marriage only when our own marriage is perfect. If the in-law relationship is affecting the marriage, it might be time to think about going to counseling. Sometimes learning a few communication techniques can help a lot. It doesn't mean that your coupling is in trouble—just that extra help is needed around this issue that is hard for everyone involved.

6. BE FORGIVING

Most things don't really matter. It really isn't worthwhile to make a big deal out of every small misstep. Maybe in your family it was tradition to order pizza on Friday nights or to spend Thanksgiving watching football instead of chatting with family members. Do not assume that your new family has the same traditions or that your family's way of doing things is superior. Think carefully about what really matters. Missteps are just that. We all make them. Figure out which traditions are "sacred" and why. Their continuation may be less valuable than the pain they cause newcomers. Understand that each individual has different needs for touching, hugging, kissing, and other expressions of intense relationships. Each of us has learned many behaviors—aggression, assertion, compliance, and withdrawal—for dealing with problems and decisions. We tend to repeat our favorites over and over. If we are aware, we can expand our repertoire and all gain.

7. BE CREATIVE

Continuing on the same path without regard for the environment or others' reactions leads to collisions. If whatever you are doing is not working, change. Try something else. Experiment. Find out some of your in-laws' interests and then use one of the many communication tools—phone, twitter, sharing cartoons, e-mail—to show them that you have found something that may connect the two of you.

Find out what each of you wants and at the very least make a compromise with that knowledge in mind. You might have a discussion or you might just observe the behavior of the other person. Some people want a lot of attention; others prefer distance. Whether at work or at play, we note this and calibrate our reactions accordingly. If you have not reached out or wished your in-law well in the past year, or if you have allowed a birthday or an event worthy of congratulations to pass unnoticed, correct those oversights now. Small gestures can pave the way for better relationships. These small gestures will not solve all of your problems, but they do provide a foundation on which to build.

8. CALL UPON YOUR MOST MATURE SELF

We all act like children sometimes, throwing tantrums or wanting things only our way. Of course, we can still do this in the privacy of our minds or complain to a close friend, but when dealing with in-laws, we need to find our grown-up selves and control both our tempers and our wants. And when we fail, we need to apologize. To make peace, we must be peaceful.

We may not find perfection, but we can strive to find more joy than sorrow in our evolving relationships. Incorporating new members into our families requires everyone to take on new roles. Each of us is only a part of the story.

We always have a choice: either let conflict destroy us and our relationships or let conflict be a signal to behave differently. We can choose to be entrapped or enriched by the inclusion of another relative. Herein lies either joy or something very different, but no matter what, the choice is ours.

9. REMEMBER THAT WE ARE ALL NEW TO THIS GAME

Do not underestimate how we can change over a lifetime. We are all living in a world we do not always understand. We don't even know ourselves fully. We don't know all of our biases or our fears until we act in ways that, at times, surprise even ourselves. We remember things through a lens of whatever emotional state we were in at the time. We act with less control of ourselves than we thought we had.[3] Some of us protect ourselves from uncertainty by building walls so that we don't have to feel pain. Others seek protection from uncertainty by surrounding themselves only with people who share similar beliefs and values—that way they do not have to question themselves. We all have reasons, though we may not know them, for acting as we do. Some look for a safe, structured world because it is comfortable. For others, that seems insular and isolating. It severely limits our ability to include in-laws into our families. We need to expand our horizons to include others, especially the in-laws whom another's choice brought into our lives.

10. BE CURIOUS

Curiosity about why we act the way we each do is a good first step in acquiring compassion, understanding, and forgiveness. We are all travelers on an unknown road just trying to figure out the way. The goal is clear: to get along. The only hard part is opening ourselves to the possibility of new relationships that are potentially loving but are, at the very least, caring and cordial. Embrace the imperfect. We are all fallible human beings. Our relationships are forever evolving.

Appendix 1: Films and Videos

Through the characters in these films, one can observe in-law interactions, even though the in-law relationship is not always the main focus. Viewing these films might lead to interesting insights and discussions.

Television Shows

All in the Family (Bud Yorkin Productions, 1968–1979). This television series spoofs fathers-in-law and sons-in-law.

In Treatment, season 3 (HBO, 2010–2011). An Indian father moves in with his American daughter-in-law who resents her husband's filial obligation.

Thirtysomething, "I'll Be Home for Christmas" (MGM/United Artists Television, December 15, 1987). A Christian woman and a Jewish man negotiate what to do during the holiday season. While this episode is about the couple, it clearly depicts the role of the past in the future.

Films

Annie Hall (directed by Woody Allen, Metro-Goldwyn-Mayer, 1977). A Jewish man and his Anglo-Saxon girlfriend interact with each other's families and customs.

Cat on a Hot Tin Roof (directed by Richard Brooks, Metro-Goldwyn-Mayer, 1958). This Tennessee Williams classic clearly shows how parents' feelings toward their own children can affect their relationships with their in-law children.

Father of the Bride (directed by Charles Shyer, Touchstone Pictures, 1991). A father copes with the fact that his daughter has grown up and is about to get married.

Guess Who (directed by Kevin Rodney Sullivan, Columbia Pictures, 2005). A contemporary remake of *Guess Who's Coming to Dinner*.

Guess Who's Coming to Dinner (directed by Stanley Kramer, Columbia Pictures, 1967). Parents' attitudes are challenged when their daughter brings home a fiancé who is black.

How to Make an American Quilt (directed by Jocelyn Moorhouse, Universal Pictures, 1995). Among other issues of marriage, this film depicts the aftermath of a sister and brother-in-law who have an episode of infidelity.

It's Complicated (directed by Nancy Meyers, Universal Pictures, 2009). This film demonstrates that ex-spouses are still part of the family constellation.

La cage aux folles (directed by Edouard Molinaro, Da Ma Produzione, 1978). Gay and straight future in-laws meet.

Lovers and Other Strangers (directed by Cy Howard, Cinerama Releasing Corporation, 1970). A depiction of divorce, affairs, and marital problems, all of which affect the entire family.

Meet the Fockers (directed by Jay Roach, Universal Pictures, 2004). A spoof of two families from different classes and political views. It is rather silly, but it does show the discomfort and misunderstandings that can result when in-laws meet.

Message in a Bottle (directed by Luis Mandoki, Warner Brothers, 1999). A man's wife dies and the in-laws blame him.

Midnight in Paris (directed by Woody Allen, Sony Picture Classics, 2011). A couple travels to Paris with her parents.

Mississippi Masala (directed by Mira Nair, MGM, 1991–1992). An African American and an Indian face cultural differences as they couple.

Mixed Blessings: The Challenges of Raising Children in a Jewish-Christian Family (directed by Jennifer Kaplan, Spencer Films, 2005). This documentary contains interviews with several intermarried families.

Monsoon Wedding (directed by Mira Nair, Mirabai Films, 2001). This movie depicts Indian wedding customs and shows the ambivalence of the younger generation between arranged and love marriages.

Monster-in-Law (directed by Robert Luketic, New Line Cinema, 2005). A wealthy future mother-in-law does not approve of the marriage between her son and a working-class woman. In the end, the two women reconcile, which is always a positive outcome.

Mrs. Miniver (directed by William Wyler, Metro-Goldwyn-Mayer, 1942). An upper class woman falls in love with a middle-class man despite her family's disapproval.

My Big Fat Greek Wedding (directed by Joel Zwick, IFC Films, 2002). A young groom copes with cultural differences in his soon-to-be new family.

National Lampoon's Vacation (directed by Harold Ramis, Warner Bros., 1983). The Griswold family travels cross-country and visits family, having adventures along the way.

Pushing Hands (directed by Ang Lee, Ang Lee Productions and Central Motion Pictures Corporation, 1992). A Chinese retired father moves in with his son and American daughter-in-law. The situation brings up culture conflict and cultural misunderstandings.

Secrets and Lies (directed by Mike Leigh, Channel Four Films, 1996). Although this film is about a young black woman who searches for her birth mother and discovers that her mother is white, it clearly depicts the havoc a sister-in-law can create between formerly close siblings.

Sex, Lies, and Videotape (directed by Steven Soderbergh, Miramax Films, 1989). The husband of a sexually repressed woman is having an affair with her sister.

Solomon and Gaenor (directed by Paul Morrison, Columbia Tristar, 2000). A Welsh girl and a Jewish boy fall in love in 1911. Their families force them to separate. The movie shows the role that parents-in-law can play in causing real trouble.

The Descendants (directed by Alexander Payne, Ad Hominem Enterprises, 2011). A man's wife is dying. His father-in-law doesn't like him, and his mother-in-law has dementia.

The Family Stone (directed by Thomas Bezucha, Fox 2000 Pictures, 2005). A young woman comes home to meet her boyfriend's family, and all sorts of sibling problems arise.

The In-Laws (directed by Arthur Hiller, Warner Bros., 1979). A silly movie that demonstrates that you do not choose your in-laws but still have to cope with them.

The In-Laws (directed by Andrew Fleming, Warner Bros., 2003). A remake of the 1979 version.

The Kids Are All Right (directed by Lisa Cholodenko, Alliance Films and Focus Features, 2010). A sperm donor enters the lives of a lesbian couple and their teenage children.

The Trip to Bountiful (directed by Peter Masterson, Island Pictures, 1985). A mother-in-law is living the end of her life in an apartment with her controlling daughter-in-law and pushover son. She must show her son and daughter-in-law that she needs an escape—one last trip home.

The Wedding Banquet (directed by Ang Lee, Samuel Goldwyn Company, 1993). A Chinese gay man arranges a marriage with one of his tenants to satisfy his parents, though he has a Caucasian American male partner.

Transamerica (directed by Duncan Tucker, IFC Films and the Weinstein Company, 2005). Although this movie is about a mother and a son, it highlights the issues in families when one person is transgendered.

Appendix 2: Suggested Websites

The following websites are places for you to begin your search for further information. For some sites, I have listed particular articles that focus on in-laws. For others, I have directed you to the main page, as the whole site is full of relevant information.

AARP (aarp.org)

This is an excellent website for any concerns about aging or grandparenting.

Good Morning America (gma.yahoo.com)

"Mending Grandmother, Daughter-in-Law Relationships" (abcnews. go.com/GMA/Parenting/mending-grandmother-daughter-law relationships/story?id=9096421&page=1>)

Babble (babble.com)

"Grandparents Just Don't Understand: I Don't Trust My In-Laws With My Baby" (http://www.babble.com/baby/baby-care/grandparenting -crying-baby-soothing/)

"What's in a Last Name?" (http://blogs.babble.com/strollerderby /2010/11/01/whats-in-a-last-name/)

"Say Hi to Grandma—through the Screen" (http://www.babble.com/CS/ blogs/strollerderby/archive/2008/11/28/say-hi-to-grandma-through -the-screen.aspx)

Bharat Moms (bharatmoms.com)

"How to Tackle MIL Problem" (http://www.blrmoms.com/forums/1 /topics/8547-how-to-tackle-mil-problem)

Boston.com Moms (boston.com/community/moms)

"Will Mother-in-Law, Daughter-in-Law Problems Ever Disappear?" (boston.com/community/moms/blogs/child_caring/2009/07/wil l_motherinla.html)

Chennai Moms (chennaimoms.com)

"Role of In-Laws" (http://www.chennaimoms.com/forums/1/topics /1172-role-of-in-laws)

Cochin Moms (cochinmoms.com)

"How to Tackle the Problems with Your Mother-in-Law" (http:// www.cochinmoms.com/blogs/8450/posts/20502-how-to-tackle-the -problems-with-your-mother-in-law)

"Personal Problem with My Kids" (http://www.cochinmoms.com /forums/1/topics/3986-personal-problem-with-my-kids-)

Daily Finance (dailyfinance.com)

"Never Mind the In-Laws, Couples Hate Discussing Money Most" (http://www.dailyfinance.com/story/investing-basics/couples-hate -discussing-money-most/19511429/)

Estranged Parents of Adult Children (www.estrangedparentsofadultchil dren.com)

This website lists resources for family members who have been estranged from one another.

Focus on the Family (focusonthefamily.com)

This is a Christian marriage resource.

GaGa Sisterhood (gagasisterhood.com)

This is a grandmothering resource.

GrandLoving (grandloving.com)

This is a grandparenting resource.

Grandparents.com

"How I Learned to Stop Worrying and Love the Other Grandmother" (http://www.grandparents.com/gp/content/opinions/adair-lara/article/ how-i-learned-to-stop-worrying.html)

Hot Flash Financial (hotflashfinancial.com)

This is a website for women who want to increase their financial security.

Hyderabad Moms (hyderabadmoms.com)

"Shall I Leave the Job?" (http://www.hyderabadmoms.com/forums/1/ topics/8543-shall-i-leave-the-job)

"Get Rid of That 'Mother Hen' Syndrome" (http://www.hyderabadmoms. com/blogs/17502/posts/41125-get-rid-of-that-mother-hen-syndrome)

India Parenting (indiaparenting.com)

"How to Be a Good Daughter-in-Law" (http://www.indiaparenting.com/ relationships/article.cgi?art_id=85&sec_id=7)

InterfaithFamily.com

This is the go-to site for Jewish intermarriage.

Kolkata Moms (kolkatamoms.com)

"Nuclear Vs. Joint Family" (http://www.bharatmoms.com/blogs/14251/ posts/37046-nuclear-vs-joint-family?from=stay_back)

Mothering21.com

"Meeting the In-Laws" (http://mothering21.com/2011/01/23/meeting-the -in-laws/)

Motherinlawstories.com

"Dr. Terri Apter Advice" (http://www.motherinlawstories.com/terri_apter _advice_page.htm)

Surat Moms (suratmoms.com)

"Binding Relationship at Home" (http://www.suratmoms.com/
forums/1/topics/5006-binding-relationship-at-home)

The Conversation Project (theconversationproject.org)

This website offers assistance in talking about end-of-life planning.

Notes

Introduction

1. In "Changing Values," *The Futurist* (January/February 1989): 8–13, Joseph Plummer corroborates this notion in commenting on the UNESCO Human Values Project. I am indebted to Mila Bronstein for the framing of families as vertical and horizontal (conversation on December 24, 2011).

2. The Kraft macaroni and cheese commercial is a prime example of the negative stereotypes of in-law prejudice: http://www.youtube.com/watch?v=LxQ-AzS38vY.

3. E. J. Graff, *What Is Marriage For? The Strange Social History of Our Most Intimate Institution* (Boston, MA: Beacon Press, 2004).

4. While I have no data supporting the extent of the tensions between mothers and daughters-in-law, on my book tour for *Don't Bite Your Tongue: How to Foster Rewarding Relationships with Your Adult Children*, questions about daughters-in-law vastly outnumbered those about sons-in-law. Also, Prof. Yan Yunxiang, *Private Life under Socialism: Love, Intimacy, and Family Change in a Chinese Village, 1949–1999* (Stanford: Stanford University Press, 2003: Loc 680, Kindle edition), writes about the vocabulary of family structure. In the 1970s, in a village in Heilongjiang Province, China, women did not say "find a husband." They said "*zhao pojia*," in which *pojia* means, as Yan puts it: "the home of a woman's future mother-in-law and the verb *zhao* means to search or look for." By the1990s, it had begun to change. However, this vocabulary confirms there is a traditional root in the primacy of the mother-in-law and daughter-in-law relationship.

5. Sarah Lamb, "Intimacy in a Transnational Era: The Remaking of Aging among Indian Americans," *Diaspora: A Journal of Transnational Studies* 11, no. 3 (2002): 299–330.

6. US Census Bureau, "America's Families and Living Arrangements: 2007," accessed March 7, 2012, http://www.census.gov/prod/2009pubs/p20-561.pdf.

7. Sarah Lamb, *Aging and the Indian Diaspora: Cosmopolitan Families in India and Abroad* (Bloomington: Indiana University Press, 2009). Also see Sarah Lamb, "Intimacy in a Transnational Era: The Remaking of Aging among Indian Americans," *Diaspora: Journal of Transnational Studies* 11, no. 3 (2002): 299. "In India, if you take a second cup, or a third cup of tea, they will object, they will object. Here, you can take even ten cups of tea, prepare yourself, any material you use, your children will never object. But, if you want their time, they will object."

8. Deborah Merrill, *Mothers-in-Law and Daughters-in-Law: Understanding the Relationship and What Makes Them Friends or Foe* (Westport, CT: Praeger Publishers, 2007), 159.

9. Dan Hurley, "Divorce Rate: It's Not as High as You Think," *New York Times*, April 19, 2005, accessed December 31, 2011, http://www.nytimes .com/2005/04/19/health/19divo.html. Exact statistics have not been collected. According to W. Bradford Wilcox, director of the National Marriage Project and associate professor of sociology at the University of Virginia (http://www .virginia.edu/marriageproject/director.html), the 41 to 43 percent range is cited by experts. The big news is that the rate is not the 50 percent regularly cited (e-mail communication, January 3, 2012).

10. Stephanie Coontz, *Marriage, a History: How Love Conquered Marriage* (New York: Viking Penguin, 2005).

11. Charles Moskos, "The Future of Greek America," *Hellenic Communication Service*, May 4, 2006, accessed December 27, 2011, http://www.helleniccom serve.com/futuregreekamerica.html; Greek Orthodox Archdiocese of America, "Department of Marriage and Family," accessed December 27, 2011, http:// www.goarch.org/archdiocese/departments/marriage.

12. The Jewish Federations of North America, "National Jewish Population Survey: Rates of Intermarriage," accessed December 27, 2011, http://www.jewishfed erations.org/page.aspx?id=46253.

13. National Healthy Marriage Resource Center, "Marriage and Intermarriage Among Asian Americans: A Fact Sheet," accessed March 7, 2012, http://acf .gov/healthymarriage/pdf/marriageamongasianamericans.pdf.

14. "After 40 Years, Interracial Marriage Flourishing," *Associated Press*, April 15, 2007, accessed December 27, 2011, http://www.msnbc.msn.com/id/18090277 /ns/us_news-life/t/after-years-interracial-marriage-flourishing/#.

15. Susan Schnur, "How Twenty-Somethings Mate Now," *Lilith* (Spring 2010): 10–15. Even among the observant, religion is becoming an individual, rather than a family, choice.

16. Melissa Barnett, Laura Scaramella, Tricia Neppl, Lenna Ontai, and Rand Conger, "Grandmother Involvement as a Protective Factor for Early Childhood Social Adjustment," *Journal of Family Psychology* 24, no. 5 (2010): 635–645.

1   Why We Make In-Laws into Outlaws

1. Definitions of *kin* vary, as demonstrated in the following source: Marvin Sussman and Lee Burchinal, "Kin Family Network: Unheralded Structure in Current Conceptualizations of Family Functioning," *Marriage and Family Living* 24, no. 3 (1962): 231–240. Some other definitions of *kin* can be found at these websites: Oregon State University, "Definitions of Anthropological

Terms," last modified February 24, 2011, accessed October 27, 2011, http://oregonstate.edu/instruct/anth370/gloss.html; Dennis O'Neil, "Cultural Anthropology Terms," last modified May 11, 2007, accessed October 27, 2011, http://anthro.palomar.edu/tutorials/cglossary.htm.

2. Deborah Merrill, *Mothers-in-Law and Daughters-in-Law: Understanding the Relationship and What Makes Them Friends or Foe* (Westport, CT: Praeger Publishers, 2007), states: "At a minimum, in-laws need to be aware that their expectations and obligations of their sons are also obligations of their daughters-in-law...perhaps temper those expectations early in the relationship," 131.

3. Karen Fingerman, *Aging Mothers and Their Adult Daughters: A Study of Mixed Emotions* (New York: Springer, 2001). Fingerman reminds us that "extended families are often based on matrilineal kinship. Therefore, young families are often closer to the wife's family than to the husband's," 42.

4. Hanna Rosin, "She Makes More Money Than He Does. So? Women Who Outearn Their Men," *Slate*, February 16, 2011, accessed October 27, 2011, http://www.slate.com/articles/double_x/doublex/2011/02/she_makes_more_money_than_he_does_so.html. About 22 percent of American marriages of people over age 30 fall into this category, up from 4 percent in 1970.

5. Merrill, *Mothers-in-Law and Daughters-in-Law*, 109. The quality of the relationship between the mother-in-law and daughter-in-law is affected by the mother–son relationship and the daughter-in-law's perception of it.

6. Norma Baumel Joseph, "From Baghdad to Montreal: Food, Gender and Identity in Two Scenarios," in *Migration, Communication, and Home: Jewish Tradition, Change and Gender in a Global World*, ed. Tania Retan-Marincheshka (Sofia, Bulgaria: LIK Publishing House, 2011), 92–104. "Food patterns communicate symbolic meanings and contain cultural codes, functioning to maintain ethnic and national identities. From communal celebrations to personal preferences, our dietary habits reveal much about who we are and how we live," 95.

7. Patricia Tjaden and Nancy Thoennes, *Extent, Nature, and Consequences of Intimate Partner Violence: Findings from the National Violence against Women Survey* (Washington, DC: US Department of Justice, National Institute of Justice, 2000, NCJ 181867).

8. I first became aware of this type of abuse at a hearing conducted by the Massachusetts Commission on the Status of Women, January 25, 2012, at the Massachusetts Maritime Academy in Buzzards Bay, MA.

9. National Center for Victims of Crime, "Spousal Rape Laws: 20 Years Later," *Victim Policy Pipeline*, Winter 1999/2000, accessed December 21, 2011, http://www.ncvc.org/ncvc/main.aspx?dbName=DocumentViewer&DocumentID =32701. "Until the late 1970s, most states did not consider spousal rape a crime....Currently, rape of a spouse is a crime in all 50 states and the District of Columbia." In some countries, spousal rape is still protected. In fact, I would argue that child marriage is legalized rape.

2 Where Do I Fit In?

1. Ernest Hartmann, *Boundaries: A New Way to Look at the World* (Summerland, CA: CIRCC EverPress, 2011). Dr. Hartmann's excellent explanation of how boundaries function in our lives is the foundation on which I have built my understanding of the different tasks of the two generations as they enter the in-law relationship.

2. Dr. Kenneth Matos, "Sandwich Generation Month: July 2011—A Council on Contemporary Families Fact Sheet," news release, July 14, 2011, http://www .prnewswire.com/news-releases/sandwich-generation-month-july-2011---a -council-on-contemporary-families-fact-sheet-125585343.html. Among people who currently only have child-care responsibilities, more than a quarter have provided elder care in the last five years, and almost half (44 percent) expect to provide elder care in the next five years. Among people with current elder- and child-care responsibilities, 86 percent expect to still be providing elder care over the next five years.

3. Judy Osborne, *Wisdom of Separated Parents* (Santa Barbara, CA: Praeger, 2011). I am indebted to Osborne for highlighting the fact that divorced families are not necessarily broken, but rather reconfigured.

4. Karen Stabiner, "For Women, Age Often Brings Isolation," *New York Times*, March 3, 2011, accessed December 21, 2011, http://newoldage.blogs.nytimes .com/2011/03/03/for-women-often-age-brings-isolation/. In this article, Stabiner quotes Dr. Ronan Factora, who is a geriatrics specialist at the Center for Geriatric Medicine at the Cleveland Clinic: "Individuals who live in isolation are more likely to be depressed, may be more likely to suffer from malnutrition and are separated from opportunities for socialization—cognitively stimulating activities and physical activities that are the hallmarks of healthy aging."

5. Phyllis R. Silverman, "Mutual Help Groups: What Are They and What Makes Them Work?" in *The Oxford Handbook of Group Counseling*, ed. Robert K. Conyne (Oxford: Oxford University Press, 2010), 511–519.

6. Merrill, *Mothers-in-Law and Daughters-in-Law*, 89.

3 How Many People Did I Marry?

1. Terri Apter, *What Do You Want from Me? Learning to Get Along with In-Laws* (New York: W. W. Norton, 2010). "When we marry, we believe the bond is between only two individuals. Few of us realize the power that in-laws will exert over our lives" (dustcover).

2. Michael Chabon, *Manhood for Amateurs: The Pleasures and Regrets of a Husband, Father, and Son* (New York: Harper, 2006).

3. Jay Albany, eulogy for Jeffrey Stamps, June 15, 2011, Unitarian Universalist Church, Newton, MA.
4. The persons mentioned in this story have given me permission to use their real names.
5. Jay Albany, eulogy for Jeffrey Stamps, June 15, 2011, Unitarian Universalist Church, Newton, MA.

4 Have I Been Displaced?

1. Claire Berman, "Peggy Is Still Mom's Favorite," *NYCity Woman*, accessed December 21, 2011, http://www.nycitywoman.com/features/peggy-still -mom%E2%80%99s-favorite?page=0,1.

5 Dueling and Other In-Law Games

1. I am indebted to Reverend Steven Maynard for contributing his experience.
2. Amelia Hill, "Healthy Food Obsession Sparks Rise in New Eating Disorder," *Observer*, August 15, 2009, accessed December 21, 2011, http://www.guard ian.co.uk/society/2009/aug/16/orthorexia-mental-health-eating-disorder.
3. Evan Osnos, "Meet Dr. Freud," *New Yorker*, January 10, 2011, 54–63. "The deeper divide, however, may be more subtle, between a theory that Freud hoped would 'disturb the world' and a Chinese philosophical tradition that values harmony and accommodation as the root to fulfillment. Will a Chinese patient be more comforted by a therapy that advocates autonomy and independence—or by one that promotes accommodation to the constraints of a system?" 60. This comment helped me understand the chasm in parental expectations.

6 In Love, but Not in Law

1. Rose M. Kreider, "Increase in Opposite-sex Cohabiting Couples from 2009 to 2010 in the Annual Social and Economic Supplement (ASEC) to the Current Population Survey (CPS)." Working Paper, Housing and Household Economic Statistics Division, US Bureau of the Census, Washington, DC, Sept. 2010, http://www.census.gov/population/www/socdemo/Inc-Opp-sex -2009-to-2010.pdf. "Between 2009 and 2010, there was a 13 percent increase, (868,000) in the number of opposite-sex couples who were cohabiting. In

2009, there were an estimated 6.7 million unmarried couples living together, while in 2010, there were 7.5 million."

2. Laura Holson, "Who's on the Family Tree? Now It's Complicated," *New York Times*, July 4, 2011, accessed November 15, 2011, http://www.nytimes.com/2011/07/05/us/05tree.html?pagewanted=all.

7 Diversity Comes Home

1. Colleen Poulin and Virginia Rutter, "Tipping Point? When Minority Families Become the Majority," Paper presented at the Council on Contemporary Families Conference, April 8–9, 2011, University of Illinois at Chicago, Chicago, IL. This paper provides statistics on racial intermarriage in America and has a full list of references to interracial research.

2. Alan Wolfe, "Cultureligion," *New York Times*, December 24, 2010, http://www.nytimes.com/2010/12/26/books/review/Wolfe-t.html. On the one hand, for many, Christmas is not a Christian holiday. In fact, its roots lie in a Yule holiday. Wolfe quotes the French social scientist Olivier Roy: "It is those defending Christmas who are not being true to their traditions and teachings. There are no Christmas dinners in the Bible."

3. Evan Osnos, "Storytelling in China and America," *New Yorker*, September 23, 2011, accessed December 21, 2011, http://www.newyorker.com/online/blogs/evanosnos/2011/09/storytelling-in-china-and-america.html#ixzz1ZlV2LDfD. Osnos discusses the subtle impact of culture on the way we think. For example, American children made twice as many references to themselves as Chinese children, thus showing the impact of emphasis on individual achievement versus collective harmony.

8 Whose Child Is This?

1. L.V. Scaramella, T.K. Neppl, M.A. Barnett, L.L. Ontai, and R.D. Conger, "Intergenerational Relationship Quality, Gender, and Grandparent Involvement," *Journal of Family Relations* 59, no. 1 (February 2010): 28–44. In addition, in an e-mail received by the author on September 8, 2011, Eve Sullivan wrote that, "Because grandparent involvement, especially in families in which grandparents do not assume primary caregiving or custodial roles, is linked to greater well-being of all generations...the results underscore the need to move beyond the nuclear family to consider how other adults, including grandmothers, influence child development." Eve Sullivan is the founder of Parents Forum; author of *Where the Heart Listens: A Handbook for Parents*

and Their Allies in a Global Society; council member of the National Parenting Education Network (NPEN, United States); and council member of the International Federation for Parenting Education (FIEP, France).

2. Merrill, *Mothers-in-Law and Daughters-in-Law*, 50.

3. I am indebted to social worker Melanie Grossman, MSW, of San Francisco for alerting me to this notion.

4. Rachel Adams, "Older Americans Month: Valuing the Contributions of America's Elders," *Council on Contemporary Families*, May 11, 2011, accessed December 27, 2011, http://www.contemporaryfamilies.org/component /option,com_fjrelated/Itemid,87/id,177/layout,blog/view,fjrelated/.

5. US Department of Defense, *Demographics 2010: Profile of the Military Community*, accessed December 21, 2011, http://www.militaryhomefront.dod .mil//12038/Project%20Documents/MilitaryHOMEFRONT/Reports/2010 _Demographics_Report.pdf. "The largest percentage of minor dependents of Active Duty members is between birth and five years old (42.3%). The next largest percentage is 6 to 11 years of age (30.7%). Almost one quarter (22.8%) of minor dependents are 12 to 18 years of age," 61. Some of these active duty members serve abroad and require grandparental assistance.

6. Barnett, Neppl, Scaramella, Ontai, and Conger, "Grandmother Involvement as a Protective Factor," 635–645.

7. Amy Chua, *Battle Hymn of the Tiger Mother* (New York: Penguin, 2011).

8. Fareed Zakaria, "Culture Is Destiny: A Conversation with Lee Kuan Yew," *Foreign Affairs*, March/April 1994, accessed December 21, 2011, http://www .lee-kuan-yew.com/leekuanyew-freedzakaria.html. Lee Kuan Yew, former prime minister of Singapore and a keen advocate of Asian values, says that the Chinese family encouraged "scholarship and hard work and thrift and deferment of present enjoyment for future gain."

9. R. B. Kanarek, "Do Sucrose or Aspartame Cause Hyperactivity in Children?" *Nutrition Reviews* 52 (May 1994): 173–175.

10. Harvey Landau, "Grandparents' Visitation Rights—To Grandfather's House We Go?" *Divorce Source*, accessed March 13, 2012, http://www.divorcesource .com/NY/ARTICLES/landau1.html.

11. Lauren F. Cowan, "There's No Place Like Home: Why the Harm Standard in Grandparents Visitation Disputes Is in the Child's Best Interest," *Fordham Law Review*, May 2007, rev. 3137. Also see Daniel R. Victor and Keri L. Middleditch, "Grandparent Visitation: A Survey of History, Jurisprudence, and Legislative Trends across the United States in the Past Decade," *Journal of the American Academy of Matrimonial Lawyers* 391 (Dec. 2009). Also see Amy Goyer, "Grandparents' Visitation Rights: Divorce, Family Misunderstandings Strain Loving Relationships with Grandchildren," *AARP*, May 28, 2009, accessed March 12, 2012, http://www.aarp.org/relationships/grandparenting /info-05-2009/goyer_grandparent_visitation.html.

12. Hope Yen, "Grandparents Play a Bigger Role in Child-Rearing," *Guardian*, August 25, 2011, accessed December 21, 2011, http://www.guardian.co.uk/world

/feedarticle/9815292. "Grandparents in recent decades have often filled in for absent parents who were ill, battled addiction, or were sent to prison. The latest trend of grandparent involvement, reflected in census figures released Thursday, is now being driven also by the economy and the graying US population, including the 78 million boomers born between 1946 and 1964 who began turning 65 this year."

13. Anne-Marie Ambert, "Relationships with Former In-Laws after Divorce," *Journal of Marriage and the Family* 50 (Aug. 1988): 679–686. Researchers have found that in-law relationships deteriorate immediately following separation, although they are likely to survive if they involve a custodial parent.

14. "One key element in effective parenting is balance. Whatever you call the two essential parenting behaviors—encouragement and guidance, affection and discipline, or, simply, love and order—any parent needs to try to strike the right balance between the two. That right balance is different at different stages of a child's life and can be different, too, for each child and for the same child on a different day," e-mail correspondence with Eve Sullivan on May 19, 2011.

15. Recently, I ran into an intergenerational group where the grandparents complained that the mothers were overprotective. A young woman piped up and said, "If I don't walk my child to the bus, I am accused of being a negligent parent." The older generation was stunned.

9   More Money, More Problems

1. Pew Charitable Trusts, "The Return of the Multi-generational Family Household," March 18, 2010, accessed December 31, 2011, http://www .pewtrusts.org/our_work_report_detail.aspx?id=57840.

2. Conversations with Charles Yanikoski, editor of the *Integrative Adviser*, and his paper inform this chapter. See http://www.retirementworks2.com/pdfs /Making_Loans_and_Gifts_to_Family_Members-UNU.pdf.

10   Until Death Do Us Part

1. National Family Caregivers Association, "Caregiving Statistics," accessed December 21, 2011, http://www.nfcacares.org/who_are_family_caregivers /care_giving_statstics.cfm.

2. Sara Zeff Geber, "Fifty Plus, Minus Kids: The Adventure of 'Solo Aging' in America," *Integrative Adviser: The Journal of the Association for Integrative Financial and Life Planning* 4, no. 4 (2011): 1–5. Nieces and nephews or

younger siblings, neighbors, co-religionists, like-minded hobbyists, professional colleagues, or friends are likely candidates.

3. E. S. Browning, "Aging and Broke, More Lean on Family," *Wall Street Journal*, December 31, 2011, accessed December 31, 2011, http://online.wsj.com /article_email/SB10001424052970203899504577128821679773752 -lMyQjAxMTAxMDMwMTEzNDEyWj.html?mod=wsj_share_email.

4. Personal conversation with Chuck Yanikoski—whose website is http://www .retirementworks2.com/support.asp?id=papers—on June 28, 2011.

5. Massachusetts Legislature, "General Laws," accessed December 21, 2011, http://www.malegislature.gov/Laws/GeneralLaws/PartIV/TitleI/Chapter273 /Section20.

6. Craig Reaves, "Ask the Expert: Parental Support and the Law," *New York Times*, February 26, 2010, accessed December 21, 2011, http://newoldage.blogs .nytimes.com/2010/02/26/ask-the-expert-parental-support-and-the-law/. "At one time, filial responsibility laws were far more common. As recently as the 1950s, 45 states and the federal government had them on the books. They began to erode during the New Deal, when the Social Security Act passed and the concept of government rather than familial responsibility started to take hold. But 28 states still have filial responsibility laws: Alaska, Arkansas, California, Connecticut, Delaware, Georgia, Idaho, Indiana, Kentucky, Louisiana, Maryland, Massachusetts, Mississippi, Montana, Nevada, New Hampshire, North Carolina, North Dakota, Ohio, Oregon, Pennsylvania, Rhode Island, South Dakota, Tennessee, Utah, Vermont, Virginia, and West Virginia. Sixteen of these impose civil penalties—these states can come after your assets or income if you fail to support your parents. In the eight states where filial responsibility entails criminal penalties, a prosecutor could actually put you in jail. Four states take both approaches. . . . But filial responsibility laws are very rarely enforced."

7. Health-care proxies and health-care powers of attorney are similar but not identical. They both direct someone else to make decisions for you when you are unable to do so for yourself. Almost all states recognize the validity of health-care proxies but not of living wills or health-care powers of attorney.

8. The Conversation Project—www.theconversationproject.org—launched a major national media campaign and movement in the spring of 2012. Its purpose is to make it easier for people to talk about death with their loved ones and to express their preferences for what kind of care they want in the course of this universal human event.

9. Roberta K. Taylor and Dorian Mintzer, *The Couple's Retirement Puzzle: 10 Must-Have Conversations for Transitioning to the Second Half of Life* (Waltham, MA: Lincoln Street Press, 2011).

10. If you have an IRA, you should consult your estate lawyer about making provisions so that your heir(s) can "stretch" the mandatory withdrawal period over his or her life expectancy (rather than yours) for maximum flexibility.

11. John F. Wasik, "A To-Do List for Estate Planning," *AARP Bulletin*, October 19, 2011, accessed December 21, 2011, http://www.aarp.org/money/estate-plan ning/info-10-2011/estate-planning-to-do-list.html#.TrWDPK8dKCI.email.

11   Do Unto Your In-Laws

1. Albert Ellis developed the concept of rational emotive behavior therapy in the 1950s. The method requires people to focus on their current lives and then take steps to change their behaviors. His methods and those of Aaron Beck are the basis for cognitive behavioral therapy. While this book is *not* therapy, the notion that one can modify one's behavior is based on their theories.
2. Ronald Eisenberg, *What the Rabbis Said: 250 Topics from the Talmud* (Santa Barbara, CA: Praeger, 2010), 89.
3. David Brooks, "Who You Are," *New York Times*, October 20, 2011, accessed December 12, 2011, http://www.nytimes.com/2011/10/21/opinion/brooks -who-you-are.html.

BIBLIOGRAPHY

Adams, Rachel. "Older Americans Month: Valuing the Contributions of America's Elders." *Council on Contemporary Families*, May 11, 2011. Accessed December 27, 2011. http://www.contemporaryfamilies.org/component/option,com_fjrelated /Itemid,87/id,177/layout,blog/view,fjrelated/.

Allinson, Bree. *How to Deal with Your Mother-in-Law: (Sisters & Family Included)*. New York: iUniverse, 2004.

Ambert, Anne-Marie. "Relationships with Former In-Laws after Divorce." *Journal of Marriage and the Family* 50 (August 1988): 679–686.

Angelich, Jane. *What's a Mother (In-Law) to Do? Five Essential Steps to Building a Loving Relationship with Your Son's New Wife*. New York: Howard, 2009.

Apter, Terri. *What Do You Want from Me? Learning to Get Along with In-Laws*. New York: W. W. Norton, 2010.

Associated Press. "After 40 Years, Interracial Marriage Flourishing." msnbc.com, last updated April 15, 2007. Accessed December 27, 2011. http://www.msnbc.msn .com/id/18090277/ns/us_news-life/t/after-years-interracial-marriage-flourish ing/#.Tu9gIVa0KSo.

Bachkoff, Patricia. *Mother-in-Law Hell: Real Stories about Real Mothers-in-Law*. New York: iUniverse, 2000.

Barash, Susan Shapiro. *Mothers-in-Law and Daughters-in-Law: Love, Hate, Rivalry and Reconciliation*. Far Hills, NJ: New Horizon Press, 2001.

Barnett, Melissa, Laura Scaramella, Tricia Neppl, Lenna Ontai, and Rand Conger. "Grandmother Involvement as a Protective Factor for Early Childhood Social Adjustment." *Journal of Family Psychology* 24, no. 5 (2010): 635–645.

Barnett, Melissa, Laura Scaramella, Tricia Neppl, Lenna Ontai, and Rand Conger. "Intergenerational Relationship Quality, Gender, and Grandparent Involvement." *Family Relations: An Interdisciplinary Journal of Applied Family Studies* 59, no. 1 (February 2010): 28–44.

Beam, Christopher. "Don't Mind the Gap: A Defense of May-December Marriages Like Hugh Hefner's." *Slate*, December 28, 2010. Accessed December 12, 2011. http://www.slate.com/articles/arts/culturebox/2010/12/dont_mind_the_gap.html.

Berman, Claire. "Peggy Is Still Mom's Favorite." *NYCity Woman*. Accessed December 21, 2011. http://www.nycitywoman.com/features/peggy-still -mom%E2%80%99s-favorite?page=0,1.

Bluper, Liz, and Renee Plastique. *Mothers-in-Law Do Everything Wrong: M.I.L.D.E.W.* Kansas City: Andrews McMeel Publishing, 2004.

Bowditch, Eden Unger, and Aviva Samet. *The Daughter-in-Law's Survival Guide: Everything You Need to Know about Relating to Your Mother-in-Law*. Oakland, CA: New Harbinger Publications, 2002.

Brooks, David. "Who You Are." *New York Times*, October 20, 2011. Accessed December 12, 2011. http://www.nytimes.com/2011/10/21/opinion/brooks-who-you-are.html.

Browning, E. S. "Aging and Broke, More Lean on Family." *Wall Street Journal*, December 31, 2011. Accessed December 31, 2011. http://online.wsj.com/article_email/SB10001424052970203899504577128821679773752-lMyQjAxMTAxMDMwMTEzNDEyWj.html?mod=wsj_share_email.

Chabon, Michael. *Manhood for Amateurs: The Pleasures and Regrets of a Husband, Father, and Son*. New York: Harper, 2006.

Chapman, Annie. *The Mother-in-Law Dance: Can Two Women Love the Same Man and Still Get Along?* Eugene, OR: Harvest House Publishers, 2004.

Chapman, Gary. *In-Law Relationships: The Chapman's Guide to Becoming Friends with Your In-Laws*. Carol Stream, IL: Boyce Shore & Associations, 2008.

Chua, Amy. *Battle Hymn of the Tiger Mother*. New York: Penguin, 2011.

Coontz, Stephanie. *Marriage, a History: How Love Conquered Marriage*. New York: Viking Penguin, 2005.

Cowan, Lauren F. "There's No Place Like Home: Why the Harm Standard in Grandparents Visitation Disputes Is in the Child's Best Interest." *Fordham Law Review*, May 2007, rev. 3137.

Cupach, William R., and Brian H. Spitzberg. *The Dark Side of Close Relationships II*. New York: Taylor and Francis, 2011.

Dr. Phil. "Son-in-Law Vs. Mother-in-Law." Drphil.com, September 31, 2010. Accessed December 22, 2011. http://www.drphil.com/slideshows/slideshow/3239/?id=3239&showID=721.

Eisenberg, Ronald. *What the Rabbis Said: 250 Topics from the Talmud*. Santa Barbara, CA: Praeger, 2010, 89.

Farouky, Jumana. "Mother-in-Law Problems: They're Worse for Women." *Time Magazine*, December 4, 2008. Accessed December 22, 2011. http://www.time.com/time/world/article/0,8599,1863282,00.html.

Fields, Douglas. "Rudeness Is a Neurotoxin." *Huffington Post*, January 5, 2011. Accessed December 12, 2011. http://www.huffingtonpost.com/dr-douglas-fields/rudeness-is-a neurotoxin_b_765908.html.

Fingerman, Karen. *Aging Mothers and Their Adult Daughters: A Study of Mixed Emotions*. New York: Springer, 2001.

Firestone, Lisa. "Are You the Cause of Your Jealousy?" *Huffington Post*, September 21, 2011. Accessed December 12, 2011. http://www.huffingtonpost.com/lisa-firestone/problems-with-jealousy_b_970592.html.

Forward, Susan. *Toxic In-Laws: Loving Strategies for Protecting Your Marriage*. Brattleboro, VT: Harper Paperbacks, 2002.

Geber, Sara Zeff. "Fifty Plus, Minus Kids: The Adventure of 'Solo Aging' in America." *Integrative Adviser: The Journal of the Association for Integrative Financial and Life Planning* 4, no. 4 (2011): 1–5.

Goldin, Judah, ed. *The Fathers According to Rabbi Nathan*. New Haven, CT: Yale University Press, 1955, 41.

Goyer, Amy. "Grandparents' Visitation Rights: Divorce, Family Misunderstandings Strain Loving Relationships with Grandchildren." *AARP*, May 28, 2009. Accessed December 21, 2011. http://www.aarp.org/relationships/grandparenting/info-05-2009/goyer_grandparent_visitation.html

Graff, E. J. *What Is Marriage for? The Strange Social History of Our Most Intimate Institution.* Boston, MA: Beacon Press, 2004.

Greek Orthodox Archdiocese of America. "Department of Marriage and Family." Accessed December 21, 2011. http://www.goarch.org/archdiocese/departments/marriage.

Hartmann, Ernest. *Boundaries: A New Way to Look at the World.* Summerland, CA: CIRCC EverPress, 2011.

Hill, Amelia. "Healthy Food Obsession Sparks Rise in New Eating Disorder." *Observer*, August 15, 2009. Accessed December 21, 2011. http://www.guardian.co.uk/society/2009/aug/16/orthorexia-mental-health-eating-disorder.

Holson, Laura. "Who's on the Family Tree? Now It's Complicated." *New York Times*, July 4, 2011. Accessed November 15, 2011. http://www.nytimes.com/2011/07/05/us/05tree.html?pagewanted=all.

Horsley, Gloria Call. *The In-Law Survival Manual: A Guide to Cultivating Healthy In-Law Relationships.* New York: Wiley, 1996.

Hurley, Dan. "Divorce Rate: It's Not as High as You Think." *New York Times*, April 19, 2005. Accessed December 31, 2011. http://www.nytimes.com/2005/04/19/health/19divo.html.

Hyman, Mark. "How Eating at Home Can Save Your Life." *Huffington Post*, January 9, 2011. Accessed December 12, 2011. http://www.huffingtonpost.com/dr-mark-hyman/family-dinner-how_b_806114.html.

Ishii-Kuntz, Masako. "Intergenerational Relationships among Chinese, Japanese, and Korean Americans." *Family Relations* 46, no. 1 (January 1997): 23–32.

Jewish Federations of North America, the. "National Jewish Population Survey: Rates of Intermarriage." Accessed December 27, 2011. http://www.jewishfederations.org/page.aspx?id=46253.

Johnson, Colleen Leahy. "In-Law Relationships in the American Kinship System: The Impact of Divorce and Remarriage." *American Ethnologist* 16, no. 1 (February 1989): 87–99.

Joseph, Norma Baumel. "From Baghdad to Montreal: Food, Gender and Identity in Two Scenarios." In *Migration, Communication, and Home: Jewish Tradition, Change and Gender in a Global World*, edited by Tania Retan-Marincheshka, 92–104. Sofia, Bulgaria: LIK Publishing House, 2011.

Kanarek, R. B. "Do Sucrose or Aspartame Cause Hyperactivity in Children?" *Nutrition Reviews* 52 (May 1994): 173–175.

Katzir, Jeannette. *Broken Birds: The Story of My Momila.* Farmington Hills, MI: Jeannette Katzir, 2009.

Kleinfield, N. R. "Baby Makes Four, and Complications." *New York Times*, June 19, 2011. Accessed December 21, 2011. http://www.nytimes.com/2011/06/19/nyregion/an-american-family-mom-sperm-donor-lover-child.html?_r=1.

Kreider, Rose M. "Increase in Opposite-sex Cohabiting Couples from 2009 to 2010 in the Annual Social and Economic Supplement (ASEC) to the Current Population Survey (CPS)." Working Paper, Housing and Household Economic Statistics Division, US Bureau of the Census, Washington, DC, Sept. 2010.

Lamb, Sarah. *Aging and the Indian Diaspora: Cosmopolitan Families in India and Abroad.* Bloomington: Indiana University Press, 2009.

———. "Elder Residences and Outsourced Sons: Remaking Aging in Cosmopolitan India." In *The Cultural Context of Aging: Worldwide Perspectives*, edited by Jay Sokolovsky, 418–442. Santa Barbara, CA: Greenwood Publishers, 2009.

———. "Intimacy in a Transnational Era: The Remaking of Aging among Indian Americans." *Diaspora: A Journal of Transnational Studies* 11, no. 3 (2002): 299–330.

Landau, Harvey. "Grandparents' Visitation Rights—To Grandfather's House We Go?" *Divorce Source.* Accessed March 13, 2012. http://www.divorcesource.com /NY/ARTICLES/landau1.html.

Lescher, Kurt, and Karl Pillemer. "Intergenerational Ambivalence: A New Approach to the Study of Parent-Child Relations in Later Life." *Journal of Marriage and the Family* 60 (May 1998): 413–425.

Lieberman, Susan Abel. *The Mother-in-Law's Manual: Proven Strategies for Creating and Maintaining Healthy Relationships with Married Children.* Austin, TX: Bright Sky Press, 2009.

Lieblich, Amia, Rivka Tuval-Mashiach, and Tamer Zilber. *Narrative Research: Reading, Analysis and Interpretation.* Thousand Oaks, CA: Sage Publications, 1998.

Lo, Alex. "Tough-Love Chinese Mother Draws Shock and Awe." *China News Watch*, January 13, 2011. Accessed December 21, 2011. http://topics.scmp .com/news/china-news-watch/article/Tough-love-Chinese-mother-draws -shock-and-awe.

Massachusetts Legislature. "General Laws." Accessed December 21, 2011. http://www.malegislature.gov/Laws/GeneralLaws/PartIV/TitleI/Chapter273 /Section20.

Matos, Kenneth. "Sandwich Generation Month: July 2011—A Council on Contemporary Families Fact Sheet." News release, July 14, 2011. http://www .prnewswire.com/news-releases/sandwich-generation-month-july-2011---a -council-on-contemporary-families-fact-sheet-125585343.html.

McAdams, Dan P. "Personal Narratives and the Life Story." In *Handbook of Personality Theory and Research*, edited by Lawrence A. Pervin and Oliver P. John, 478–500. New York: Guilford Press, 1999.

Merrill, Deborah M. *Mothers-in-Law and Daughters-in-Law: Understanding the Relationship and What Makes Them Friends or Foe.* Westport, CT: Praeger Publishers, 2007.

Milardo. Robert. *The Forgotten Kin: Aunts and Uncles.* New York: Cambridge University Press, 2010.

Mirfin-Veitch, Brigit, Anne Bray, and Marilyn Watson. "We're Just That Sort of Family." *Family Relations* 46, no. 3 (July 1997): 305–311.

Montgomery, Rhonda. "In-Law Relationships." *jrank.org*, 1995. Accessed December 22, 2011. http://family.jrank.org/pages/892/In-Law-Relationships.html.

Moore, Meg Mitchell. *The Arrivals.* New York: Little, Brown and Company, 2011.

Moskos, Charles. "The Future of Greek America." *Hellenic Communication Service,* May 2006. Accessed December 27, 2011. http://www.helleniccomserve.com /futuregreekamerica.html.

National Center for Victims of Crime. "Spousal Rape Laws: 20 Years Later." *Victim Policy Pipeline,* Winter 1999/2000. Accessed December 21, 2011. http://www .ncvc.org/ncvc/main.aspx?dbName=DocumentViewer&DocumentID=32701.

National Family Caregivers Association. "Caregiving Statistics." Accessed December 21, 2011. http://www.nfcacares.org/who_are_family_caregivers/care_giving _statstics.cfm.

National Healthy Marriage Resource Center. "Marriage and Intermarriage Among Asian Americans: A Fact Sheet." Accessed March 7, 2012. http://acf.gov/hea lthymarriage/pdf/marriageamongasianamericans.pdf.

"New KRAFT Macaroni & Cheese Commercial: 'Impromptu In-Law Visit.'" YouTube video, 0:32. Posted by "kraftmacncheese," October 17, 2011. Accessed December 21, 2011. http://www.youtube.com/watch?v=LxQ-AzS38vY.

Okun, Barbara, and Joseph Nowinski. *Saying Goodbye: How Families Can Find Renewal Through Loss.* New York: The Berkeley Publishing Group, 2011.

O'Neil, Dennis. "Cultural Anthropology Terms." Last modified May 11, 2007. Accessed October 27, 2011. http://anthro.palomar.edu/tutorials/cglossary.htm.

Oregon State University. "Definitions of Anthropological Terms." Last modified February 24, 2011. Accessed October 27, 2011. http://oregonstate.edu/instruct /anth370/gloss.html.

Osborne, Judy. *Wisdom of Separated Parents.* Santa Barbara, CA: Praeger, 2011.

Osnos, Evan. "Meet Dr. Freud." *New Yorker,* January 10, 2011: 54–63.

———. "Storytelling in China and America." *New Yorker,* September 23, 2011. Accessed December 21, 2011. http://www.newyorker.com/online/blogs/evanos nos/2011/09/storytelling-in-china-and-america.html#ixzz1ZlV2LDfD.

Pans, A. E. M. J. "The Mother-in-Law Taboo." *Ethnology* 37, no. 1 (1998): 71–97.

Parry, Alan, and Robert E. Doan. *Story Re-Visions: Narrative Therapy in the Postmodern World.* New York: Guilford Press, 1994.

Peters-Davis, Norah D., Miriam Moss, and Rachel A. Pruchno. "Children-in-Law in Caregiving Families." *Gerontologist* 39, no. 1 (1999): 66–75.

Pew Charitable Trusts. "The Return of the Multi-generational Family Household." March 18, 2010. Accessed December 31, 2011. http://www.pewtrusts.org/our _work_report_detail.aspx?id=57840.

Plummer, Joseph. "Changing Values." *Futurist* (January–February 1989): 8–13.

Poch, Dina Koutas. *I (Heart) My In-Laws.* New York: Owl Books/Henry Holt, 2007.

Poulin, Colleen, and Virginia Rutter. "How Color-Blind Is Love? Interracial Dating Facts and Puzzles." *Council on Contemporary Families*, March 30, 2011. Accessed December 27, 2011. http://www.contemporaryfamilies.org/marriage-partnership -divorce/how-color-blind-is-love.html.

Reaves, Craig. "Ask the Expert: Parental Support and the Law." *New York Times*, February 26, 2010. Accessed December 21, 2011. http://newoldage.blogs .nytimes.com/2010/02/26/ask-the-expert-parental-support-and-the-law/.

Reytan-Marincheshka, Tania, ed. *Migration, Communication & Home: Jewish Tradition, Change & Gender in a Global World*. Sofia, Bulgaria: LIK Publishing House, 2011.

Rosin, Hanna. "She Makes More Money than He Does. So? Women Who Outearn Their Men." *Slate*, February 16, 2011. Accessed October 27, 2011. http://www.slate.com/articles/double_x/doublex/2011/02/she_makes _more_money_than_he_does_so.html.

Roy, Oliver. *Holy Ignorance: When Religion and Culture Part Ways*. New York: Columbia/Hurst, 2010.

Sands, Roberta, Dorit Roer-Strier, and Susana Strier. "Family Coping with Religious Intensification: The Case of Argentinean/Baalot Teshuvah." Working Paper, School of Social Policy and Practice, University of Pennsylvania, Philadelphia, PA, 2011.

Schnur, Susan. "How Twenty-Somethings Mate Now." *Lilith* (Spring 2010): 10–15.

Silverman, Ilena. *I Married My Mother-in-Law: And Other Tales of In-Laws We Can't Live with—and Can't Live Without*. Boston: Riverhead Trade, 2007.

Silverman, Phyllis R. "Mutual Help Groups: What Are They and What Makes Them Work?" In *The Oxford Handbook of Group Counseling*, edited by Robert K. Conyne, 511–519. Oxford: Oxford University Press, 2010.

Spencer, Liz, and Ray Pahl. *Rethinking Friendship: Hidden Solidarities Today*. Princeton, NJ: Princeton University Press, 2006.

Stabiner, Karen. "For Women, Age Often Brings Isolation." *New York Times*, March 3, 2011. Accessed December 21, 2011. http://newoldage.blogs.nytimes. com/2011/03/03/for-women-often-age-brings-isolation/.

Stone, Douglas, Bruce Patton, and Sheila Heen. *Difficult Conversations: How to Discuss What Matters Most*. New York: Penguin Books, 2010.

Sussman, Marvin, and Lee Burchinal. "Kin Family Network: Unheralded Structure in Current Conceptualizations of Family Functioning." *Marriage and Family Living* 24, no. 3 (1962): 231–240.

Taylor, Roberta K., and Dorian Mintzer. *The Couple's Retirement Puzzle: 10 Must-Have Conversations for Transitioning to the Second Half of Life*. Waltham, MA: Lincoln Street Press, 2011.

Tjaden, Patricia, and Nancy Thoennes. *Extent, Nature, and Consequences of Intimate Partner Violence: Findings from the National Violence against Women Survey*. Washington, DC: US Department of Justice, National Institute of Justice, 2000, NCJ 181867.

Ullman, Paul S. "A Sample of Married College Students and Aspects of Their In-Law Relationships." *Coordinator* 4, no. 2 (1955): 18–21.

US Department of Defense. *Demographics 2010: Profile of the Military Community.* Accessed December 21, 2011. http://www.militaryhomefront.dod.mil//12038 /Project%20Documents/MilitaryHOMEFRONT/Reports/2010 _Demographics_Report.pdf.

Vera-Sanso, Penny. "Dominant Daughter-in-Law and Submissive Mother-in-Law? Cooperation and Conflicts in India." *Journal of the Royal Anthropological Institute* 5, no. 4 (1999): 577–593. Accessed December 29, 2011. http://www .jstor.org/pss/2661149.

Victor, Daniel R., and Keri L. Middleditch. "Grandparent Visitation: A Survey of History, Jurisprudence, and Legislative Trends across the United States in the Past Decade." *Journal of the American Academy of Matrimonial Lawyers* (December 2009): 391–409.

Wasik, John F. "A To-Do List for Estate Planning." *AARP Bulletin*, October 19, 2011. Accessed December 21, 2011. http://www.aarp.org/money/estate-plan ning/info-10-2011/estate-planning-to-do-list.html#.TrWDPK8dKCI.email.

Wolf, Arthur. "Adopt a Daughter-in-Law, Marry a Sister: A Chinese Solution to the Problem of the Incest Taboo." *American Anthropologist* 70, no. 5 (October 1968): 864–874.

Wolfe, Alan. "Cultureligion." *New York Times*, December 24, 2010. Accessed December 21, 2011. http://www.nytimes.com/2010/12/26/books/review/Wolfe -t.html.

Yen, Hope. "Grandparents Play a Bigger Role in Child-Rearing." *Guardian*, August 25, 2011. Accessed December 21, 2011. http://www.guardian.co.uk/world /feedarticle/9815292.

Zakaria, Fareed. "Culture Is Destiny: A Conversation with Lee Kuan Yew." *Foreign Affairs*, March/April 1994. Accessed December 21, 2011. http://www.lee-kuan -yew.com/leekuanyew-freedzakaria.html.

INDEX